Teaching Adult Learners with Dyslexia and English as an Additional Language

Packed full of practical tips to use in the classroom, case studies to provide theoretical grounding and ideas to improve inclusion, *Teaching Adult Learners with Dyslexia and English as an Additional Language* covers all the key areas necessary to ensure inclusive and effective teaching practice in higher and further education settings.

This book provides a coherent framework for those looking to develop their knowledge and skills in this challenging area and explores key areas such as: teaching and learning strategies, differentiation, assessment, feedback and supporting students using technology. It provides a unique insight into how to develop a thorough understanding of the needs of learners and the principles and practices of how to meet those needs within a classroom setting.

This is an essential introductory book for anyone working or training to work in either Further or Higher Education and who wishes to develop knowledge and skills in the challenging area of supporting and teaching adult EAL learners with learning differences.

Paul Demetriou is an experienced teacher/education consultant and journalist specialising in working with young people and adults who are educationally excluded because of their socio-economic backgrounds or learning disabilities in the secondary, post-secondary and higher education sector. He currently works in teacher education in Further Education and has worked on the post-graduate teaching programmes of several British universities for the past 20 years.

Teaching Adult Learners with Dyslexia and English as an Additional Language
Practical Tips to Support Best Practice

Paul Demetriou

LONDON AND NEW YORK

Designed cover image: © Getty Images

First published 2023
by Routledge
4 Park Square, Milton Park, Abingdon, Oxon OX14 4RN

and by Routledge
605 Third Avenue, New York, NY 10158

Routledge is an imprint of the Taylor & Francis Group, an informa business

© 2023 Paul Demetriou

The right of Paul Demetriou to be identified as author of this work has been asserted in accordance with sections 77 and 78 of the Copyright, Designs and Patents Act 1988.

All rights reserved. No part of this book may be reprinted or reproduced or utilised in any form or by any electronic, mechanical, or other means, now known or hereafter invented, including photocopying and recording, or in any information storage or retrieval system, without permission in writing from the publishers.

Trademark notice: Product or corporate names may be trademarks or registered trademarks, and are used only for identification and explanation without intent to infringe.

British Library Cataloguing-in-Publication Data
A catalogue record for this book is available from the British Library

Library of Congress Cataloging-in-Publication Data
Names: Demetriou, Paul, author.
Title: Teaching adult learners with dyslexia and English as an additional language : practical tips to support best practice / Paul Demetriou.
Description: Abingdon, Oxon ; New York, NY : Routledge, 2023. | Includes bibliographical references and index.
Identifiers: LCCN 2022041211 (print) | LCCN 2022041212 (ebook) | ISBN 9781032013725 (hardback) | ISBN 9781032020433 (paperback) | ISBN 9781003181583 (ebook)
Subjects: LCSH: English language--Study and teaching (Higher)--Foreign speakers. | Dyslexics--Education (Higher) | Adult students. | Adult education.
Classification: LCC PE1128.A2 D433 2023 (print) | LCC PE1128.A2 (ebook) | DDC 428.0071/1--dc23/eng/20221004
LC record available at https://lccn.loc.gov/2022041211
LC ebook record available at https://lccn.loc.gov/2022041212

ISBN: 978-1-032-01372-5 (hbk)
ISBN: 978-1-032-02043-3 (pbk)
ISBN: 978-1-003-18158-3 (ebk)

DOI: 10.4324/9781003181583

Typeset in Times New Roman
by SPi Technologies India Pvt Ltd (Straive)

To my son for keeping me grounded
To my dog (RIP) for entertaining me
To my students for motivating me

And especially to everyone who collaborated with me in writing this book

Contents

List of Boxes   xi

1 Introduction   1

Aims of the book 1
The background to the book 2
Some of the main impacts of dyslexia on language learning and studying 4
Supporting the needs of EAL students with dyslexia 7
Inclusive teaching and the Universal Design for Learning (UDL) 9
The major teaching and learning themes of the book 11
The main structure of the book 12
The book as a toolbox 12
References 14

2 Independent learning skills   16

Pre-reading 16
Overlearning 18
Multi-sensory teaching 19
Accelerated Cognition (AC) 20
Building self-confidence 22
Building Locus of Control 25
Self-questioning 28
Thinking aloud 29
Dialogic teaching 31
Automatisation 34
Anchor Charts 36
Conclusion 38
References 39

3 Critical reading, critical writing and critical thinking — 42

Critical reading 42
Small group reading 50
DARTs (Directed Activities Related to Texts) 51
Critical writing 53
Do Nows 56
Critical writing and reading 59
Critical thinking 60
Enquiry-based learning 65
Conclusion 66
References 67

4 Assessment and feedback — 69

Comprehension tasks 69
Questioning 72
Dictogloss 76
Cued Spelling 78
Using rubrics 80
Peer assessment 82
Conclusion 85
References 86

5 Self-assessment and feedback — 88

Self-assessment 88
Some of the most effective approaches to self-assessment 88
Ipsative assessment 94
Feedback 97
Feedback and motivation 107
Using teachers' feedback effectively 108
Conclusion 112
References 112

6 Differentiated teaching and learning — 115

Scaffolding 115
Small group work and differentiation 117
Peer teaching and learning 119
Reciprocal Teaching (RT) 120
Paired thinking 122

Experiential learning 124
Differentiation and Self-Regulated Learning (SRL) 126
Gamification 128
Metalinguistic awareness 130
Differentiating teaching of terminology 135
Translanguaging 138
Conclusion 140
References 141

7 Assistive technology 143

Using technology to differentiate 143
Types of blended learning 144
Active Blended Learning (ABL) 146
Using interactive online facilities 149
Content Acquisition Podcasts (CAPs) 152
Remote teaching 154
Virtual learning 155
Mobile learning (aka M-learning) 156
Social media and differentiation 158
Conclusion 168
References 168

8 Developing academic skills 172

Academic writing 172
Writing frames 178
Using academic sources 180
Note taking 182
Making notes from texts 189
Visual note making 194
Handwriting 197
Effective proof-reading 199
Conclusion 201
References 202

9 Reading comprehension 203

Barriers to reading comprehension 203
The five steps of SQ3R 204
Differentiating the learning of specialist vocabulary 209

Game ideas 211
Using mnemonics 217
Literature circles 219
Critical Analysis skills 222
Conclusion 228
References 229

Afterword	232
Index	235

Boxes

1.1	Some of the main challenges faced by students who have EAL and Dyslexia	5
1.2	Developing learner independence	8
1.3	Over to you!	13
2.1	An example of pre-reading used in a GCSE History class	18
2.2	A Case study of AC used in an A Level Psychology class	21
2.3	A teaching example of how to develop LOC in students	27
2.4	Using a Think Aloud in a Fashion class	30
2.5	Using recorded comments as the basis for an essay draft	31
2.6	An example of dialogic teaching used in a biology class	33
2.7	An example of Automatisation in an Early Years Class	34
2.8	An example of cut-up reviewing in a Film Studies class	35
2.9	Using a Content chart in a dance class	38
2.10	Over to you!	38
2.11	Take away self-reflective questions	38
3.1	Reading checklist	43
3.2	Critical Reading checklist	44
3.3	Teaching resource critical reading example	45
3.4	Here is an example of a teacher's use of small reading groups	51
3.5	An example of using DARTs in an Early Years Level 2 class	53
3.6	A health and Social Care lecturer's example of how she used a serial map	55
3.7	A Geography teacher's example of how a concept map can be used as self-assessment tool	56
3.8	A Media Studies teacher's example of how they used a graphic organiser	56
3.9	Using a Do Now in a science class	58
3.10	The 5Hs and W model	59
3.11	A Critical reading, thinking, and writing exercise	60
3.12	An example of how The IMPROVE framework could be used (adapted from Mevarech and Kramarski (1997)) in a sports science class	62
3.13	Using ideas storming in an English class	64
3.14	Using PBL in a business class	66

3.15	Over to you!	66
3.16	Take away self-reflective questions	67
4.1	Using summary by deletion	70
4.2	An example of how to use comprehension exercises	72
4.3	Using the Big Question technique in a Sociology class	75
4.4	An example of how a Dictogloss can be used in an English class	76
4.5	10 steps to cued spelling	79
4.6	Using the Cued spelling approach on a Hair and Beauty course	79
4.7	An example of how an analytical rubric can be used in a business class	81
4.8	I, You and We table	84
4.9	An example quote	85
4.10	Over to you!	86
4.11	Take away self-reflective questions	86
5.1	An example of self-assessment in Biology using the traffic light system	89
5.2	An example of Video self-assessment in a Dance class	93
5.3	Using self-assessment in an English class	93
5.4	A RAG Rating table for self-assessment	94
5.5	An example of League table Ipsative assessment used in a Sports class	95
5.6	An example of how FR is used in an Access to Sociology class	99
5.7	Using minute papers in a drama class plenary	101
5.8	Using structured questions designed to stimulate self-reflection	104
5.9	A self-assessment checklist for students	104
5.10	An example of a feedback podcast in a catering class	106
5.11	A feedback priorities checklist table	109
5.12	A completed student self-evaluated action plan	110
5.13	Over to you!	112
5.14	Take away self-reflective questions	112
6.1	An example of scaffolding used to support a student who is learning how to paint a door	117
6.2	An example of using a fishbowl activity in a childcare class	119
6.3	An example of using Reciprocal Teaching in an Economics class	121
6.4	An example of experiential learning used in a marketing course	126
6.5	An example of building SRL in a Science class	127
6.6	An example of gamification used in formative assessment in Media theory	129
6.7	The checklist approach	131
6.8	The triple section approach	132
6.9	An example of using metalinguistic awareness in an engineering class	133
6.10	A meaning triangle for a catering class showing the stages of making bread	134
6.11	An example of breaking down terminology in a Business Studies class	136

6.12	An example of terminology teaching from an Anatomy class	138
6.13	Over to you!	140
6.14	Take away self-reflective questions	140
7.1	An example of using RASE in a hotel management class	148
7.2	Some reflections of using the chat facility in MS Teams	149
7.3	Using Moodle Forum in a Child Care class	151
7.4	Using Mark the Words in a functional Skills session	152
7.5	An example of a CAP session for some students with Dyslexia on a Level 3 Sport and Exercise Science class	153
7.6	An example of using Instagram in a performing arts class	160
7.7	Grading Tik Tok videos	161
7.8	An example of how Pinterest can be used in GCSE Film Studies	163
7.9	An example of using Pinterest in a politics class	163
7.10	An example of how Snapchat was used in a health care class	165
7.11	how using Twitter has made students with Dyslexia more autonomous and self-directed as learners	167
7.12	Over to you!	168
7.13	Take away self-reflective questions	168
8.1	An example of how to teach descriptive writing within a chemistry class	173
8.2	An example of how to teach analytical writing in a music class	174
8.3	An example of how to teach persuasive writing in a marketing class	174
8.4	An example of how to teach critical writing in a psychology class	175
8.5	Paragraph checklist	177
8.6	Writing frame	179
8.7	Some different ways of developing students' use of academic sources	181
8.8	Self-reflection task	183
8.9	The triple section approach to note making	192
8.10	A checklist for analysing a research article	193
8.11	Some ways in which you could help your students develop their handwriting skills	197
8.12	Over to you!	201
8.13	Take away self-reflective questions	202
9.1	A SQR3 template	206
9.2	Using game starters to develop your students' vocabulary	211
9.3	Here is an example of a literature circle conducted in a class of EAL students on a Level Two Nursing course	221
9.4	Description and Critical Analysis comparison exercise	222
9.5	Theory checklist	223
9.6	Task prompts/sentence starters for Critical Analysis	224
9.7	Over to you!	229
9.8	Take away self-reflective questions	229

1 Introduction

Aims of the book

In Further and Higher Education (FE and HE) there are increasing numbers of adult learners with academic writing/literacy issues. Many of these are learners who have English as an Additional Language (EAL) and an additional learning difference. Many teachers in FE and HE are struggling to support the needs of these learners in the classroom because this area receives very little coverage on standard teaching training programmes and, thus, they tend to rely upon their own research and occasional Continuing Professional Development (CPD) sessions for information and guidance. There is much research about how to teach children who have EAL and learning differences but very little regarding adult learners.

This book intends to fill the gap on research as it is an introductory textbook for anyone who is working or training to work in either FE or HE and who wishes to develop knowledge and skills in the challenging area of supporting and teaching adult EAL learners with learning differences. It contains a fusion of theoretical discussion and practical examples and aims to develop a thorough understanding of the needs of these learners and the principles and practices of how to meet those needs within a classroom setting. The book provides a coherent framework for reflection and practice which encourages you to make connections between the various aspects of teaching and to develop a more inclusive and detailed approach to teaching and learning minority groups. Each chapter contains vital teaching tips and many exercises which can be used in your own teaching.

It can be read cover to cover or theme to theme, but it is more likely to be 'dipped' into by a variety of people involved in teaching and learning, including:

- Experienced teachers who have students who have EAL and dyslexia
- Trainee teachers who need to develop an understanding of the issues as art of their training
- Early Career Teachers (ECT) who are encountering students with these barriers for the first time

DOI: 10.4324/9781003181583-1

2 Introduction

- Experienced teachers who want to develop expertise in this area as part of their CPD
- Teacher trainers who need appropriate resources to develop their own teaching and to support their own trainees
- Teachers of EAL who need resources to help in teaching students with dyslexia
- Special Needs teachers who need resources to develop their own strategies in supporting students with dyslexia
- Special Educational Needs and/or Disabilities Coordinator (SENDCO), Learning Support Assistants and Teaching Assistants who need to investigate different ways to support students in their classrooms
- Independent trainers who provide CPD support courses during INSET days to teachers in schools and colleges

The background to the book

Who are the students?

The term generally used for our subject throughout the book is "adults who identify with the term EAL". This term carries no specific implication about the level of as an adult's proficiency in either their first language (L1) or their second (L2). The statistics from the Office for National Statistics states 20.6% of adults in the UK education system are known to speak English as an additional language (ONS, 2019). In addition, research suggests that it may affect as much as 20% of the population (Wagner et al. 2020). Considering this evidence, we can assume that a teacher is likely to be presented with an adult learning EAL with dyslexia at some point in their teaching career.

EAL students are not a homogenous group; they can include students who:

- have spent most of their lives in England and had a long history of education using English as the language of instruction
- have newly arrived in the country
- have studied English as a foreign language for varying parts of their educational career or have had no grounding in English at all.
- enter the mainstream classroom with very limited English, and are literate in their own language
- are fluent in English but speak one or more languages at home
- have had extreme difficulty acquiring literacy skills, because of their dyslexia or lack of educational opportunity.
- may not realise that they have an underlying difficulty because their first language is highly transparent
- speak English only outside the home. speak, hear, read, and access television and digital media only in their mother tongue.

(Norton and Toohey, 2011)

There is little research and guidance relating to the complexities of identifying and supporting dyslexia surrounding children with dyslexia learning EAL (Hutchinson et al., 2014; Mortimore et al., 2012). There is even less research surrounding young people and adults (Tudhope, 2014a), despite the increasing numbers of students in FE and HE. Much of the material, guidelines and recommendations that have been written about supporting EAL students with dyslexia is designed for EL teachers and teachers of students with Dyslexia (Tudhope, 2014a).

According to recent research dyslexia is thought to affect around 10% of the population, 4% severely (Wagner et al., 2020). If dyslexia is present in all language groups, then it is possible that the same percentage is true of EAL students entering FE and HE in the UK (Tudhope, 2014b).

Dyslexia cannot be clearly defined in isolation, and it can have several interconnecting issues; in many cases dyslexia is overlapped with other learning issues, like dyscalculia, dyspraxia, and ADHD. Issues with transfer between languages were noted by Geva (2016), who suggested that, in general terms, pupils who have decoding and spelling problems in their first language, such as phonemic awareness, speed of processing and visual processes, also have difficulties in their second language. Therefore, the greater the difficulties in the first language, the more challenging it may be to acquire the additional language (Schneider and Crombie, 2009). All students have a unique profile of strengths and weaknesses, and teachers need a clear understanding of these to work effectively with them and to provide support on an individual level. For example, the nature and extent of their difficulties and strengths, the particular interference and proficiency issues relating to their L1.

According to Bell and Tudhope (2016), the main indications of fluency in literacy include the following:

- Automatic identification skills of the visual features of print, letter and word, letter pattern recognition and letter identification and phonological awareness and the ability to remember a number of verbal units (L2 phonemes, morphemes, words, clauses) while reading a text.
- Knowledge of language structure, including syntax morphology and the understanding of the uses, purposes and conventions of literacy, and the generic conventions of different texts, knowledge of vocabulary and lexical memory.
- Understanding new content and being able to draw upon background knowledge and the ability to activate relevant concepts and synthesise prior knowledge.
- The ability to synthesise textual information and to evaluate it against other information and knowledge and metacognitive skills which include the ability to monitor own response to the text. For example, to recognise own problems of comprehension.

Arguably, all these elements are required both by students with dyslexia and students who have EAL but with differences in emphasis. For example, a student with dyslexia might struggle with letter identification and an EAL student might need more support with linguistic knowledge (Tudhope, 2014a).

Some of the main impacts of dyslexia on language learning and studying

According to Inoue (2018), some of the main areas of language learning which dyslexia could affect include the following:

Processing ability

Students with dyslexia tend to take time to read, respond to questions and to process information which can impact on their ability to decode text and the processing of new vocabulary, spelling, recalling, and organising information.

Metacognition

When students with dyslexia struggle with metacognition this can create problems for the development of independent learning and autonomous learning skills. By developing metacognition, they will be able to master the most effective ways of learning and be able to tailor them to meet their individual needs

Concentration span

Students with dyslexia tend to have a shorter concentration span and hence it is more difficult for them to focus for long periods. In particular, visual attention issues can impact on single word identification, and complex reading comprehension (Chen et al., 2016).

Memory

Students with dyslexia tend to have difficulties with Long-Term Memory (LTM). This can result in problems with representing, storing, processing and retrieving sounds and with visual word processing. This can affect spelling and reading. They also tend to have weak Working Memories (WM) which affects their ability to manipulate and retain information over short periods. This can have an impact on their complex reasoning, multi-tasking, organisation, recall, concentration, and general phonological learning. When students with Dyslexia have verbal Short-Term Memory issues (STM), this can affect their ability to access phonological and graphemic information which can affect their reading speeds and their vocabulary and syntactical knowledge (Majerus and Cowan, 2016).

Self-organisation

When students with dyslexia display this difficulty it can affect their verbal fluency, their letter recall and their ability to generate and execute problem-solving strategies even when given goal-directed tasks (Levin, 1990).

Self confidence

Some studies suggest that students with dyslexia often struggle with a lack of self-concept and self-esteem. This is the result of their previous educational experiences which impact on their motivation and their ability to achieve (O'Byrne et al., 2019).

Box 1.1 Some of the main challenges faced by students who have EAL and dyslexia

These could be present in the following areas:

Reading

Problems can manifest themselves in reading and understanding words, texts, and speed of reading. This can be impacted upon by possible dyslexia difficulties such as:

- The decoding and reading of individual words
- Slow speed of cognitive processing
- Ineffective visual processing
- Problems with working memory

And can also be impacted upon by possible EAL difficulties such as:

- Unfamiliar vocabulary in texts
- Unfamiliar phonics
- Lack of knowledge of language structure
- Lack of familiarity with generic conventions of the text

The reduced working memory capacity of students with SLDs could potentially impact on comprehension by limiting the number of verbal units (L2 phonemes, morphemes, words, clauses) they could recall while reading a text.

Writing

This can be evidenced in issues with spelling, sentence construction, planning, and organisation of writing, proof reading, handwriting and the speed and production of written texts and can be impacted upon by possible dyslexia difficulties such as:

- Processing speech sounds
- Phonics
- Speed of processing
- Problems with motor skills and penmanship
- Difficulties with organisation and time management
- Retrieval difficulties of using subject specialist vocabulary from working memory

And can also be impacted upon by possible EAL difficulties such as:

- Unfamiliar vocabulary
- Lack of understanding of selling conventions
- Issues with syntax and word order
- Lack of knowledge over grammatical conventions
- Difficulties with generic textual conventions

It is also worth noting that reduced phonological awareness and difficulties with rapid word naming can also lead to L2 word-decoding problems (Mortimore et al., 2012).

Oral skills

This can be seen in issues related to understanding spoken English and producing oral English and can impact on following instructions, lectures, practical classes, discussions, oral exams, communicating when on work placements. It can be impacted upon by possible dyslexia difficulties such as:

- Speed of processing and retrieval of phonological information
- Inability to concentrate for long periods
- Lapses in auditory working memory which can mean that students with dyslexia show struggle to learn new skills implicitly.
- Poor self-confidence in speaking in public
- Issues with retrieving subject specialist vocabulary from working memory

And by possible difficulties associated with EAL such as:

- Lack of understanding of language structure
- Lack of subject specialist vocabulary
- Lack of self confidence in speaking in L2
- Adjusting to a more student-centred approach to teaching and learning than they were previously used to

Academic skills

This can be evidenced in problems such as attention and focus, time management and organisation and can be impacted upon by possible dyslexia difficulties such as

- Speed of processing information, which can impact, for instance, on note taking
- Difficulties in retrieving subject specialist vocabulary from LTM which can affect comprehension
- Inability to concentrate for long periods and problems with multi-tasking which can affect assignment completion and is aligned with difficulties with organisation and time management

And by possible EAL difficulties such as:

- Adjusting to differing academic expectations such as teaching methods, level of student independence (Tudhope, 2014b)
- Difficulties in comprehending longer texts can result from either word-level reading problems or from a global language comprehension deficit).

Supporting the needs of EAL students with dyslexia

Hutchings and Mortimore (2016) reviewed literacy programmes for monolingual dyslexic children, dyslexic learners acquiring a modern second language and EAL programme materials. They prescribed a structured, reinforced, cumulative and multi-sensory programme, including: phonological processing skills, verbal memory and processing speed, oral language development, explicit strategies to develop comprehension skills and vocabulary and the teaching of morphemes.

According to NALDIC (1999), the core principles for supporting EAL students include:

- Activating prior knowledge in the pupil. Examples of this include the use of questioning, thought storming, Think Pair and Share, encouraging the use of L1 in class

- The provision of a rich contextual background to make the input comprehensible. This can be achieved through the use of relevant visuals and graphic organisers which summarise information but also structure it within a context.
- Students should be encouraged to use the widest variety of different forms of oral and written communication such as via peer teaching, questioning, group reading, collaborative learning, oral feedback and scaffolding. Whilst drawing the students' attention to the relationship between form and function; key grammatical elements should be pointed out and made explicit. Students should also be supported to understand forms, functions and structures of language via modelling, genre analysis, comprehension and critical analysis of texts exercises

---

Box 1.2 Developing learner independence

Teaching strategies

Students should be encouraged to be more self-reliant and autonomous in their approach to studying by developing their skills in comprehension, research, note taking, Dictogloss and small group work. Other researchers have suggested a series of approaches, which include:

- Utilising the main principles of the Universal Design of Learning as a set of underpinning principles to planning.
- Using a multi-sensory teaching approach and organising learning to meet the varied learning preferences of the students and drawing upon the students' prior knowledge of subjects and their specific social and cultural understanding to develop group inclusion.
- Developing over learning and structured approaches to recapping within a framework of cumulative and sequential teaching.
- Incorporating previous ways of learning into current teaching methods to help the transition of some students from teacher-centred to learner-centred approaches and scaffolding learning to enable all students to develop their individual potential.
- Using a range of differentiated questioning techniques to develop orality and to stretch and challenge more capable students, but also reducing the learning load of the student by breaking down the content into bite-sized segments and working towards the atomisation of teaching content.
- Being mindful of the overtaxing of attention as writing in a second language demands a high level of composting and linguistic encoding processes and contextualising using examples so that it is relevant and meaningful.

- Exposing students to a range of comprehension texts in order to develop their lower-level decoding skills but also developing skills in critical analysis and deconstruction of texts and using peer teaching and peer assessment to develop collaborative skills.
- Using different methods to make language skills more automatic, especially the use of vocabulary and subject specialist vocabulary and culturally appropriate materials to create a more diverse learning environment, prioritising the accuracy of written and oral communication.
- Helping students to develop independent study skills such as note taking and note making, comprehension and academic writing and utilising small group work to develop self-regulating learning within a range of metalinguistic approaches to teaching including translanguaging.
- Using varied teaching methods to raise levels of self-confidence and locus of control including using technology in a variety of different forms to provide differentiating support and to develop visual creativity and creating problem solving opportunities for students to develop metacognition.
- Building upon some of the cognitive and linguistic advantages associated with bilingual and multilingual students such as the following, cognitive control and supervisory attentional system, problem solving and creative thinking, metalinguistic awareness, and conceptual transfer (Bialystok, 2001; Kormos and Smith, 2012; O'Byrne et al., 2019; Peer and Reid, 2016; Tudhope, 2014b).

Inclusive teaching and the Universal Design for Learning (UDL)

The Universal Design for Learning is a framework based on a series of differentiation principles that aims to provide all learners with equal opportunities to learn, regardless of their diverse needs. It is intended to provide a blueprint for the curriculum design based on the learners' requirements (Meyer et al., 2013). It has been a key influence for me on the design and the selection of many of the strategies selected in the book. There are three main overriding principles that suggest that inclusive teaching should provide the following: Multiple means of engagement; multiple means of representation; and multiple means of action and expression.

Multiple means of engagement

The teacher should:

- Provide options for self-regulation, including promoting motivational expectations, facilitating coping skills and developing and supporting self-assessment and reflection

- Provide options for sustaining effort and persistence, including the understanding of goals, varying challenges and demands, promoting collaboration and increasing mastery-orientated feedback and for promoting different levels of interest, including optimising autonomy, learning relevance and value.

This could be achieved by some of the following:

- providing learners with as much discretion and autonomy as possible by providing choices in such things as: the level of perceived challenge; the type of rewards or recognition available; the context or content used for practicing and assessing skills; the tools used for information gathering or production; and the colour, design, of graphics or layouts, etc.
- varying the learning activities and sources of information so that they can be more personalised and contextualised to reflect the lives of the students and also culturally, ethnically, and socially relevant.

Multiple means of representation

The teacher should:

- Provide varying options for comprehension, including background knowledge, critical features, guiding the processing of information and visualisation.
- Provide options for language, mathematical expressions, and symbols through the classifying of language, syntax and structure, the decoding of text and mathematical symbols, and the development of understanding across languages using multiple media and options for perception, including customising informational displays and visual and auditory alternatives.

This could be done through

- using different audio-visual media such as text, speech, drawing, illustration, comics, storyboards, design, film, music, dance/movement, visual art, sculpture, or video and combining different media to support each other to produce clearer understanding e.g. an expository text with an animation.
- using audio feedback rather than text whenever possible, or using captions or voice recognition software as an alternative to spoken language.
- providing visual diagrams, charts and tables, written transcripts for videos or auditory clips, British Sign Language for spoken English if needed and using visual analogues to represent emphasis and prosody (e.g., emoticons, symbols, or images).
- designing visual and/or emotional description for musical interpretation and descriptions (text or spoken) for all images, graphics, video, or

animations, illustrating points with more graphics and less text and modifying material so that it can embed support for vocabulary and symbols within the text (e.g., hyperlinks or footnotes to definitions, explanations, illustrations, previous coverage, translations).

Multiple means of action and expression

The teacher should:

- Provide options for the development of executive functions including individual goal setting, supporting the planning of self-development and self-monitoring of progress and options or expression and communication including multiple design media and communication to support practice and performance with options for physical action include varying methods for response and navigation, tools and assistive technologies.

This can be achieved by doing some of the following:

- showing students how to solve problems using a variety of strategies and using a range of different scaffolding techniques (both offline and online) and providing digital alternatives to non-digital activities, including non-text-based options such as presentations or seminars for formative assessment for those who struggle with literacy.
- providing differentiated models of teaching, learning, and resources and differentiated feedback on a variety of different bases such as face to face, online, written, audio and differentiated mentors (including peers) to deliver individual support.
- encouraging understanding across languages by: writing all key information in the dominant language and making it also available in first languages of the student groups; linking key vocabulary words to definitions and pronunciations in both dominant and home languages; breaking down specialist vocabulary using both specialist and non-specialist terms; and promoting the use of multi-lingual translation tools which are both web-based and print-based.

The major teaching and learning themes of the book

Some of the major areas covered in the book include:

- Using a variety of different teaching strategies to appeal to a variety of learning preferences
- Replacing text-based activities with alternatives whenever possible
- The importance of developing metacognition
- The role of peer teaching and peer assessment
- The significance of Self-Regulated Learning

- Prioritising different and diverse forms of assessment in the classroom
- Using a range of different technologies
- The importance of developing academic skills

The main structure of the book

The book is structured into four areas: Teaching and Learning, Assessment and Feedback, Differentiation and Academic Skills. Each area is superficially stand alone in content; in reality, however, each cross over because teaching and learning never exist in isolation. Each chapter is prefaced by an individual contents page listing the strategies available in each chapter. I have tried to provide in each chapter practical examples of teaching strategies drawn from literature and also designed by colleagues and former PGCE students and advice and some of the theory underpinning them.

I have also tried to include templates that can be used or adapted and examples of these that have been used already in a classroom setting. I chose many of my own favourite strategies and those which have been recommended by friends and colleagues but obviously cannot guarantee that they will be effective for every student in every classroom. I have also included quotations from interviews taken by me from experienced and enthusiastic teachers discussing their own good practices because I believe that I can always learn from other people. This book is less an arsenal of magic teaching bullets and more a box of tools that can help to find answers to individual problems.

The final chapter of the book is dedicated to the development of a range of academic skills including note taking, critical reading, summarising, and research skills. It is intended, to some extent, to bring together many of the teaching strategies mentioned in the previous chapters and to focus them onto a single area of learning that has proved particularly problematic for students who have EAL and dyslexia. It contains specific strategies and suggestions drawn mainly from my own experiences in embedding academic skills in my own classes.

The book as a toolbox

The book is a teaching toolkit which should be seen a collection of authoritative and adaptable resources for teaching professionals that enables you to learn about an issue and identify approaches for addressing them. Toolkits can help translate theory into practice, and typically target one issue or one audience. Arguably, this book, like all good toolkits, should be open and flexible. It should enable, not constrain your ideas and provide a basis for your own professional development. The main premise of the book is to offer practical advice and guidance regarding pedagogical issues of concern or importance, especially when the issue is emerging or evolving, and well-established processes for addressing them are not yet widely adopted.

It should help individual classroom teachers and also to facilitate widespread adoption of a particular best practice or concept across the profession so that learners are better served. The intention behind the book is not to reinvent the wheel. It does not want to recreate the wheel, but instead wants to create tools that support resources you already use in class and fills in gaps in what's available.

All the content within the book has been selected using the following criteria: relevancy, currency, reliability/authoritative, evidence-based, easy to understand and adaptability. The book draws upon neuroscience, psychology and sociology and provides an overview of evidence-based innovations in teaching and presents over 50 different teaching strategies techniques for all subjects at FE level with many practical ideas for developing independent learning skills, improving critical reading, and writing and promoting the use of learning technology. It also presents ideas and teaching resources for enhancing your approaches in areas such as assessment, feedback and managing group work activities.

In order to allow focus on individual areas that you might need some guidance upon, the book has been broken down into nine central areas of teaching learners who have EAL and who have literacy difficulties: independent learning skills; critical reading and writing; assessment (both peer and self-assessment); assistive technology; academic writing; and reading comprehension. Many of the sections contain templates to be used in teaching activities and some provide detailed breakdowns of teaching tasks. Many of these you may already be aware of. You are encouraged to build on these and to adapt them to meet the needs of your own students.

The book is based upon the key notion that the quality of teaching and learning improves most readily when practice and theory inform each other. We need to know why things work, or do not and it is helpful to have principles to guide the design of lessons; and to know how students learn so we don't always operate unthinkingly from expediency or unquestioningly from policy directive. So, it could also be helpful for your own professional development to use the theoretical discussions in the chapters as a foundation for further research.

Box 1.3 Over to you!

Write a short reflective note to yourself answering the following three questions:
How many students in your class have English as an Additional Language?
How many have dyslexia?
How many fit both categories?
Do you differentiate effectively for both needs in your lesson planning?

References

Bell, S., and Tudhope, E. (2016). Theory and practice in the support of young people and adults with English as an additional language and dyslexia in further and higher education. In L. Peer, and G. Reid (Eds.), *Multilingualism, Literacy and Dyslexia* (pp. 148–164). London: Routledge.

Bialystok, E. (2001). *Bilingualism in Development: Language, Literacy, and Cognition.* Cambridge: Cambridge University Press.

Chen, C., Schneps, M. H., Masyn, K. E., and Thomson, J. M. (November 2016). The effects of visual attention span and phonological decoding in reading comprehension in dyslexia: A path analysis. *Dyslexia*, 22(4), 322–344. DOI: 10.1002/dys.1543. Epub 2016 Oct 14. PMID: 27739162.

Cline, T., and Shamsi, T. (2000). Language needs or special needs? The assessment of learning difficulties in literacy among children learning English as an additional language: A literature review. DFE special report.

Elden, M., & Levin, M. (1991). Cogenerative learning. Bringing participation interaction research. In W. F. Whyte (Ed.), *Participatory Action Research* (pp. 127–142). Newbury Park, CA: Sage Publications.

Geva, E. (2016). Second-language oral proficiency and second-language literacy. In D. August, and T. Shanahan (Eds.), *Developing Literacy in Second-Language Learners: Report of the National Literacy Panel on Language-Minority Children and Youth* (pp. 123–139). New York: Lawrence Erlbaum Associates Publishers.

Hutchings, M., and Mortimore, T. (2016). Lessons from the dyslexia and multilinguist project. In L. Peer, and G. Reid (Eds.), *Multilingualism, Literacy and Dyslexia* (pp. 124–137). London: Routledge.

Hutchinson, J., Whitely, H., Smith, C., and Connors, L. (2014). The early identification of dyslexia: Children with English as an additional language. *Dyslexia*, 10, 179–195.

Inoue, L. (2018). Looking at dyslexia from a second language point of view. Unpublished MA Thesis.

Kormos, J., and Smith, A. M. (2012). *Teaching languages to students with specific learning differences.* Bristol: Multilingual Matters. London: Routledge.

Majerus, S., and Cowan, N. (October 2016). The nature of verbal short-term impairment in dyslexia: The importance of serial order. *Frontiers in Psychology*, 7(1522), 3. DOI: 10.3389/fpsyg.2016.01522.

Meyer, A., Rose, D., and Gordon, D. (2013). *Universal design for learning: Theory and practice.* 1st edition (17 December 2013). Wakefield, MA: Cast incorporated.

Mortimore, T., Hansen, L., Hutchings, M., and Northcote, A. (2012). Dyslexia and multilingualism: Identifying and supporting learners who might be at risk of developing SpLD/dyslexia. Available at: http://www.bdadyslexia.org.uk/common/ckeditor/filemanager/userfiles/About_Us/Projects/Big_Lottery_Research_Report_Final_Version.pdf. Accessed: 24 March 2016.

National Association For Language development in the Curriculum (NALDIC) Working Paper 5: The Distinctiveness of EAL: A Cross-Curriculum Discipline. (1999). Watford: NALDIC.

Norton, B., and Toohey, K. (2011). Identity, Language Learning, and Social Change. *Language Teaching*, 44, 412–446. DOI: 10.1017/S0261444811000309

O'Byrne, C., Jagoe, C., and Lawler, M. (2019). Experiences of dyslexia and the transition to university: A case study of five students at different stages of study. *Higher Education Research & Development*, 38(5), 1031–1045. DOI: 10.1080/07294360.2019.1602595

Office of National Statistics (ONS). (2019). Available at: https://www.ons.gov.uk/peoplepopulationandcommunity/culturalidentity/language.

Peer, L., and Reid, G. (Eds.) (2016). *Multilingualism, Literacy and Dyslexia*. London: Routledge.

Schneider, E., and Crombie, M. (2009). *Dyslexia and Foreign Language Learning*. London: David Fulton Publishers.

Tudhope, E. (Summer 2014a). How can dyslexia negatively impact upon acquiring English as an additional language and what can dyslexia/SpLD tutors do to address these issues? *PATOSS*, 7(1), 7–19.

Tudhope, E. (April 2014b). *Identifying Dyslexia in International Students for Whom English Is an Additional Language*. InForm, Issue 13. University of Reading.

Wagner, R. Zirps, F. A., Ashley A., Edwards, A. A., Wood, S. G., Joyner, R. E., Becker, B. J., Liu, G., and Beal. B. (2020). The prevalence of dyslexia: A new approach to its estimation, *Journal of Learning Disability*. 53(5), 354–365. DOI: 10.1177/0022219420920377

2 Independent learning skills

Developing independent learning skills is central for all students, including those who have EAL and dyslexia, so that they can become confident in organising their own learning, studying what they want or need to study in order to achieve their long-term goals and work independently with confidence. These can be developed using many different strategies. In this chapter I want to highlight the following:

- Pre-reading
- Accelerated Cognition (AC)
- Building self-confidence
- Thinking Aloud
- Dialogic Teaching
- Anchor Charts

Pre-reading

Pre-reading is the activation of students' prior knowledge before they start reading a text. It helps them to connect what they already know with the new information. Although the majority of research regarding its effectiveness has been conducted at primary and early secondary level, it has been used effectively with older EAL students and those who struggle with literacy (Al Rasheed, 2014).

Pre-reading can have a variety of benefits. It can develop a greater comprehension of the text and build vocabulary and the meaning of the vocabulary. It can help develop more fluent and faster reading via using skills in skimming and scanning texts more efficiently. It can develop knowledge of the generic conventions of different types of text and students uncover gaps in their own understanding. It can develop the skills of self-regulation in students, building self confidence in reading and comprehension. It can improve skills in collaborative learning, peer teaching and peer support (Topping and Bryce, 2004). It can also enable students to learn how to connect their prior knowledge to new knowledge to produce a deeper understanding of concepts (Marinaccio, 2012; Lailiyah et al. 2019).

DOI: 10.4324/9781003181583-2

There are many ways in which pre-reading can be used in class. These include:

Identifying the textual features

Teachers can model the key features of the text and students could complete a rubric where they have to identify the features before they start reading.

Think Pair, Share (TPS)

In pairs students think pair and share their ideas about the text to the whole class before they start reading.

Fishbowling

After teacher models how to deconstruct the text, the students collaborate and in small groups replicate the deconstruction.

List, label, group

This has three stages: List – During this stage, the students should thought shower all the topic words they know associated with the text. Group – they should arrange words in subcategories. Label – they should then choose a label or a title for each group.

Mind mapping

Students skim the text for overall meaning and then scan for detailed concepts and draw up a mind map of the text. They then read the text in detail.

Concept mapping

Students mind map their prior learning and then add extra material to it as they read the text. When they have finished, they swop it with another student who adds to it.

Quotations

The teacher reads selected quotes form the text and the students discuss the implications of them in small groups and then are given the full text to read.

Know, Would like to Know and Learned charts (KWL)

Students complete these in three stages. In the first stage, they list what they already know about the subject of the text. In the second, they list what they would like to know more about and then, after having read the text, they analyse what they have learned.

True or false

The teacher chooses a series of contentious statements from the text and asks a series of 'True' or 'False' questions to the group. They are not given the correct answers. The group then have to read the text and discover what they have answered correctly.

First paragraphs

Ask the group to read the opening paragraph of the text and then to discuss what they anticipate being its key arguments.

Listen, read and discuss

During the **listen** stage – students take notes from a teacher's presentation using a graphic organiser of the main themes of text. Then they **read** the text and supplement their notes with extra material. Finally, they **discuss** their notes, either with the whole group or in smaller groups.

Box 2.1 An example of pre-reading used in a GCSE History class

Teaching example

All my students struggle with accessing information directly from texts so I decided to use a constructing sentences pre-reading approach. I read out key ideas from a text about the English Civil War and asked my students in groups to prepare a mind map of all the ideas that they associated with it, such as Royalist, Parliamentarians, New Model Army. They were then asked to define the words and create sentences and paragraphs using them. Once they were finished, they were allowed to read the text and compare the text with their sentences. They could amend their content if necessary and then feed back to the whole class.

(Angela, History Teacher)

Overlearning

Overlearning is basically the use of a range of teaching approaches to change long-term memory by teaching the same range of skills and ideas in different situations with the ultimate aim of repeating the task so that almost no thought is required in its completion (Christodoulou, 2017). Arguably, long-term performance increases in line with the amount of overlearning during targeted practice which can mean better retention and performance. Rohrer et al. (2005) argued that that overlearning needed to include deliberate practice, activity directed specifically to enhance performance and the development of mental representations of success to be effective. Driskell et al. (1992) suggested that it was most effective when teaching cognitive tasks, but that its impact decreased over time.

There are several benefits to overlearning. It can help to make specific learning activities automatic and develop skills in new areas, confidence in performance and improve recall over a short period.

How to use overlearning as part of teaching

Overlearning can be used as part of a package of multi-sensory activities to provide enough repetition for automaticity to be reached using such tasks as:

- Quizzes and tests, both online and offline
- Card matching concept tasks
- Wordsearches
- Crosswords
- Scrambled sentence activities
- Cloze exercises
- Building glossaries and then using them as the basis for revision quizzes
- Starters designed to test recall of previous sessions
- Using homework to test recall of work completed in class
- Practice timed essays for examination revision
- Small group Think Alouds to reinforce learning of concepts

Multi-sensory teaching

Multi-sensory teaching techniques and strategies stimulate learning by engaging students on multiple levels. It was originally developed specifically for teaching primary reading and spelling but is now used in a variety of teaching subjects and at different levels to support students who struggle with literacy and to develop critical thinking and advanced comprehension skills. Multi-sensory strategies encourage students to use some or all their senses. It can enable students to consolidate information about an activity or task, linking information and concepts to previous knowledge and enabling them to evaluate relationships between concepts and also to synthesise ideas and apply them in different contexts. They can also solve problem-solving tasks using a variety of skills and deconstruct the logic involved in solving problems, ultimately developing more effective non-verbal reasoning skills which are essential for those learners who have barriers with literacy.

Among the teaching techniques used to provide multi-sensory teaching are:

- Using audio-visual devices to create a more holistic stimulus. For example, record an audio track on PowerPoint slides so students can refer back to the lesson at their own leisure and ask students to create presentations, or videos as research exercises

- Using interactive game and puzzles as starters or as formative assessment methods
- Introducing realia into the classroom to make learning more concrete and encourage students to produce concrete examples of texts that they can use for their own studying such as posters and handbooks or use scenarios and case studies as the basis for role playing or dramatisation activities and organise relevant visits or field trips to locate learning
- Developing the use of graphic organisers to provide visual stimulation and promote the use of visual note taking to reduce writing stress and Think Alouds to prompt communication and self-reflection
- Promoting the use of paired reading and literacy circles to develop confidence in reading and criticality and initiate small-group and whole-group discussions as advance organisers

Accelerated Cognition (AC)

AC (aka Cognitive Acceleration through Science Education (CASE) originated via the work of Piaget (1975) and Vygotsky (1978) and focusses on the development of cognition which, it argues, is the result of an interaction between internal and external dynamic factors and social context. Its aim is to increase students' semi-abstract and abstract thinking by designing specific interventions which challenge thinking, develop social construction and understanding and increase metacognition.

According to Adey and Shayer (2007), the teacher is a mediator; if learners given a challenge without preparation, they will fail. If a teacher gives the answers, learners may remember the facts. If learners develop the answers themselves, they will understand the learning and if they are then asked to discuss how they could apply the thinking process they have just undertaken to other areas, they have truly learned. This finding is based on the principle that learners should persist with the learning of a particular area only until they have reached mastery of it.

Embedded across all five stages of AC are goal setting and planning, self-monitoring and self-control and self-evaluation and reflection. There are five stages to Accelerated Cognition.

The five stages of AC

Concrete preparation

Students need initial introduction to any intellectual problem they face as they need to recognise the context of the problem and some vocabularies to discuss it. Therefore, the first stage in Cognitive Acceleration is designed to involve students in the task.

Cognitive conflict

The theory suggests that these processes work as follows. Students mentally compare new situations with prior experiences. They construct expectations of what may happen when they act in these new situations. They comfortably assimilate observations when these are consistent with expectations, but where there are inconsistencies and contradictions, there is a perturbation, or 'cognitive conflict' (Piaget, 1975). This may produce an emotional response of disappointment, surprise or anxiety. The need to reduce such 'dis-equilibration' is a basic, powerful human motivator that may lead the student to revisit and review characteristics of the situation in order to analyse the cause of the inconsistencies. The initial situation is thus observed more intently.

Social construction

The emphasis in AC is on working in groups, with no more than four students per group. Cognitive Acceleration also adheres to the other core instructional practices of using prompting questions and modelling (which is done by peers in this case). It is vital that the problem or cognitive conflict the students are attempting to solve is achievable with support and guidance. This can be done most effectively via the use of open questions and providing more thinking time for the learners.

Metacognition

Students develop awareness of their own thinking and through developing vocabularies which are crucial in describing the different tools of thinking by discussion amongst themselves (Baratta, 2020).

Bridging

Students are encouraged therefore to contextualise their learning and to apply it to their everyday lives and to other forms of learning beyond their classrooms in a wide range of new contexts which serve to develop the new ideas.

Box 2.2 A case study of AC used in an A Level Psychology class

Case study

At the start of the session the teacher probed the prior knowledge of the learners with a series of open questions about the psychodynamic school of Psychology to contextualise the new learning as 'concrete preparation'. The students were taught nothing new; nor were they even made aware of some of their gaps in understanding. The aim of the starter was to make them aware of their own intuitive interpretations and methods. The learners were then sent to the library to specifically investigate the work of psychodynamic counsellors Karen Horney and Alice Millar.

When the groups returned after an hour, the teacher initially gave them feedback in to provoke and create 'cognitive conflicts' as they began to realise and confront the inconsistencies in their own interpretations and methods. Students were asked to make notes and reflect in their individual groups. The teacher then asked students to compare their responses with those made by other students by asking them to present their findings to the group and peer-assessing their conclusions. The students were given time to write down questions to pose to their peers before the presentations started. This led to conflict and debate amongst the whole class as the groups were encouraged to articulate conflicting points of view and reformulate their own opinions about the two theorists' work in a process of 'social construction'.

Students were then given new areas to research and extra reading to expand their understanding of the issues and another opportunity to consolidate their metacognition and to reflect on their own contributions through small-group discussion Quigley et al. (2013). The teacher facilitated the new discussions and challenged their ideas.

Students were given new questions to research and extra reading to expand their understanding of the issue. The presentations were also uploaded onto the virtual learning environment (VLE) for the student groups to access them later in order to develop their independent learning. The teacher also obtained from the group a list of new terminology which had arisen during the session; this was also uploaded as part of an ongoing online glossary. To conclude the session, the teacher set them homework to apply Horney and Walker's theories of parenting and childhood to the lives of three famous people so as to 'bridge' their learning.

Building self-confidence

Creating an inclusive and welcoming learning environment can help build EAL students' self-confidence and allow them to develop an internal Locus of Control (LOC) in which they feel that they own their learning. According to Kane Lewis et al. (1989), these are some of the key underpinning practices and practices:

Activating students' prior knowledge

This will enable teachers to plan classes more effectively and support those who may be struggling. Use small-group work, mind mapping and self-reflective tasks to produce the information (Trehan, 2014).

Providing a rich contextual background to make the input comprehensible

This is vital to make the unfamiliar more familiar for EAL students. This can be done most effectively through the use of graphic organisers and visual activities which can be linked to first language and home culture.

Actively encouraging discussion

This will help students in their cognitive and their linguistic development which should help to improve their self-confidence and their feeling of belonging in the class. This could be done through a variety of activities: small-group work, role play, debates, and group presentations.

Drawing the learner's attention to the relationship between form and function

By encouraging students to deconstruct the structures, forms, and functions of the language, this can provide opportunities for translanguaging, which will help students develop their mastery of new subject specialist vocabulary. This can be done by the use of an electronic thesaurus, building word banks, comprehension passage activities.

Developing learner independence

Independence and self-confidence often operate as self-supporting concepts in the classroom. Teachers need to develop strategies that provide opportunities for students to become more self-directed and autonomous as learners. Teachers can develop these skills through providing tasks which develop academic skills, such as note taking, summarising and essay planning.

Praise and acknowledge accomplishments

Use the praise sandwich in feedback, whether in groups or individually, to ensure that students draw encouragement from it. Use peer feedback to help reinforce confidence in students.

Embrace a growth mindset

Dweck (1986) and Molden and Dweck (2006) argue that confidence and academic achievement is related to how students view their own capabilities (e.g., intelligence), and whether they view these capabilities as fixed or flexible. Students that believe the latter tend to be more self-assured, more flexible, and more resilient in their studies. There are many ways in which a growth mindset can be developed:

Conduct activities that give students the chance to practice phrases that promote growth mindset

For example, students could complete an anchor chart of phrases that motivate or complete a contrasting card game where they have to group phrases as either Fixed mindset words or Flexible mindset words.

Display visible reminders of growth mindset vocabulary using inspirational posters and bulletin boards

Display motivational posters either on classroom walls or as screen savers on classroom PCs or laptops, or have students design their own using their own role models. This could also be embedded in the lesson by using relevant case studies of individuals who have overcome obstacles to succeed.

Have students turn in growth mindset exit tickets

Growth mindset exit tickets could be issued at the end of every session in which students need to reflect briefly on what they have achieved in each session. This could also help them to formulate targets for the next session.

When giving feedback to students, use prompts that facilitate a growth mindset

Ask students questions about how and why they did something and prompt them into self-evaluation rather than feedback on the strengths and weaknesses of the work itself. This will develop their own understanding of how they find solutions and refine their self-talk strategies.

Model growth mindset as an educator

Teachers can use their own experiences to encourage students how to think through situations using a more expensive mindset. This could be done as a starter involving small group discussions and collective problem solving (Mills and Alexander, 2013).

Develop a community of practice approach to learning

Students who may feel isolated because of linguistic barriers will benefit from a collaborative and inclusive approach to teaching. For example, teaching could centre on small-group activities where knowledge is acquired, shared, and then applied and evaluated as practices by the students.

Create realistic individual expectations

During tutorials individual targets should be set by negotiation with the student based on their past performances and their current aspirations and ideally expressed as SMART targets.

Use scaffolding strategically

According to Jumaat and Tasir (2014), there are four main types of scaffolding. Firstly, there is Procedural scaffolding, which helps students use the tools available to them. Secondly, Conceptual scaffolding, which helps students prioritise the key concepts of their learning. Thirdly, there is Metacognitive scaffolding, which guides students in the thinking process and helps them self-assess during learning. Finally, there is Strategic scaffolding, which suggests alternative ways for students to tackle the learning problems they encounter. All four methods can be used effectively in tandem, but it is the latter with its emphasis on finding alternative solutions which is arguably the most powerful in developing autonomy and self-confidence in learning.

Develop buddy systems in the class

Pairing students who struggle with confidence issues with a More Knowledgeable Other (MKO). This can have various benefits for learners. It can help the students to feel valued and supported, teach important leadership skills to both parties, reduce feelings of isolation, and create greater social integration and provide opportunities for peer tutoring. It can also enable EAL students to develop second language skills via one-to-one peer discussions and help to erode language barriers and develop responsibility for learning (Thurston and Cockerill, 2016).

Building Locus of Control

The theory behind Locus of Control (LOC) dates to the 1950s. LOC is a personality dimension that is said to help to explain an individual's traits and behaviour. It refers directly to an individual's belief about whether their successes or failures are the result of their efforts or due to external factors (Rotter, 1966). Individuals with an internal LOC would tend to believe the former; those with an external LOC, the latter.

Although it has been suggested that individuals can switch from one stance to the other depending on the circumstances and that there is not one right LOC set of beliefs, some studies suggest that students with an internal LOC achieve greater than those with an external LOC for several reasons (Tyler et al., 2020; Nowicki and Duke, 2017; Hill, 2016).

Students with internal LOC tend to be more proactive and effective during the learning process and more self-reliant and independent in their approach to study. They tend to be better at problem-solving, setting their own SMART targets autonomously and developing their own means to achieve them. Furthermore, because they attribute success to internal factors, they are more likely to expect future success. They are flexible learners and can adapt their learning preferences to different conditions. Whereas students with an external LOC tend to be less proactive and less effective in class, more dependent on the teacher's direction and struggle with setting SMART targets; they need direction to achieve them. They are more likely to attribute failure to external successes and hence more likely to expect future failure since they are more rigid in their learning preferences and struggle to adapt them to different circumstances (Nowicki and Duke, 2017).

Some research seems to indicate that students who have a learning disability tend to develop an external LOC partly because of their previous learning experiences and, in addition, that when they develop an internal LOC, it is programming for failure rather than for success. These students tend to believe that the failure they encounter is a result of their own behaviour, while the success they may experience is due to chance or the action of others (Hill, 2016; Nowicki and Duke, 2017).

Developing Locus of Control in students

There are many strategies that can be used to develop a sense of ownership of learning in students. These include:

Varying learning contexts

Because students with external LOC tend to prefer more structured and supportive classes and students with internal LOC the opposite, teachers might vary the context of learning to ensure that all their needs are being met.

Strengthening internal Locus of Control

Encourage students to believe they have more control over their education and academic achievement. A common method is known as Attributional Retraining (AR), which is designed to enhance motivation and encourage achievement by changing how students think about their academic successes and failures so that their beliefs work for, rather than against, their chances for academic success. Some practical examples of using AR as a strategy include:

Self-reflection

Encourage students to evaluate their strengths and weaknesses as a learner by analysing the feedback given in each assignment and then to focus their energies on overcoming the weaknesses by setting learning targets.

Role play

Write role play scenarios which can be used to show students how to cope with poor performance in tasks and how to move on from it. Alternatively, students could write their own scenarios based on their own experiences and act them out in front of the class.

Teacher modelling

Teachers could draw from their own experience and tell the class how they have had to overcome struggles in their own academic road.

Student modelling

Asking former students, who have completed the course and gone on to bigger and better things, to discuss their own academic triumphs and failures with current students can be very motivating and inspiring.

Develop independent mindset

Alternate classroom activities and homework tasks between individual and group work to build a flexible approach to studying and to develop self-confidence.

Encourage students to internalise positive messages

Teachers could provide students with a positive affirmation each session to discussion as a starter and then to note down in their books. Students could also be encouraged to find positive statements online and to tweet them to each other as part of peer support culture in the class.

Feeding back on teachers' feedback

As part of the formative and summative feedback process, provide students with the opportunity to feed back on the feedback they have been given. This will give teachers an insight into how the feedback has been understood and how it has impacted on the way that the student sees the strengths and the weaknesses of their own learning and also those areas in which they believe they need further support.

Box 2.3 A teaching example of how to develop LOC in students

I taught a group of adult learners on an Access course in Childcare. The majority of the group had been in the UK under five years and over half of the group had literacy difficulties. They were all desperate

> to succeed because they had all made applications to go onto to university but were all very anxious about their forthcoming examinations because for many of them it was the first time they had to do examination for many years. Several weeks before the exams I invited several former students from the programme to come on several occasions and speak to the group about their own struggles and experiences on the programme and how they were now succeeding in university and at work. The students then were encouraged to make individual action plans based on the discussions with the former students and to set revision targets for themselves. This seemed to do the trick as all the group passed and during feedback to me many of them commented upon how they were motivated by the sessions with the former students.
>
> (Samantha, Childcare Teacher)

Self-questioning

Self-questioning is built on the early work of Wong (1985), who investigated reading techniques amongst primary school children but has since been applied in different learning contexts and to develop independent reading and analytical skills in older students, especially those who have EAL and dyslexia (Wray, 2003).

It is based on a self-questioning procedure that needs to accompany the reading process which aims to promote an enhanced awareness of the learning process and to develop students' abilities to monitor their comprehension and to isolate gaps in their understanding.

According to King (1992) self-questioning functions most effectively when it follows a three-stage cycle. Firstly, the student focusses upon the major concepts of the text. Secondly, they analyse the content of the text using their prior knowledge and, finally, to evaluate their learning during the self-questioning and answering process.

Some research recommends that students need to receive training in this process if it is to be effective (Ogle, 1986). One way that it can be modelled is if the teacher reads aloud and asks their own questions about a short section of the text and then gives the students' time to answer them. The teacher moves onto to the next short segment of the text; on this occasion, however, students ask the questions. The teacher and students continue through the text, taking turns asking questions and making sure to model questions that move through the various levels of Bloom's taxonomy.

The type of questions that need to be modelled include the following:

What does the author mean here?
What is the definition of this word?
Am I following the author's argument?
If not, why not? What am I not understanding?

Are the arguments in a logical order?
Why do I agree/disagree with these arguments?
Does what the author say compare with what I have read about the same subject?
Which sections of the text can I use in my assignment?
If I looked at his evidence in a different way, would I have come up with similar conclusions?

Thinking aloud

Thinking aloud has been combined with verbalising, suggesting that students benefit in several ways. They are better able to summarise information and develop responsibility for learning and more critical and thoughtful in their information processing. They ensure they have understood each section before jumping ahead to the next and, therefore, they are less impulsive in jumping to critical conclusions. They tend to monitor their comprehension while reading more thoughtfully and are more mindful about detecting errors in the text and leaps in argument.

Bereiter and Bird (1985) analysed protocols of adults' think alouds during reading and identified four strategies:

- restatement (paraphrasing and summarising),
- backtracking (looking back and re-reading),
- demanding relationships (self-questioning and inferring unstated information),
- problem formulation (hypothesising and predicting). There are two types of think alouds: concurrent and retrospective think aloud.

Concurrent

The former is elicited while a learning task is being performed. The participant typically either voices aloud thoughts, feelings, and reasoning as the primary learning activity is going on, or stops the primary task every now and then, usually at the prompt of a visual, acoustic or semantic reminder, so that s/he can tell the researcher what has been going on in his/her mind.

Retrospective or reflective think aloud

Retrospective think aloud happens at the end of a learning task and is meant to collect the participants' thinking and reasoning processes while they are still in the short-term memory of the learner.

The process

Choose a textbook that is grade-level-appropriate for the topic of study.
Preview reading material to find any unfamiliar vocabulary or parts in the story that can confuse students.

Give background knowledge on the topic at hand. Then take a book walk (flipping through the pages) to look at illustrations and nonfiction features.

While reading, pause and make comments about what you are thinking in order to clarify for students how comprehension is taking place.

Verbalise predictions, confusing parts, or connections with prior knowledge to help show comprehension of the text (to lead students to make predictions).

Close the lesson with a strong connection to the book, or short review of the purpose of the session.

Box 2.4 Using a think aloud in a fashion class

Teaching example

I have a large number of students with statemented literacy issues and who are multi-lingual, and I have found that using think aloud is an effective way of briefing them about their assignments. I provide my students with a copy of the learning outcomes of the module and the indicative content when they are given the assignment brief. Then I give them 20 minutes in pairs to discuss how they are going to meet the learning outcomes in their assignment drawing from the indicative content and any areas or terminology they are unfamiliar with. The pairs feed back to the group and as a class we discuss their problems collectively and then I provide them with previous students' work. I take a section from one essay and model my thinking out aloud of how I think the student has approached the learning outcomes and how I feel they could have been done better. I highlight any new vocabulary and define any new terms. The students are then given time to think out their own model answers and how to meet the learning outcomes themselves in their pairs. This allows students to focus both on process and product at the same time and to develop their understanding of what is expected of them in the assignment. Finally, we discuss their deliberations as a group.

(Karin, Fashion Lecturer)

In this study, students write about the task first and recognise their problems in writing then models are introduced, and students try to solve their writing problems by studying a model essay and thinking aloud about what they notice. In this case, process and product are focused on the same time.

Verbalising can often be found at the centre of thinking aloud and is often also discussed as an effective means of self-teaching (Wong, 1985). This can be problematic for students who have EAL, depending upon the level of English spoken. Many students with dyslexia also find it difficult to sequence words to verbalise their thoughts because of their struggles with phonological processing (Snowling, 1995).

Verbalising could help learners in in various ways. It could enhance their motivation and focus on intrinsic goals. It could operate as a form of self-instruction and direct their attention towards the task and minimise distraction. It could prompt self-reflection and enable students to evaluate their own understanding and operate as a tool of self-positive reinforcement and feedback to be used when the student is struggling with reading a text.

Box 2.5 Using recorded comments as the basis for an essay draft

Teaching reflection

At the beginning of the academic year, I met a mature student on an A Level course in Psychology whose first language was Turkish and who was dyslexic. She told me she had always struggled with reading and note taking and therefore summarising the information for her assignments was hard work. I suggested that she verbalised her thoughts and analysis of the texts whilst reading them and that she recorded her comments on her phone and played them back when she was ready to work on her assignments. At first, she found this very embarrassing and was very self-aware because her family could hear her comments as she studied in her bedroom. After a while, however, she became used to this and now finds that she has a much more detailed understanding of her material and writes more fluently.

(Marcus, Psychology Lecturer)

Dialogic teaching

Dialogic teaching is a comprehensive approach to talk in teaching, learning and assessment. It is not a single method but draws on a range of strategies and techniques concerned with teacher and student talk (Alexander, 2017). It is an especially powerful method to support students who struggle with English as it can help to harnesses the power of talk to stimulate and extend students thinking and advance their learning and understanding (Mercer, 2019).

The main principles of dialogic teaching

Dialogic talking is collective as students work together to develop collective relevant knowledge. It is also reciprocal because students listen to each other, share ideas, and respect and consider alternative viewpoints and supportive as students can be open in their responses because there are no wrong answers. It is also cumulative as students build on their peers' responses and answers and other oral contributions and chain them together to produce a deeper understanding (Mercer and Dawes, 2014). The overall goal of the class is joint sense making. It is purposeful as talk and discussion is structured by the teacher and directed to meet specific learning outcomes.

The six repertoires of dialogic teaching

There has been much debate over the range of strategies to be included as Dialogic teaching, but in broad terms it combines six repertoires (Mercer, 2019). There is talk for everyday which includes transactional, expository, interrogatory, exploratory, expressive, and evaluative talk, questioning which comprise the use of open, closed, and leading questions, volunteer and nominated, variations of thinking time, extensions, and feedback. There is extending, which is the logical follow-on from questioning, and it includes approaches such as sharing, expanding, and clarifying thinking, listening carefully, deepening reasoning, and thinking with others.

There is learning talk, which encourages students to narrate, explain, analyse, speculate, imagine, explore, evaluate, discuss, argue, justify, and pose questions of their own, but which also needs to include listening, reflecting, and allowing other students time to think and respecting alternative opinions. There is also teaching talk which consists of rote, recitation, instruction, exposition, and dialogue, but which should focus more upon discussion and scaffolded dialogue which involves interaction and can lead to uptake (taking peers' ideas forward) and handover (assimilating ideas to create new learning) (Alexander, 2018).

Classroom organisation

There are five ways of organising dialogic classroom talk: whole-class teaching, group work (teacher-led), group work (student-led), one-to-one (teacher and student) and one-to-one (student pairs) (Mercer and Dawes, 2014). Any of these variations can help students to develop a range of high-level cognitive and communication skills.

Impacts of dialogic teaching

Dialogic teaching could encourage the students to express ideas and stimulate their courage to dialogue and in this way improve their self-confidence. Engaging with alternative points of view may challenge own understanding and perspectives and help them develop open-mindedness and greater acceptance of other cultures (Alexander, 2020). For EAL students in particular, it can develop the ability to ask more concise and structured questions and improve their participation in class and encourage students to prepare more for class.

It can also help to develop critical self-reflection and the evaluation of own understanding of a topic, a sense of autonomy in students and a greater willingness to take responsibility for their own learning. Dialogic teaching can help to develop stronger learning bonds between students, especially those who feel linguistically or culturally excluded and therefore change teaching into a more cooperative, interactive and partnership relationship with students via discussion and debate (Alexander, 2018).

Using questions to scaffold dialogic teaching

There are many different types of questions used in a dialogic classroom (Alexander, 2020). Deferring questions can be used to check students' meanings by pausing before giving answers. Follow-up questions can be used to promote deeper thinking. Questions that ask for examples to support ideas. Connected questions can be prompted by visual or audio stimuli or built on students' interests and stretch students' understanding. Open, closed, leading, short, and long, narrow, and discursive questions can be used that encourage students to model the subject-specific language but are also differentiated to meet the differing needs of students. These include the following types:

- Discursive questions which prompt discussion and encourage students to think, and to think in different ways, and which invite analysis and reflection rather than simple recall and provide opportunities for in depth extended answers and further research as homework.
- Personalised questions which enable students to bring their own experiences into the discussion to enrich the group's understanding or generated by the group which enable self-generating discussion. These can prompt feedback from the teacher and the students leading to thinking forward and provide scaffolding into the next level of understanding via new concepts or ideas by challenging and stretching current level of understanding.
- Cross-over questions which can be used to link cross curricula knowledge and to draw upon cross cultural knowledge (Mercer, 2019).

Box 2.6 An example of dialogic teaching used in a biology class

Teaching example

In order to encourage oral communication and verbal responses among EAL students in my group, I used visual description which is an effective strategy to motivate students to respond verbally. It allows students to talk without concern for syntax, grammar, pronunciation or other mechanics of writing. It engages them to interact in a meaningful way in a small-group situation. Small groups provide non-threatening environment to students for practice before putting EAL students on the

> spot in front of the entire class. I gave them four different pictures of different types of cells, epithelial cells, nerve cells, muscle cells and connective tissue cells, and asked them to describe and discuss their characteristics amongst themselves. They were encouraged to look up online any appropriate scientific vocabulary and to note down new key words they had learned. The activity provided a structured environment for them to engage in short discussions. Finally, they were given an opportunity to present their ideas to the rest of the group.
>
> (Tajat, Science Teacher)

Automatisation

Automatisation is the process of learning and assimilating a task or skill so completely that it can be consistently completed with little or no conscious attention (Savage, 2004). It is composed of two parts: speed and accuracy. Students need to automatise a skill or task so they can remember it and use it as a foundation for the completion of new tasks.

According to some researchers (Van der Leij and Van Daal, 1999; Savage, 2004), automatisation is a central concept in fluent reading. Students need to have automatic word recognition to be able to understand a text. Students who are dyslexic and whose first language is not English often struggle with decoding the word and constructing the meaning of the sentence with speed and accuracy which impacts on their comprehension when reading individually (Wolff et al., 1991).

According to Bottle Neck theory (Van der Leij and Van Daal, 1999), students who find word identification problematic will have issues with the development of their reading. This could potentially impact upon their speeds in word identification, and their abilities both to deal with higher phonological complexity in tests and to decode unfamiliar words.

Box 2.7 An example of automatisation in an Early Years class

Teaching example

Many of the students in the class are adult learners who have EAL and who struggle with reading academic texts in class. In order to develop their reading fluency, I make sure that I give them at least one reading task per session containing new vocabulary and an exercise which involves them researching, annotating, or manipulating the text in some way. Sometimes I give them an editing exercise. For example, I ask them to break the text up into paragraphs using a paragraph

> symbol (//) and to write appropriate subheadings for the text. This tests their understanding of the structure of the text and the subject-specific components of the material. I then give them an answer copy from which they could correct their own work. I do all these on a regular basis so after a while it becomes second nature to them and they become more confident readers.
>
> (Donna, Early Years Lecturer)

What to do

The teacher must create opportunities to repeat tasks and renew learned material. Students must be supported to repeat and review the same material until the skill or content has been familiarised to them without scaffolding. This can be done through the following methods. Unfamiliar words can be made more familiar to students on the course using continually updated word banks. Opportunities can be created for students to use the words in context to develop an understanding of their meaning in the context of other words via discussions for instance. Students can be encouraged to use text-to-speech software when reading online texts and to research the definitions of new terminology and apply it to their assignments. This can be reinforced by gapped handouts to challenge their recognition and usages of words.

This can be useful for students who struggle with understanding the sequencing of argument in a text. The object of the process is to deconstruct and then to reconstruct the sequence to gain a stronger practical understanding of the flow of an argument. This can be done as an independent or a paired activity in the following way:

Box 2.8 An example of cut-up reviewing in a Film Studies class

Teaching example

My students were given a text about Film Noir to read and asked to find the topic sentences in each paragraph and then to write them on separate slips of paper. They then shuffled the slips and tried to restructure the text by sequencing the topic sentences in their correct order using their recall of the text and their understanding of the sequencing in the original text. Once they had completed the exercise, they compared it with the original text and made changes accordingly. Then I extended it a stage further by asking them to summarise the text in a single paragraph of about 30 words using only the topic sentences.

(Richard, Media Studies Teacher)

Anchor Charts

Anchor Charts are visual summaries and reinforcers of learning. They are normally created after a skill has been demonstrated and modelled by a teacher. They contain the most relevant content, strategies, cues, and processes and are placed in a prominent student-friendly part of the teaching setting so that students can access them independently and expand upon them in their individual and collaborative work (Bauer, 2014). They can be designed by the teacher, but are most effective when they are the result of a collaboration of teacher and student. They are especially effective as learning tools for visual learners and for students who struggle with literacy (Croasdell et al., 2003).

Anchor Charts make thinking visible and create a culture of literacy in the classroom. Students can refer to them whist they work on answering questions, expanding on their ideas, and solving problems in class. They supplement class notes by providing visual points of reference in the classroom by summarising aspects of lessons and in doing so can reinforce learning, minimising cognitive loads and building vocabulary and conceptual understanding (Gregory and Cahill, 2010).

Purposes of Anchor Charts

Anchor Charts have many purposes. They can serve as a quick reference so that students do not lose momentum while writing or reading and scaffold learning and enable students to feel increasingly confident, capable, and competent. They can make learning visually interesting linking the learning to the real world from past to present to future because of their physical presence (Trehan, 2014). They can serve as reminder learning paths and also help to link learning across modules providing a foundation for new cross-curricular learning.

They can help to prepare students for examinations or tests and remind students of the most significant vocabulary and meaning of terms to be used in their assignments and of criteria for assignments and help them keep on track. They can develop literacy skills and motivate students to advance their vocabulary and to apply it in new contexts. If they are produced by students and then reviewed by teachers, they can become a formative assessment of learning or used as peer assessment in a collaborative learning session (Fontanez, 2017).

Some characteristics of effective Anchor Charts

They should be simply and clearly designed, visual and colourful, contain only the most relevant and important information and clearly linked to assignments or learning outcomes, so students are constantly reminded of their importance. They should provide differentiated tools for learning to meet all learning needs and should be referred to, and modelled in, lessons, so students understand their relevance and, ideally, they should be the result of collaborative process involving discussions with students (Jones et al., 2012). They should also allow space for cumulative learning allowing new learning to incorporated into them.

How to implement an Anchor Chart

Identify the learning target for which having a posted Anchor Chart will be useful for students. Create the Anchor Chart where every student can see it and, during or after a lesson, engage students in identifying relevant content, strategies, cues, processes, and/or guidelines that were modelled.

Subcategories of Anchor Charts

Strategy charts

Strategy charts are a form of Anchor Chart that seek to, "demonstrate strategic thinking so that kids know when, how, and why to use a strategy in their reading and can refer to the chart for support" (Harvey and Goudvis, 2007, p. 51). Strategy charts are a great option to integrate into a read-aloud lesson and the more opportunities to include visual learners and give them a boost as well can only be positive.

Content chart

Content charts are a form of Anchor Chart that is aimed at pulling out the most important information being taught or read about. Harvey and Goudvis (2007) describe the process of creating a content Anchor Chart when they write, "Sometimes we record new learning, how our thinking has evolved and changed, or new information we have acquired during a content area study" (p. 51).

Genre charts

Genre charts are often used to introduce text features and elements (Harvey and Goudvis, 2007, p. 51). This is also helpful when students are struggling with a particular type of literature or text feature. The visual will help jog their memories and put their thinking into action for the work that needs to be done.

Procedural charts

Mraz et al. (2013) present another use for Anchor Charts beyond the conventional curriculum uses. They suggest using Anchor Charts to present or reinforce classroom procedures, such as ground rules, appropriate voice levels, and even using materials in the proper way.

An example using an Anchor Chart for a Performing Arts class.

> **Box 2.9 Using a content chart in a dance class**
>
> **Teaching reflection**
>
> My Dance group struggle with note taking because they have a range of literacy issues so I decided to collaborate with my group in producing a Content chart to summarise a series of Hip Hop moves that we had just practiced. In pairs, the students had to explain a single move on paper and then photograph themselves performing it. Once all of the pairs had completed their tasks, I download the work and edited it into a poster which was put up in the studio and on the students' Virtual Learning Environment (VLE). This provided them with a visual reminder of what we had just learned and a foundation for practicing the moves before next week's class.
>
> (Jessica, Dance Teacher)

Conclusion

In this chapter we have discussed how we can develop our students' independent learning skills. We have examined how through the incorporation of teaching techniques such as Dialogic Teaching and Accelerated Cognition our students can become more confident and more autonomous, with greater levels of self-efficacy. These themes will be developed in the next chapter where we will look at building critical skills and metacognition in our students,

> **Box 2.10 Over to you!**
>
> **Self-analysing success**
>
> Encourage your students to film reflective vlogs about their strengths and the strategies they use to achieve success and how they could use these gifts in contexts in which they struggle.

> **Box 2.11 Take away self-reflective questions**
>
> How will you know your students are becoming more confident in their studies?
> Do confident students necessarily achieve better than less confident students?
> Could some of the strategies discussed in the chapter be more effective with male students or female students?

References

Adey, P., and Shayer, M. (2007). Cognitive acceleration comes of age. In M. Shayer, and P. Adey (Eds.), *Learning Intelligence: Cognitive Acceleration across the Curriculum from 5 to 15 Years* (pp. 1–17). Buckingham: Open University Press.

Al Rasheed, H. S. (2014). Examining the effectiveness of pre-reading strategies on Saudi EFL college students' reading comprehension. *English Language Teaching*, 7(11), 79–91.

Alexander, R. J. (2017). *Towards Dialogic Teaching: Rethinking Classroom Talk*. (5th ed.). York: Dialogos.

Alexander, R. J. (2018) Developing dialogic teaching: Genesis, process, trial. Research papers in education, 2018. DOI: 10.1080/02671522.2018.1481140.

Alexander, R. J. (2020). *A Dialogic Teaching Companion*. London: Routledge.

Baratta, A. (2020). *Read Critically*. London: Sage Publications Ltd.

Bauer, L. B. (2014). Concept mapping: Developing metacognitive awareness in a post-secondary reading and writing classroom. *Journal of College Literacy and Learning*, 40, 35–44.

Bereiter, C., and Bird, M. (1985). Use of thinking aloud in identification and teaching of reading comprehension strategies. *Cognition and Instruction*, 2, 131–156.

Chiou, C. (2008). The effect of concept mapping on students' learning achievements and interests. *Innovations in Education and Teaching International*, 45(4), 375–387.

Christodoulou, D. (2017) *Making Good Progress? The Future of Assessment for Learning*. Oxford University Press. Oxford Comprehension in Dyslexia: A Path Analysis. Dyslexia First published: 14 October 2016. DOI: 10.1002/dys.1543.

Croasdell, D. T., Freeman, L. A., and Urbaczewski, A. (2003). Concept maps for teaching and assessment. *Communications of the Association for Information Systems*, 12, Article 24. DOI: 10.17705/1CAIS.01224. Available at: https://aisel.aisnet.org/cais/vol12/iss1/24.

Driskell, J. E., Willis, R. P., and Copper, C. (1992). Effect of overlearning on retention. *Journal of Applied Psychology*, 77, 615–622.

Dweck, C. S. (1986). Motivational processes affecting learning. *American Psychologist*, 41(10), 1040–1048. DOI: 10.1037/0003-066X.41.10.1040.

Gregory, A., and Cahill, M. (2010). Kindergartners Can Do It, Too! Comprehension strategies for early readers. *Reading Teacher – READ TEACH*, 63, 515–520. DOI: 10.1598/RT.63.6.9.

Flavell, J. H. (1979). Metacognition and cognitive monitoring: A new area of cognitive-developmental inquiry. *American Psychologist*, 34(10), 906–911.

Fontanez, K. I. (2017). Examining the impact of art-based anchor charts on academic achievement in language arts. Walden Dissertations and Doctoral Studies, 4625. Available at: https://scholarworks.waldenu.edu/dissertations/4625.

Harvey, S., and Goudvis, A. (2007). *Strategies That Work: Teaching Comprehension to Enhance Understanding*. London: Heinemann.

Hill, R. (2016). Locus of control, academic achievement, and discipline referrals. Murray State Theses and Dissertations. Available at: https://digitalcommons.murraystate.edu/etd/1.

Jones, B. D., Ruff, C., Snyder, J. D., Petrich, B., and Koonce, C. (2012). The effects of mind mapping activities on students' motivation. *International Journal for the Scholarship of Teaching and Learning*, 6(1), 1–21.

Jumaat, N. F., and Tasir, Z. (2014). Instructional scaffolding in online learning environment: A meta-analysis. *Proceedings of the IEEE*, 74–77. Available at: https://www.researchgate.net/publication/269033099_Instructional_Scaffolding_in_Online_Learning_Environment_A_Meta-analysis.

King, A. (1992). Comparison of self-questioning, summarizing, and notetaking-review as strategies for learning from lectures. *American Educational Research Journal*, 29(2), 303–323. DOI: 10.2307/1163370.

Lailiyah, M., Wediyantoro, P., and Yustisia, K. (2019). Pre-reading strategies on reading comprehension of EFL students. *EnJourMe (English Journal of Merdeka): Culture, Language, and Teaching of English*, 4(2), 82–87. DOI: 10.26905/enjourme.v4i2.3954.

Marinaccio, J. (2012). The most effective pre-reading strategies for comprehension. Education Masters. Paper 208.

Mercer, N. (2019). *Language and the Joint Creation of Knowledge: The Selected Works of Neil Mercer*. Abingdon: Routledge.

Mercer, N., and Dawes, L. (2014). The Study of Talk between Teachers and Students, from the 1970s until the 2010s. *Oxford Review of Education*, 40, 439–445. DOI: 10.1080/03054985.2014.934087

Mills, D., and Alexander, P. (2013). *Small Group Teaching: A Toolkit for Learning*. Higher Education Academy Publication. Available at https://www.advance-he.ac.uk/knowledge-hub/small-group-teaching-toolkit-learning

Molden, D. C., and Dweck, C. S. (2006). Finding "meaning" in psychology: A lay theories approach to self-regulation, social perception, and social development. *American Psychologist*, 61(3), 192–203. DOI: 10.1037/0003-066X.61.3.192.

Mraz, M., Nichols, W., Caldwell, S., Beisley, R., Sargent, S., and Rupley, W. (2013). Improving oral reading fluency through readers theatre. *Reading Horizons*, 52(2), 163–180. Available at: http://dbsearch.fredonia.edu:2048/login?url=http://search.ebscohost.com/login.aspx?direct=true&db=eric&AN=EJ1098232&site=ehost-live

Nowicki, S., and Duke, M. P. (2017). "Foundation of locus of control: Looking back over a half-century of research in locus of control of reinforcement," in J. W. Reich and F. J. Infurna (Eds.), *Perceived Control: Theory, Research, and Practice in the First 50 Years* (pp. 147–170). Oxford: Oxford University Press.

Ogle, D. (1986). K-W-L: A teaching model that develops active reading of expository text. *The Reading Teacher*, 39, 564–570. DOI: 10.1598/RT.39.6.11.

Piaget, J. (Fall 1975). Contemporary education. *The Terre Haute Journal*, 47(1), 5.

Quigley, A., Muijs, D., and Stringer, E. (2013). *Metacognition and Self-Regulated Learning Guidance Report*. Education Endowment Foundation (EEF). Available at https://educationendowmentfoundation.org.uk/education-evidence/guidance-reports/metacognition

Rohrer, D., Taylor, K., Pashler, H., Cepeda, N. J., and Wixted, J. T. (2005). The effect of overlearning on long-term retention. *Applied Cognitive Psychology*, 19, 361–374.

Rotter, J. B. (1966). Generalized expectancies for internal versus external control of reinforcement. *Psychological Monographs: General and Applied*, 80(1), 1–28. DOI: 10.1037/h0092976.

Savage, R. (2004). Motor skills, automaticity and developmental dyslexia: A review of the research literature. *Reading and Writing*, 17, 301–324. DOI: 10.1023/B:READ.0000017688.67137.80.

Snowling, M. J. (1995). Phonological processing and developmental dyslexia. *Journal of Research in Reading*, 18(2), 132–138. DOI: 10.1111/j.1467-9817.1995.tb00079.x.

Thurston, A., and Cockerill, M. (2016). *Peer Tutoring: Cross-Age Paired Reading* (4th ed.). Belfast: Queen's University Press.

Topping, K. J., and Bryce, A. (2004). Cross-age peer tutoring of reading and thinking: Influence on thinking skills. *Educational Psychology*, 24, 595–621.

Trehan, D. M. (2014). The impact of concept mapping as a learning tool on student perceptions of and experiences with introductory statistics. Unpublished Doctoral Thesis, Kent State University College.

Tyler, N., Heffernan, R., and Fortune, C.-A. (2020). Reorienting locus of control in individuals who have offended through strengths-based interventions: Personal agency and the good lives model. *Frontiers in Psychology*, 11, 553240. DOI: 10.3389/fpsyg.2020.553240

Van der Leij, A., and Van Daal, V. H. P. (September/October 1999). Automatization aspects of dyslexia: Speed limitations in word. *Journal of Learning Disabilities*, 32(5), Health Research Premium Collection, 417.

Vygotsky, L. (1978). *Mind in Society*. Massachusetts, US: Harvard University Press.

Wolff, P. H., Michel, G. F., and Ovrut, M. (1991). Rate variables and automatized naming in developmental dyslexia. *Brain and Language*, 39(4), 556–575. DOI: 10.1016/0093-934X(90)90162-A.

Wong, B. Y. L. (1985). Self-questioning instructional research: A review. *Review of Educational Research*, 55(2), 227–268. DOI: 10.2307/1170191.

Wray, A. (2003). Formulaic language and the lexicon. *Journal of Pragmatics*, 35. DOI: 10.1016/S0378-2166(03)00079-1.

3 Critical reading, critical writing and critical thinking

Critical reading and writing are both vital to the development of academic study skills and to critical thinking, understanding and analysis. They present particular difficulties for students who have problems with literacy because they are complex and time-consuming to master (Manarin et al., 2015). In this chapter I will suggest techniques to support the development of each one in turn.

Critical reading

Critical reading is an investigation into, and critique of the validity of arguments expressed in reading passages (Walz, 2001). It's the job of the critical reader to read between the lines, sift through the rhetoric and interrogate the arguments and ideas contained within the text. Critical reading is always a struggle for students who have difficulties with literacy. According to Manarin et al. (2015), reading critically for academic success consists of the following key skills:

Identifying patterns of textual elements

Students could be given a lot of exposure to varied reading examples to understand the three patterns of text organisation (McCarthy, 1991; Holland and Johnson, 2000): Problem-Solution, which constitutes a simple narrative flow of the four main parts: Situation → Problem → Response → Evaluation found newspaper editorials; General-Specific, which is centred on an initial general statement, followed by a series of (progressively) more specific statements, culminating in a further generalisation such as in a magazine or newspaper feature; and Claim Counterclaim, which consists of a series of claims and contrasting- counter claims, which is presented on a given topics as in a news article (Nelson, 1984).

Distinguishing between main and subordinate ideas

The ability to identify main ideas in text is a key reading comprehension skill. Here is an example of how to support students identifying ideas in a text.

DOI: 10.4324/9781003181583-3

> **Box 3.1 Reading checklist**
>
> **Teaching resource reading checklist**
>
> **I teach a group of eight students journalism on a Level 2 part-time course.** Many of them have lived in the UK for only a few years and all of them have additional literacy problems. I gave them this checklist to help them separate the wheat from the chaff when reading for their assignments:
>
> Step One
>   Read the title of the study and the subheadings.
> Step Two
>   Look for clues in the introductory paragraph. How is the author setting the scene?
> Step Three
>   Study the topic sentences of every paragraph
> Step Four
>   Look out for the signposting of arguments normally conveyed through phrases like:
>   Most importantly, Significantly, It is vital that, Unquestionably
> Step Five
>   Underline the key terminology.
> Step Six
>   Focus on those sections of the text where there are the most examples used to support arguments or where there are the most in-text citations
> Step Seven
>   Delete most details and examples, unimportant information, anecdotes, examples, illustrations, data etc.
> Step Eight
>   Colour code the main ideas from the subordinate ideas and read the main colour-coded ideas together and see if the argument flows
> Step Nine
>   Compare the concluding paragraph to the introduction. How has the author wrapped up?

Evaluating credibility

Credibility in academic writing is normally associated with the following concepts: accuracy, authority, objectivity, currency, and coverage/scope.

Here is a teacher's example of how she developed her students' abilities to evaluate textual claims and arguments:

> My Level Three Health Care Students have a variety of literacy issues and find it difficult to substantiate the findings of a text, so I designed this checklist to support their critical reading for assignments.

Box 3.2 Critical reading checklist

Teaching resource

Components of Credibility	Questions to be answered	Comments
Accuracy	Is the content free from errors? Can the information be verified elsewhere?	
Authority	Can you check the author's credentials? Is the author established in this field? Can you identify their previous work in this field? Which institution are they currently associated with?	
Objectivity	Has the writer a particular axe to grind?	
Currency	How current is the information in the source? Check the dates of facts and statistics especially. Are they relevant today?	
Coverage/scope	How much detail does the text contain? Can you see any major areas that are not covered adequately?	

Making judgements about how arguments in a text are supported

Students need to be made aware of the three basic tools and how they can be used in textual analysis:

- Facts, which are among the best tools to involve the reader in the argument. Since facts are indisputable, the writer automatically wins the reader's mutual agreement by utilizing them. Facts are used primarily to get the reader to stand on the writer's plane of reasoning.
- Judgements, which are assumptions that the writer makes about his/her subject after carefully considering the facts. The success or failure of the entire argument rests on whether or not the writer can utilise adequate reasoning in coming to the right judgements
- Testimony, which constitute both eyewitness and expert witness accounts which both lend credibility to an argument.

Here is an example of a critical reading class exercise for a Politics class on the government's policy on vocational education and training.

Box 3.3 Teaching resource critical reading example

Teaching resource

Critical reading example
Read the following article and follow the steps:

1. *Identify the conclusion and the premises.*
2. *Summarise the arguments briefly.*
3. *Decide if the argument is deductive or non-deductive. (A deductive argument is one that is offered to provide logically conclusive support for its conclusion. A non-deductive argument is one that is offered to provide probable support for its conclusions, but not conclusive.)*
4. *Determine whether the argument succeeds logically.*
5. *If the argument succeeds logically, assess whether the premises are true.*

For premises that are backed up by a sub-argument, repeat all the steps for the sub-arguments.

6. *Make a final judgement: are the arguments valid or invalid?*

The best way to grow sunflowers; in praise of BTECs

On Wednesday 12 October 2021, the government's latest attempt to 'defund' most BTEC and diploma courses through the Skills and Post-16 Education Bill passed through the House of Lords despite opposition from some Labour, Lib Dem and Conservative peers. This is part of a long line of Conservative policies reaching back to the Wolf Report of 2011 and the Sainsbury Review of 2016 which has aimed at reducing the range of vocational courses available to young people and to replace them with more specialist work-related qualifications.

In spite of the results of a government consultation exercise staged between January and July 2021 where it emerged that over 86% of respondents opposed the policy (DFE, 2021), the current bill aims to cull most technical qualifications from August 2023 and August 2024 in order to ensure that they do not conflict with the, arguably, more academic, more specialised, and less inclusive T-Levels which were piloted last year.

Over the decades many millions of young people have passed through the BTEC and vocational qualification systems. In 2021 over 25% of students entering Higher Education had a BTEC qualification (ukas.com) Many of these students have also gone on to become teachers in

Further Education and have taught on BTEC programmes. I spoke to three trainee and recently qualified teachers from our PGCE programme and asked them about their own experiences as students on BTEC programmes.

In the first instance they all agreed that they gravitated towards vocational qualifications because they found academic work at school problematic:

> I used to struggle all the time with spelling and written work and I had no self confidence in my ability to finish a course. During those days, dyslexia wasn't really well known so I had no had proper support from school, either.
>
> (Alicia)

> I struggled with writing English because it wasn't my first language, so I hated having to write course work. I just got further and further behind and in the end, I just stopped turning up at school and really had no direction as to my future and so I drifted around from one dead end unskilled job to another.
>
> (Josephine)

> It has been suggested in the consultation results of July 2021 that students from minority ethnic backgrounds may struggle if BTECs are replaced by the new T-Levels because they are likely to have achieved lower GCSE grades than their peers who progress on to A-Level.
>
> (DFE, 2021)

> I suppose I wanted to be a grown up, really. I found course work really restricting. I suppose it didn't fit in with my learning style and I thought I was being held back to some extent.
>
> (Simone)

> Their actual routes into vocational education were quite different however but were all initiated by the flexibility of their BTEC programmes which have always been an attractive feature of them for students.
>
> (youthemployment.org.uk/)

> A friend of my mum's was a care worker and she suggested to her that if I got a college qualification it would give me openings to different types of careers.
>
> (Josephine)

> I had always been 'arty' and 'crafty' at school and always enjoyed designing cards and invitations for my friends. A Level Art at school was too academic for me because it involved a lot of writing critical essays about artists which I knew that I couldn't cope with. I decided to do a college course in Graphic Design that was more hands on and more commercial.
>
> (Alicia)

> The only option for me at school was at school was A Level Dance which was very dull and a bit straightforward. It was focussed on just contemporary dance and the teaching was a bit static. It was more like 'watch this video and copy this dance'. I wanted to do something where I could learn a variety of different styles and do something more creative, so I decided to go to college.
>
> (Simone)

According to Sir David Blunkett (*The Guardian*, 13 October 2021) the current potential replacements for BTECs and diplomas would be 75% academic and 25% practical. This would not have benefited the learning of any of the three teachers. They all felt that they flourished as a result of the 'hands-on' teaching they received on their courses:

> I got to work on real briefs using up to date computer software which really stretched me creatively. I never felt so enthusiastic about learning. It was like I was in areal design studio and I used to go in at 8.00 and finish at 8pm some days.
>
> (Alicia)

> The BTEC course in Health and Social Care totally changed the way I thought education was. I learned that it could be about the real world and real things. We did a lot of case study work and presentations and poster making and the teacher used to cite examples form her own practice all the time to bring sessions to life.
>
> (Josephine)

> When I was at college we did a real range of styles of dance such as Tap, Ballet, Ballet and Jazz. We did a lot of practical assessments such as group numbers and even worked on shows.
>
> (Simone)

(During the 2021 consultations concerns were also raised about the lack of transferable skills development in the new qualifications (DFE, 2021). All of the teachers felt that they benefited from learning about time management, teamwork, self-reliance, and personal presentation in addition to their subject specialisms.)

A central criticism of the new qualifications is that because they are so specialised, they could potentially tie young people into making rigid career decisions at an early age. Two of the teachers I spoke to felt that their qualifications opened up a variety of career avenues which they had never hitherto considered:

> After doing my BTEC in Health and Social Care I went on to do a Degree in Occupational Therapy I never thought I would be doing that in a million years. The course opened up my eyes to different options which was helped by the placements I did in hospitals.
> (Josephine)

> I had never used computer design technology before going on the course and t helped me completely change direction from Art and Design. I went on to do a Degree in Digital Design and to set up my own digital design and advertising agency.
> (Alicia)

Over 25% of students who started university in 2023 had a BTEC. All the teachers believed that the qualification provided a strong foundation for the kind of self-directed learning expected on their degree courses:

> I think if I had come from an academic course I would have been completely overwhelmed. You had to use your own initiative all the time and organise yourself and work with a team to get the work completed. There was no spoon feeding.
> (Simone)

> I felt totally prepared for the forms of assessment and the placements from doing BTECs.
> (Josephine)

> At uni you were just expected to take the briefs and run with them with not much guidance from your tutor. I had already done this so I was more confident about working on my own initiative than some students who had come straight from A Levels.
> (Alicia)

Critics of the skills policy are suggesting there should be no immediate changes to BTEC and other technical qualifications and that they should be run alongside T-Levels for four years to be able to measure their impact (*The Guardian*, 13 October 2021). Many teachers also fear that the current legislation is going to throw the baby out with the bathwater. According to Simone, 'this would be a crazy move. A teacher one said to be that academic course explain the theory of growing sunflowers and provide you with the instructions and the seeds to grow them. Vocational courses just tell you to go away and grow. Students shouldn't lose this independence.'

References

Review of post-16 qualifications at level 3 in England Government consultation response. July 2021. HMSO

The Guardian. 13 October 2021. Sir David Blunkett article. Ministers are trying to sneak through a cull of post-16 qualifications. In the Lords we are taking a stand to protect vocational training.

Question the author's assumptions

Questioning new material is often an ideal way of increasing students thinking about the potential relationships between the new content and their prior knowledge and enabling them to make relevant inferences about the text. It also improves their understanding of the new material because it requires them to think beyond the text. One of the most effective ways to enable critical reading is to encourage the students to break the text down into paragraphs and deconstruct the argument paragraph by paragraph.

Here are some question prompts that I give to Access to Education students to guide the process of understanding:

What is the paragraph about?
What is the author's point of view?
How does this impact on his/her argument?
What evidence does he/she use to support his argument?
How valid is this evidence?
Who would agree with his/her arguments and why?
Who would disagree with his/her arguments and why?
Are you convinced by his/her arguments?
If so, why?
If not, why?

It can also be done using peer questioning. This also increases learning in both parties as in doing so, they must recall previous knowledge, clarify, and organise the new material and also identify any gaps in their own understanding. When teachers model this process, research has suggested that the benefits to students' understanding of the text are even greater and enable the student to apply the text to their own work more readily.

Identify power relations within the text

According to sociolinguistic theory texts hail their readers and invite their readers to learn lessons, and accept certain values, or to take on certain positions in response to the text (Althusser, 1979). Through their surface ideology texts ask the reader to patiently internalise a lesson while enjoying the text. They ask the reader to consider a certain idea, to imagine a particular thing, or to respond to the text in a particular way. Students need to be aware that the writer could position themselves in several different ways: as an expert, friend, opponent, and victim. Your students might benefit from posing the following questions to the text:

> *Who is the implied reader of the text?*
> *How does the writer address the implied reader? In familiar or unfamiliar terms?*
> *Do you think the writer is writing to you as an equal?*
> *How does the author respond to other people's arguments in the text?*
> *How does the writer want you to respond to his arguments?*
> *Does he make a convincing case for his arguments?*

Small group reading

Students that struggle reading independently can also benefit from reading in a small group. This style of reciprocal reading has been well researched in the primary and secondary sector in spite of its effectiveness, but there has been scant research in FE and HE (Hall and Burns, 2018). Collaborative reading involves and develops many skills in readers who lack confidence or who struggle because of a disability or language barrier. These skills include: co-operative teaching and learning, talking, learning and discussion, comprehension, and analysis, deconstruction, and synthesis of ideas, creating collective meaning by discussion from the text and autonomous learning.

The benefits of small group reading

Students will be more engaged and motivated for several reasons:

- They won't be reading alone in silence. They could have a wider understanding of the text because they will be able to draw from a range of ideas.
- Interacting and communicating with others will help develop their confidence in understanding texts. They will be able to use their own first language if there are similar students in the group who will be able to help them with problematic vocabulary.
- Less confident readers will be able to benefit from the support of stronger readers and they will be able to make notes from the discussions and use the collective knowledge to improve their assignment or revise for their examinations.

> **Box 3.4 Here is an example of a teacher's use of small reading groups**
>
> **Case study**
>
> Most of my Level 3 Business students have EAL and reading and writing issues. In order to motivate them to read in more depth for their assignments sometimes I bring selected texts from the required reading list into the session. I organise them in preselected groups of three or four students and ensure a balance between strong readers and less able readers. They are each given a loosely defined role as note taker, presenter, or mind map designer. In their groups they then choose which text they want to consult for their assignment. They are then given 30 minutes to read a section from the book or printed article, discuss what they have read and make notes about how relevant it is for their assignment as a large mind map.
>
> I go around from table to table to help them with terminology and with decoding some of meanings of the text but most of the time they discuss it amongst themselves. When they have finished, each group presents their analysis to the rest of the class on a finished mind map which they tape to their table. Each group then visits each table to annotate each mind map by drawing reference to their own reading and take photographs of their peers' work for future reference.
>
> We then have a full class discussion pulling all the students' analysis together and collectively evaluating the importance of each text. We discuss how we can use these in their assignment by mapping them against the learning outcomes. As homework, the students are encouraged to read the texts which they haven't read on the reading list more carefully and to expand their notes and use them when they write their assignments. (Lilah, Business Studies Teacher)

DARTs (Directed Activities Related to Texts)

Directed Activities Related to Texts (DARTs) are a range of strategies for analysing and understanding texts developed by Lunzer and Gardner (1984). DARTs encourage students to read texts, including visual texts in detail, to go beyond literal comprehension and reflect upon what they read. They can also provide an alternative to traditional comprehension questions as a way of assessing and encouraging understanding. DARTs motivate students to engage with texts by using active reading strategies. They can be used in working with both fictional and non-fictional texts.

DARTS can encourage students to read in depth and challenge students to use higher-order thinking to analyse texts and to contextualise meaning.

They can support students who struggle with literacy because they provide a framework for understanding and can empower students to take control of their own learning if they are encouraged to design their own DARTs. They can enable students to learn new vocabulary more quickly and to understand new concepts within context and can form the basis of paired or group activities and help support discussion and collaborative learning. There are two main types of DARTs, DARTs using modified and unmodified texts (Holden, 2004):

> DARTs using modified texts are DARTs where the teacher has modified the original text, for example by taking out words, phrases, or sentences or by cutting the text into segments. This works particularly well for students who struggle with literacy when the activities can highlight the misspelling of subject specialist terms, for instance.
> (Shamsulbahri and Zulkiply, 2021)

Modified text activities could include any of the following: filling the gaps in texts with missing words, phrases, or sentences, sequencing words, sentences, or short paragraphs, grouping segments of text according to categories, completing a table, grid, flow chart, etc, labelling a diagram, writing the next step or an end to the text, punctuating texts where the punctuation has been removed and correcting deliberate SPAG errors. Here is an example from an A Level Biology teacher:

> My students often struggle with using scientific language in their lab reports, so I provide sentence stems to them in pairs to discuss from the Manchester University word bank. This starts them off in their writing as they then can complete the sentences using their own examples and structure them into paragraphs.
> (Christiana, Science teacher)

DARTs using unmodified text are where the teacher provides a copy of the original text, so the student can adapt it to their own interests by annotating or manipulating it (Ichwan et al. 2015). Examples of activities using this form of DARTs include True/False analysis of textual statements, changing text into a flow diagram or other genres such as letters, posters, leaflets or into graphic organisers like mind maps, pyramids, tree diagrams. It can also involve asking students to write new topic sentences/subheadings for texts or colour coding, comparing, and contrasting texts using a criteria table either created by the teacher or by the students. Alternatively it can involve designing a cause-and-effect grid which the students complete by using information from the prescribed text.

> **Box 3.5 An example of using DARTs in an Early Years Level 2 class**
>
> **Teaching example**
>
> My group normally struggle with organising their writing because of dyslexia and language issues so I found that segmenting is very effective in developing text organisation and structuring. I gave them a text about safeguarding that had no paragraphs. In pairs, the students were asked to break the text into paragraphs and to write subheadings for each section of the text. Then they were told to write new topic sentences for each paragraph. Then they tested each other's knowledge by posing questions to each other from the text. For homework the students were asked to write a summary of the text in 50 word or fewer.
>
> (Alicia, Early Years Teacher)

Critical writing

Critical writing is a difficult skill as it involves weighing up the arguments and evidence of other writers and then synthesising them to developing a fresh argument. It implies that the student can recognise the limitations of evidence: either their evidence or the evidence provided by other writers. It is particularly difficult for students with literacy issues as they sometimes struggle to move themselves outside of the comfort zone of descriptive writing (Mevarech and Kramarski, 1997).

Graphic organisers

Graphic organisers are a tool to enable students to learn how to integrate knowledge and to build meaning by understanding relationships between concepts. They help students to organise and represent ideas visually so that they can reflect on their learning, leading to a deeper understanding. There is much research to suggest their effectiveness as instructional, learning and assessment tools to increase knowledge integration and meaningful learning across a range of disciplines and levels (Kim et al., 2004).

They have a variety of different names, such as Concept Maps, Information Maps, Relationship Chart, Planning Diagram, but they all have the same function which is to represent linear statements into nonlinear graphical information.

There are many different designs of graphic organisers on the internet such as Clock, Cluster/Word Web, Idea Wheel, KWL/KWHL Chart, Spider Map,

Timeline, Tree Chart, and Venn Diagram. The choice of which would depend on function, purpose, the nature of the material/information, the classroom activity and the personal preference of the teacher.

Their basic structure consists of:

- a focus verb or themes
- linking verbs
- cross-links
- propositions
- different types of geometric shapes

Here are some of the most common designs:

- Spider/Web design: the main theme is at the corner of the page and words spread and connect to form links in a spider web
- Hierarchical design: information is presented in order of importance
- Flowchart: where the information is represented in a linear fashion.
- Landscape structure: this shows information as a panorama across the page
- Mandala: information is presented in geometric forms such as squares, triangles, hexagons
- Ideas wheel: where information is placed in concentric circles and can be used to show hierarchy of ideas or as a record of ideas that are placed within different sections

Graphic organisers can be used in the class as a completed template to model learning. They can be either partially completed so that students can fill them in as an activity or a blank template so students can decide themselves how the information fits into it and what are the key connections (Ballanca, 2017). They can also function as an activity in which students have to design their own graphic organiser.

Benefits of using a graphic organiser

The benefits to students' learning from using a graphic organiser include the following:

- It can help students who struggle with literacy: describe, compare and contrast, classify concepts, sequence ideas or events, show cause and effect and progression and organise disjointed information.
- They present a different way for students to see and think about information and can enable students to visualise the relationships between different concepts and the hierarchical structures and organisation of the relationships.
- In the case of EAL students they can remove some of the language barriers, such as grammar and complex terminology, so they can focus on

key information and connections between the information and the visual representation of information makes it easier to understand quickly and showing how it is structured makes it easier to understand.

(Miranda, 2011)

It helps to develop critical thinking and planning because students must engage on a high cognitive level of understanding to deconstruct the central theme, identify and summarise key terms/concepts, identify and examine the meanings and the relationships between topics/concepts and prioritise the material and decide its position on the graphic. These steps will all help to develop strategic thinking. It can help students to revise from because it compresses information into a visual display (Kim et al. 2004). It can provide an essay plan structure to work from for students with dyslexia who may struggle with organising material for their essays.

It can also provide a 'big picture' of the topic and show how each area is connected. It can be easily edited and updated by students as new perspectives arise from the group or from teachers and it can help trigger ideas during the process of placing them as part of the graphic and, in doing so, it can help develop metacognition (Sam and Rajan, 2013).

There are a multitude of uses for graphic organisers which would include the following approaches. They can help to structure students writing and be used to plan and research. They can be used by students to summarise texts and to store and organise subject specialist vocabulary (Croasdell et al., 2003). Some examples of how they were used are discussed below.

Using serial maps to show students' work in progress

Serial maps are concept maps drawn by students at different stages during the learning. They can help teachers to monitor their students' progress and to give constructive and timely feedback.

Box 3.6 A Health and Social Care lecturer's example of how she used a serial map

Teaching reflection

My students are encouraged to produce a mega mind map of each unit so that every time that we complete a course learning outcome, I tell my students to write it on the mind map itself. The mind maps are displayed on the classroom walls so they can see where they are in each unit and so they can easily add to them every lesson. They also take photos of them on their phones so they can review their learning at home as well. I think that this motivates the students to work hard and to progress. This also enables to give formative feedback every lesson to every student.

(Natasha, Health and Social Care Lecturer)

Using graphic organisers for formative assessment:

Box 3.7 A Geography teacher's example of how a concept map can be used as self-assessment tool

Teaching reflection

When I have finished a particularly tricky part of a module, I give my EAL students a blank concept map to fill in individually. This helps me to test their recall and especially their understanding of how ideas are interlinked and how they develop from each other. It is much more effective than using a linear quiz as it measures much more than just rote learning. It is also a powerful method of develop their skills in self-assessment and ultimately it can be used by them as a revision aim when it comes to examination time.

Using graphic organisers for essay planning

Box 3.8 A Media Studies teacher's example of how they used a graphic organiser

Teaching reflection

When I give my students a new assignment brief, I discuss it with them orally and explain the learning outcomes they will have to meet. Then I tell them to work in groups as I think this approach lends itself to group work, and to produce a graphic organiser to show how each task fits together and how they intend to meet the assignment outcomes. This makes them work together and examine the assignment in much more depth than they would normally and to star to plan in advance how they are going to approach it. I actually took this idea from one of my Dyslexic students who always took notes in class in this way.

(Lucy, Media Teacher)

Do Nows

The "Do Now" is an individual, pen-to-paper activity done at the start of each class The activities usually last between three to ten minutes, ranging from responding to prompts to asking questions, and existing in formats such as writing, discussion, quizzes, or games. Do Now activities are rooted in constructivist theory (Dewey 1916, 1938) and student-centred learning, both active learning theories. Do Now activities are widely used across elementary, secondary, and HE classrooms.

They can have many functions, including the following strategies. They can be used to review previous learning, providing opportunities for reflections on learning and introducing new subject content. Thus, they can create a bridge between the old learning and the new. They can set the tone for new learning and keep the students on task from when they first arrive in the class, reinforcing classroom management. They can develop early opportunities for the teacher to provide individual support to students who are struggling with learning and provide a non-threatening space for students who struggle with literacy to write. This can also motivate students into wanting to move onto the session's topic.

Some examples of Do Nows

Five

Students could look up five new vocabulary words on their phones and write the definitions into their notebooks.

Swopsies

They could also thought shower a list of at least five concepts they learned in previous classes and swop them with their neighbour building a widening vocabulary.

Skill self-assessment

They could write down the skill which they wish to improve today.

Assessing the criteria

They could write down four things their assignment needs in order to meet the criteria in the brief.

Lesson recapping

They could be asked to summarise three main points from yesterday's class.

Punctuate

They could be given a paragraph from a text with missing punctuation and asked to punctuate it.

Mind the gap

Learners have to read a passage which previews some of the content in the new class and fills in the missing words.

Quick quizzes

Learners must complete either a short crossword puzzle or a short word-search based on the previous lesson's content.

Targets for today

Learners should write three learning targets for today's session based on previous feedback from you. They should then tape them under their chairs and review them as part of the plenary later.

Find the missing link

The teacher could draw a picture of three different things on the whiteboard (use images) and have students identify not only the three items but also the link between them.

Amazing anagrams

Learners to unscramble the letters of five words to find the key concepts of the forthcoming lesson.

Do it yourself

Ask your students to design two subject-specific Do Nows for their peers and swop them.

Piece the Puzzle

Box 3.9 Using a Do Now in a science class

Teaching example

Piece the puzzle is really a long Do Now, but I find it really effective to get them going before the class starts. This is what I do. I organise the students into groups of three. I then deconstruct the content from the previous sessions into four or five sections and isolate the key points from each section and make them into jigsaw puzzles, one puzzle for each section, with five or six pieces per puzzle. I then jumble the pieces and give a set of puzzles to each group of students. I ensure that I print each puzzle in a different colour which helps me to differentiate. Each group should complete all the puzzle and then write a short summary based on the puzzles. The first table to complete all the puzzles correctly wins a prize. Each group should then feedback

> their summary to the rest of the group. I find that this activity helps those learners who are struggling with spoken and written English benefit the most.
>
> (Marnie, Science Teacher)

Roundtable review

Students write a list of numbers from one to 20 on a sheet of paper. They are then told to put one important idea from the previous session on the first line. They then pass the sheet to the person on the left. Each time the paper is passed, the person receiving the paper writes a different idea. When they have completed the exercise by writing down 20 points the papers go back to the original writer. Each student individually then reads out to the rest of the class and explains an interesting point made by one of their peers from their sheet of notes.

Critical writing and reading

This is often a more problematic relationship. One way it can be done is using the 5Ws and H and the following questions, What If? So What? What Next? together, to produce a model like this which you could encourage your learners to use to structure their work:

Box 3.10 The 5Hs and W model

Teaching resource

Description	What? When? Who? Where?
Analysis	Why? How?
Evaluation	What if? So what? What next?

Another way of doing this is to encourage your students to stand back from their writing and step into the shoes of a reader and look at it from their point of view.

They should think about and then try to write down answers to the following questions about their work:

What is the paragraph about?
Where is the writer coming from?
What is their argument?

What kind of evidence does the writer use to support it?
How valid is this evidence?
How does it relate to the writer's main arguments?

When they are writing answers to each question, if they have no answer, they should leave it blank and rewrite the paragraph accordingly and fill in the blank later.

Box 3.11 A critical reading, thinking and writing exercise

Teaching reflection

I have used the following critical reading, thinking and writing exercise (adapted from Baratta, 2020) with GCSE History students who struggle with reading and textual analysis to great effect:

Ask your students to select a sentence, or indeed a small paragraph of text, which they have taken from any source (online news report, magazine, etc.). They need to read it critically, circle the words which they believe are key and interpret these. They then prepare a short response to the original text consisting of their interpretations, agreement, disagreement, illustration and explanation, regarding the original text. They should then take a break and return to the work later and review their work again considering any ways that they can improve it and making the changes.

Critical thinking

Metacognition

Metacognition was originally developed in 1976 and has been explained in a variety of ways such as thinking about thinking, learning how to learn, learning to study. But it has always been deemed to be a higher-order thinking skill that involves monitoring and controlling though processes (Flavell, 1976).

The benefits of metacognition include the following suggestions. It encourages students to think about how they learn best and it can develop students awareness of their own capabilities by reflecting on their learning. It can increase motivation to learn and develop their ability to problem solve. Ultimately, It can encourage them to become independent learners by developing their self-confidence and self-efficacy.

One central metacognitive technique is metacognitive questioning which can be applied to the student, the task, the strategy, the experiences, or the goals. Students are asked to focus upon how they have learned as well as what they have learned and to understand the processes that inform their learning (Flavell, 1979).

The IMPROVE method

Mevarech and Kramarski's (1997) IMPROVE method has traditionally been used in developing effectiveness in improving mathematics achievement in several studies such as Gidalevich and Kramarski (2019), but it can also be used in many subject specialisms to develop metacognitive learning and learning in those students who struggle with literacy-based tasks. The method draws upon Constructivist and Cooperative learning theories to develop new levels of verbal reasoning (Mevarech and Kramarski's (1997).

IMPROVE consists of three interdependent components: Metacognitive questioning; cooperative learning consisting of students of different abilities; and the systematic provision of feedback-corrective-enrichment. It uses three distinct types of metacognitive questions. These questions centre on the following concepts: the structure of the problem; connections between the new and existing knowledge; and specific strategies/tactics/principles that are appropriate for solving the new problem (Quigley et al., 2013). They have been categorised as: comprehension questions, strategic questions, and connection questions.

Comprehension questions

Comprehension questions introduce students to the problem and relevant concepts, test their initial knowledge, and identify possible gaps in understanding. Students could then be provided with an acronym to remember the comprehension questions.

Strategic questions

Strategic questions asked students what strategies could be used, why certain strategies could work, and how to use different strategies to solve the problem at hand.

Connection questions

Connection questions prompted students to find problems similar to the current task in order to identify additional strategies that could be employed, drawing on their prior knowledge of solving similar problems.

The three questions in combination can guide students through the planning and problem-solving process and provide them with multiple approaches to solving the problem. They can alert them to their previous successful strategies and bring in previous understanding. They can provide them with proximal goals to move forward from and support students with peer teaching and develop more autonomous thinking skills (Topping and Bryce, 2004).

Box 3.12 An example of how The IMPROVE framework could be used (adapted from Mevarech and Kramarski (1997)) in a sports science class

Case study

1. Introducing new concepts
   In groups learners were given detailed case studies of individual sportspeople, a footballer, a powerlifter, a rower, an 800-meter sprinter, and a tennis player, and asked to design a weekly diet sheet for them which itemised and justified all their individual requirements.
2. Metacognitive questioning
   The teacher recapped on the functions of the various food groups and broke down the problem by modelling the answers to the three metacognitive questions: (a) comprehension question: 'What's in the problem?'; (b) connection question: 'What are the differences between the problem you are working on and the previous problem?' (s); and (c) strategic question: 'What is the strategy/tactic/principle appropriate for solving the problem?'
3. Practicing
   The students were given opportunities to practice using the questions in a group-wide question-and-answer session. The teacher differentiated for the class by using a range of case studies of sportspeople of different difficulty levels and using the questions and providing answers in different depths and in different ways.
4. Reviewing and reducing difficulties
   The students were then given the opportunity to work on their own case studies. The teacher had designed a series of individual handheld strategy prompt cards and students used these cards in their groups to prompt their discussions. Each student, in turn, tried to solve a problem and explain their reasoning by answering the questions printed on the cards and the rest of the group would feedback to their answers. If the group failed to reach a consensus, they were encouraged to use the three metacognitive questions printed on the back of the cards When they agreed on the answers, they wrote them down on their work sheets.
5. Obtaining mastery
   The students found that by working in their groups, discussing their case study, explaining, and exploring their ideas to one another, comparing it to their prior understanding of the sports, approaching it from different perspectives, comparing and contrasting their individual perspectives against one another, and

> reaching consensus, they had used the diversity in their own prior knowledge to self-regulate their learning.
> 6   Verification
>   The role of the teacher was to support their discussions as she worked with the team as an additional team member. When her turn arrived, she modelled again the use of the metacognitive questioning in solving the problems. The teacher read the problem aloud, used the metacognitive questions, and explained each step of the solution. The teacher listened to how the students coped with the problems and aided when needed but avoided unnecessary intervention.
> 7   Enrichment
>   At the end of the session students were given a formative Multiple-Choice Test (MCT) to complete based on the case studies of different sports people. They were given 30 minutes to complete it individually and were marked out of 20. Those students who failed to reach the pass mark of 10 were given an opportunity to look at the questions they had got wrong and to discuss their difficulties with their peers. Those students who had achieved then pass mark were provided with more advanced case studies to discuss in their groups.
>
>   (Rachael, Sports Lecturer)

Small group seminar activities

Seminars are small group learning opportunities which enable students to interact with each other and support each other's learning. They are normally organised by the teacher and are most effective when they are differentiated.

The impacts of seminar learning include the following: They can develop group cohesion and facilitate peer teaching and peer assessment, encouraging a free flow of ideas amongst students facilitating independent problem-solving skills and helping to develop self-confidence in speaking and asking questions in students that struggle with language(Thurston and Cockerill (2016). There are many different types:

Crossover groups

The class is sub-divided into two or more smaller groups with transfers of some students between groups at appropriate times. E.g., Students begin part A of a task in groups of four; after completing this, two people from one group swap places with two people from a second group – to form a new group of four. The task then continues to part B. This is similar to Snowballing, in which individuals, then pairs, then fours etc. generate wider views on a topic progressively. You effectively grow the size of the working group and draw in an increasing range of views. For example, this could be done in discussing a subject like bulimia in Health and Social Care.

Ideas storming

> **Box 3.13 Using ideas storming in an English class**
>
> **Teaching reflection**
>
> I find ideas storming really useful to develop students free writing skills they are writing to explain. I write down a statement, a word, or a question on the board. Then I ask the students to shout out their thoughts and ideas and write them down without comment, on the board or flip chart. I don't stop to analyse any of the suggestions, I just produce the list of comments. When suggestions or time has been exhausted, we organise, and critique the list together. This enables the group to develop interesting and well-developed themes for their written pieces.
>
> (Mohamed, English Teacher)

Role play

Students take on specific roles and act out the views or actions associated with those roles. This could involve experiencing different points of view or putting into practice certain skills and approaches. E.g., Taking a patient history, or interviewing a witness, supporting a service user etc.

Simulations

The teacher provides the students with a set of 'briefs' that provide information and background to the simulation. The students often work in small teams to adopt different roles within the simulation (Mills and Alexander, 2013). E.g., groups taking the stance of different European countries in a European Union strategy negotiation.

Fishbowl

In this approach a sub-group of students are observed (in the 'fishbowl') by the rest of the students. The student in the bowl is asked to argue a case, debate, or role play a situation. The observing students are then called upon to feedback, summarise the discussion, or take the reverse role. For example, in a counselling course session, a student could be supporting a client.

Project-based seminars

The small group work can also form the basis of small-scale project work such as in enquiry-based learning.

Enquiry-based learning

Student-centred learning is a powerful technique to use when teaching students who have language and literacy issues because it can enable them to learn according to their own strengths. One of the most structured and research approaches to student-centred learning is enquiry-based learning (EBL).

In EBL learning is driven by a process of enquiry owned by the student. Its central characteristics are as follows. Learning starts with an open-ended 'scenario' or case and students identify their own issues and questions with support from the teacher in the first instance learning becomes essentially student-centred, and an emphasis on group work and use of library, web, and other information resources (Velez et al. 2011). In this, lecturers become facilitators, providing encouragement and support to enable the students to take responsibility for what and how they learn, and students become motivated through active learning to find solutions to problems (Kahn and O'Rourke, 2004).

Benefits of EBL

There can be many benefits of EBL. Students can be more engaged with the subject. Learning is perceived as being more relevant to their own needs; thus, they are enthusiastic and ready to learn. They can expand on what they have learned by following their own research interests.

It allows students to develop a more flexible approach to their studies, giving them the freedom and the responsibility to organise their own pattern of work and work at their own pace within the time constraints of the task enhancing students' sense of self-efficacy and confidence in self-learning. Because it is a flexible learning approach it can benefit students who struggle with literacy-based activities and students who have EAL and dyslexia can use their first language to help them in their research activities. EBL covers a spectrum of approaches, for example: problem-based learning (PBL), small-scale investigations and project work.

Problem-based learning (PBL)

Problem-based learning (PBL) is one of the largest categories of EBL. It tends to use 'triggers' within the initial briefing which help to direct students towards particular lines of inquiry (Kahn and O'Rourke, 2004).

Each 'problem' will operate on a cycle roughly as follows. The student group identifies the learning outcomes and discusses, examines, and defines the problem. They arrange ideas systematically, consider them in depth and make decisions about the method of approach to the problem. The group then – research roles and tasks and responsibilities for the production of sections of outcomes (written or oral) are allocated. They gather key information in self-directed study and clarify unclear terms and concepts; the group then come together and feedback to each other the results of their research activities reassessing the problem in the light of research findings. They then decide whether there is a need for further research, collate the research findings, decide, and finally present on outcomes and cite their resources.

Box 3.14 Using PBL in a business class

Teaching reflection

I use this technique a lot in my commerce classes as it helps my students who have dyslexia to engage in depth with research by working with others. I normally give them a case study of a business that has a real problem such as customer service and give each group a different aspect of the problem to find a solution to. When they have all researched and presented their solutions, we can come together and discuss a collective package of changes to solve the original problems.

(Angela, Business Studies Lecturer)

Small-scale investigations and projects

These can include field work, case studies, and workshops of differing durations. These are common in most subject areas and can vary in scope from a module to a programme. Project work can include individual and group projects and long- and short-term research activity. These tend to be targeted more towards summative activities at the end of a module or academic year.

Conclusion

In this chapter, we have focussed on developing our students' criticality. We have examined critical reading and different strategies for understanding texts, critical writing using graphic organisers and critical thinking via the use of seminar learning and enquiry-based learning. In Chapter 4, we begin to examine some of the issues associated with the core of teaching and learning, assessment, and feedback.

Box 3.15 Over to you!

Jigsawing a topic

Produce two sets of cards giving two sets of alternative variables or situations. The students would be given one card from each set to generate a unique set of circumstances. E.g., for a Politics session one set of cards could include the names of different historic figures and the second set a number of political issues – the students have to discuss or present on the connections between the person and the issue.

Box 3.16 Take away self-reflective questions

How do you assess criticality in your teaching?
How important is critical thinking in your subject area?
How critical are you of your own teaching strategies?

References

Althusser, L. (1979). *For Marx*. Trans. B. Brewster. London: Verso.
Bellanca, J. A. (2007). *A Guide to Graphic Organizers: Helping Stu-dents Organize and Process Content for Deeper Learning* (2nd ed.). Thousand Oaks, CA: Corwin Press.
Croasdell, D. T., Freeman, L. A., and Urbaczewski, A. (2003) Concept maps for teaching and assessment. *Communications of the Association for Information Systems*, 12, Article 24. DOI: 10.17705/1CAIS.01224. Available at: https://aisel.aisnet.org/cais/vol12/iss1/24.
Dewey, J. (1916). *Democracy and Education: An Introduction to the Philosophy of Education*. New York: Macmillan.
Dewey, J. (1938*). Experience and Education*. New York: Macmillan Company.
Dexter, D. D., and Hughes, C. A. (2011). Graphic organizers and students with learning disabilities: A meta-analysis. *Learning Disabilities Quarterly*, 34, 51–72.
Flavell, J. H. (1976). Metacognitive aspects of problem-solving. In L. B. Resnick (Ed.), *The Nature of Intelligence*. Hillsdale, NJ: Lawrence Erlbaum.
Flavell, J. H. (1979). Metacognition and cognitive monitoring: A new area of cognitive-developmental inquiry. *American Psychologist*, 34(10), 906–911.
Gerrard, J., Collette, D., and Elowson, S. (2005). Using cooperative learning techniques with adults. Presented at *NW Regional ASTD Conference*, November 2005 Orlando, Florida, USA.
Hall, M., and Burns, M. K. (February 2018). Meta-analysis of targeted small-group reading interventions. *Journal of School Psychology*, 66, 54–66.
Holland, R., and Johnson, A. (2000). Patterning in texts. In R. Holland, and A. Lewis (Eds.), *Written Discourse* (pp. 11–28). Birmingham: School of English Centre for English Language Studies.
Ichwan, Z., Susilawati, S. M. E., and Bintari, S. H. (2015). The development of workbook DARTs-based to increase students' critical thinking skill on the contaminated environment. In Sutikno, A. Widiyatmoko, Masturi and A. Purwinako (Eds.), *International Conference on Mathematics, Science and Education 2015* (pp. 40–44). Semarang State University.

Kaddoura, M. A. (2013). Think pair share: A teaching learning strategy to enhance students' critical thinking. *Educational Research Quarterly*, 36, 3–24.

Kim, A. H., Vaughn, S., Wanzek, J., and Wei, S.(2004). Graphic organizers and their effects on the reading comprehension of students with LD: a synthesis of research. *Journal of Learning Disabilities*, 37(2), 105–118.

Manarin, K. C. M., Rathburn, M., Ryland, G., and Hutchings, P. (2015). *Critical Reading in Higher Education: Academic Goals and Social Engagement*. Indiana University Press. http://www.jstor.org/stable/j.ctt18crz3s.

McCarthy, M. (1991). *Discourse Analysis for Language Teachers*. Cambridge: Cambridge University Press.

Mevarech, Z. R., and Kramarski, B. (1997). IMPROVE: A multidimensional method for teaching mathematics in heterogeneous classrooms. *American Educational Research Journal*, 34(2), 365–394. DOI: 10.2307/1163362.

Mills, D., and Alexander, P. (2013). *Small Group Teaching: A Toolkit for Learning*. Higher Education Academy Publications. Available from https://www.advance-he.ac.uk/knowledge-hub/small-group-teaching-toolkit-learning

Miranda, J. N. W. (2011). Effect of graphic organizers on the read-ing comprehension of an English language learner with a learn-ing disability. *Second Language Studies*, 30, 95–183.

Nelson, G. (October 1984). Reading: A student-centered approach. *English Teaching Forum*, 2–5, 8.

Quigley, A., Muijs, D., and Stringer, E. (2013). *Metacognition and Self-regulated Learning Guidance Report*. Education Endowment Foundation (EEF). Available from https://educationendowmentfoundation.org.uk/public/files/Publications/Metacognition/EEF_Metacognition_and_self-regulated_learning.pdf

Sam, P. D., and Rajan, P. (2013). Using graphic organizers to improve reading com-prehension skills for the middle school ESL stu-dents. *English Language Teaching*, 6, 155–170. DOI:10.5539/elt.v6n2p155

Shamsulbahri, M. M., and Zulkiply, N. (2021). Examining the effect of directed activ-ity related to texts (DARTs) and gender on student achievement in qualitative anal-ysis in chemistry. *Malaysian Journal of Learning and Instruction*, 18(1), 157–181. DOI: 10.32890/mjli2021.18.1

Thurston, A., and Cockerill, M. (2016). *Peer Tutoring: Cross-age Paired Reading* (4th ed.). Belfast: Queen's University.

Topping, K. J., and Bryce, A. (2004). Cross-age peer tutoring of reading and thinking: Influence on thinking skills. *Educational Psychology*, 24, 595–621.

Velez, J., Cano, J., Whittington, M. S., and Wolf, K. J. 2011. Cultivating change through peer teaching. *Journal of Agricultural Education*, 52(1), 40–49. DOI: 10.5032/jae.2011.01040.

Walz, J. (2001). Critical reading and the internet. *The French Review*, 74(6), 1193–1205.

4 Assessment and feedback

Selecting the right types of formative assessment is a crucial decision when teaching learners who have literacy and language issues. Assessments should be varied and use strategies that incorporate collaborative activities like group discussion, group reading and group writing in order to differentiate for individual needs. There are many ways that this can be accomplished but in this chapter, I would like to focus on some of the main ones such as comprehension tasks, questioning, Dictagloss, Cued Spelling, the use of rubrics and peer assessment.

Comprehension tasks

Comprehension activities are one of the language teaching techniques most frequently used to train students in reading. Generally, they are based on a series of questions that direct students' attention to a reading text, but audio and video texts can be just as effective and occasionally some questions are answerable from the students' own experiences.

The questions can take many forms, namely pronominal questions, yes/no questions, true/false statements, multiple-choice items and blank-filling or completion exercises. A question can check vocabulary, sentence structure, inference, supposition, the ability to understand the question itself, and many other things.

Comprehension questions are local rather than general. They focus attention on the message of a particular text although they may require the students to use more generalisable knowledge (like the interpretation of reference words or modal verbs).

Different comprehension activities

Literal comprehension of the text. This involves understanding what the text explicitly says. At their easiest, such questions could be answered by quoting parts of the text. These questions would be more demanding if the students were not allowed to look at the text while answering the questions.

DOI: 10.4324/9781003181583-4

Drawing inferences from the text. This involves taking messages from the text that are not explicitly stated but which could be justified by reference to the text. This can involve working out the main idea of the text, looking at the organisation of the text, determining the writer's attitude to the topic, interpreting characters, and working out cause and effect and other conjunction relationships which might not be explicitly stated.

Using the text for other purposes in addition to understanding. This involves applying ideas from the text to solve problems, applying the ideas in the text to personal experience, comparing ideas in the text with other ideas from outside the text, imagining extensions of the text, and fitting the ideas in the text into a wider field, as in a review of the literature.

Responding critically to the text. This involves considering the quality of the evidence in the text, evaluating the adequacy of the content of the text, evaluating the quality of expression and clarity of language of the text, expressing agreement or disagreement with the ideas in the text, and expressing satisfaction or dissatisfaction with the text.

Some teaching activities using comprehension texts

Information transfer

The students must design a graphic organiser to represent the information in the text. Alternatively, they should write a paragraph describing the information given in a graphic organiser like a chart or a table.

Summary

Comprehension tasks can be done as group work. The students are divided into small groups. Each group makes a list of the main ideas in the passage. Then the class as a whole discusses the main points and the teacher writes. Then each group writes the complete summary.

Summary by deletion

Box 4.1 Using summary by deletion

Teaching reflection

I have used this strategy a lot when teaching Law because it helps them to summarise cases. I demonstrate how to systematically delete unimportant parts of the text and then use what is left as the text for a summary. I tell them to firstly read the passage and delete all the sentences that merely elaborate the main sentences; next, to delete all unnecessary

> clauses and phrases from the main sentences; thirdly, to delete all unnecessary words from what remains; and then replace the remaining words with their own expressions; and finally write their own summary out neatly.
>
> (Tina, Law Lecturer)

Mind the gaps

In this activity, the student must find the missing words in the comprehension text questions. Some of the words could be found directly in the text and others not, so the students must use their knowledge of vocabulary to fill the empty spaces. This task could be differentiated by giving those students that struggle with literacy the first letter of each word.

Theory to practice

Students who are on a vocational course can benefit from reading a text that explains the theory of a particular technique or work practice and then being given the opportunity to apply this in practice in class as a written task or as a role play. For example, students on a business course could read a text about Hertzberg's theory of motivation and then apply it to their own placement.

DIY

Students are given a text to read and asked to write five questions based on their understanding of the text. They give their questions to their partner and given a limited amount of time to write answers to the questions which are then marked by their partner as part of peer assessment.

Comprehension tweeting

In this exercise students read the text or watch the video and then tweet questions to each other as teams.

Concept comparison

Students are given two texts and asked to compare and contrast them; then, as an extension exercise, they could summarise the main points of the texts in 100 words.

Question time

In groups of three, students would be given a text to read and explore its ideas. Then, the rest of the group would be given the opportunity to ask them oral questions which they would have to respond to without having access to the text. This would help assess their understanding of the text and their ability to synthesise its ideas and also help those students who struggle with reading on their own.

Box 4.2 An example of how to use comprehension exercises

Teaching example

This activity was devised for a Level One Health Care group that consisted predominantly of students who struggle with literacy.

"Coronally"

i was angry when i heard about the virus which seems to scare the whole world and dictate to all how to live their lives you can't kiss you can't hug oh no you can't give even a handshake she sadly walked away as she was welcomed with a cold look when she attempted to greet me just few minutes after sneezing and coughing she had no clue that everyone was looking at her 'coronally' they said it originated from a dirty market where big sales of all sorts of animals took place the golden rule remains the old rule for you to be free from covid19 your hands your house and clothes must be clean no more night clubbing no more birthday parties no more boring lessons to attend because anywhere that is crowded is an invitation to covid19 funny, isn't it i i recon were going to be wearing masks for at lest the next six months because the goverment scientists say that the viros is caried in the air and that you can brethe it in if you are in the same rom as someone who alreddy has the virus.

Read the passage, answer the questions, and complete the tasks:

A   How can you catch the Coronavirus?
B   How can you protect yourself from catching it?
C   How many punctation and spelling mistakes can you identify? Now punctuate the passage and correct the spelling errors.
D   Identify and underline regular adjectives in the written passage below. The first one has been done for you.
E   Change the regular adjectives into extreme adjectives.
F   Summarise the main points of the passage in 100 words or fewer

---

Questioning

Some of the many varieties of types of oral questions

High-challenge questioning

Phrasing questions carefully to concentrate on Bloom's Taxonomy of higher-challenge areas. Questions must be pre-planned, as they are very difficult to invent during a lesson. Teachers must focus questions to address analysis, synthesis, evaluation, and creativity, based on Bloom's Taxonomy. This method can be particularly effective during revision classes such as in Physics or Chemistry.

Staged questioning questions

Teachers need to increase the level of challenge with each question, moving from low- to higher-order questioning.

The big question

The setting of a substantial and thought-provoking question. Big questions cannot be easily answered by students when the question is posed. They are often set at the beginning of the lesson and can only be answered by the end of the lesson, using all of the thinking based on all of the contributions to the lesson. For example, a question like 'Is global warming man-made?' could be posed in a science class and then asked again to the group at the end of a session on the causes of global warming.

Focus and funnel questioning

When students struggle to answer bigger or more complex questioning, the teacher can model or lead the thinking by asking Focus questions to lead the student through the steps of the thinking to the larger questioning. Funnel questions are the opposite of focus questions. These types of questions can start with a narrow focus and then develop into a wider discussion, or vice versa. They are very useful for assessing specific knowledge or enabling students to show a wider understanding of issues.

Hinge questions

These are questions designed to assess students' knowledge at the 'hinge point' of a class and to help the teacher decide whether the group have understood enough about a topic or a learning objective to move onto a new area.

Thick questioning and thin questioning

Students have to answer a question using a minimum of 15 words or using a particular word or phrase. They must give an extended answer or make a complete sentence/phrase. Thin questioning is the opposite to thick questioning and often linked to closed questioning. Students can answer 'yes' or 'no' to a skinny question or give a number or knowledge-based response.

Eavesdropping questioning

When using this approach, the role of the teacher is to deploying specific targeted questions. As the teacher moves around the room, they listen in on each group and contribute to the discussion by providing questions that are appropriate to the discussions.

Metacognitive questioning

These types of questions are useful to assess the process of understanding in student groups. When teachers use these types of questions, they are trying to examine the process of cognition and to assess how their students have arrived at their answers to the question. This also helps students to develop their ability to be reflective on the way they learn and to think metacognitively. They are particularly useful in teaching social sciences and the teacher should use a lot of questions that begin with 'why?' and 'how?'

Using translanguage questioning

This approach could ideally be used across many examples of questioning. There is much research that attests to the effectiveness of this strategy (Lewis et al., 2012). Teachers could utilise their students' fluency in their first language by giving them the opportunity to respond in both first and second language. This can also build confidence and help to develop an inclusive environment.

Questioning techniques

The precise questioning strategy that a teacher adopts can make a big difference to the proportion of students who participate, both mentally and verbally, in their lessons. Here are some alternative strategies that could be used to assess the students of students who have EAL and dyslexia. You might want to consider which ones would be the most effective with your own students, possibly in combination.

Question and answer: volunteers answer

Students volunteer to answer questions posed verbally by the teacher. This could be done with hands raised sometimes students call out their answer. If more than one student volunteers the teacher chooses who will answer. The 'thinking time' between asking a question and the answer being delivered is usually less than a second here. There is often a low 'participation' rate because students learn that if they do not answer, they will not be asked to contribute. If some students call out the answer, they reduce the thinking time of the others.

Question and answer: nominees answer

Students nominated by the teacher answer questions asked by the teacher. "Pose, pause, pounce." That is, the teacher poses the question, pauses for thought, and then 'pounces' on an individual to answer. (Optionally, the teacher can choose students who appear to be not listening or not engaging to answer questions.)

Buzz groups: volunteers answer

Students work in small groups, or pairs, to answer a thought-provoking question, or do a calculation or similar task. The teacher asks each group in turn to contribute part of the answer. E.g., "Can you give me one advantage of using email? Can this group give me another?" A volunteer answers for their group. They are called 'buzz groups' because of the buzz of conversation created while they work.

Buzz groups: nominees answer

Box 4.3 Using the big question technique in a sociology class

Teaching reflection

This is a favourite questioning technique of mine, and it is very effective when discussing complex issues in Sociology as it gives them time to discuss things in depth and support those students who may be struggling. I give my students a big question to discuss in groups and then I choose which student will give the group's answer after their group discussion. This way all members of the group will have to get involved in the discussion and to try to get their head around the group's answer, as any of them may be asked to explain it. Sometimes I choose students who do not appear to be taking part or engaging with the class to explain their group's answer.

(Zara, Sociology Teacher)

Assertive questioning

Groups work on a thought-provoking general question. Teacher asks individuals to give their group's answer, and then asks the rest of the class in groups to come up with their own answer. These are fed back to the whole group until a consensus class answer can be agreed. The teacher then reveals the (real) answer and the whole class discuss their answers in relation to it.

Pair checking

The teacher asks a question to the whole class. Then students work alone to answer it. In pairs they then compare their answers, giving their partner one good point and one way their answer could be improved while the teacher observes. The teacher then gives the correct answer. Pairs now suggest another improvement to their partner's answer. Pairs can then be combined to fours to compare their answers.

Dictogloss

A Dictogloss is a supported dictation strategy developed by Ruth Wajnryb (1990) for use with US high school students, but it can be adapted for use with students of all ages. It combines dictation, paraphrase, and interpretation. In it, students reconstruct a text by listening, noting down key words, and then synthesising it collectively through small-group discussion. It is especially effective with English language students because the strategy focuses on fluent academic language and supports students in listening and recalling good English language models (Gibbons, 2009).

It can have the following benefits. It can develop skills in writing notes and in paraphrasing and subject specialist vocabulary. It can develop close listening skills and focus by promoting noticing, i.e., the conscious attention to the form and the use of words and grammatical structures and, thus, can help to develop a stronger understanding of academic writing and grammatical structures (Richards and Schmidt, 2009). It can help to develop skills in recall and problem-solving skills and can encourage self-reflection when students discuss the accuracy of their summaries. This can also improve their understanding of subject matter and also to promote student autonomy and the ability to set own learning targets (Ellis, 2003). It can reduce anxiety in less confident students via working in small groups and therefore can encourage peer teaching, peer assessment and peer marking. It allows the teacher to assess their knowledge in context and can develop creativity and self-confidence in working with new genres.

Box 4.4 An example of how a Dictogloss can be used in an English class

Case study

I have several students who struggle with reading in my class and are often afraid to step out of their comfort zones, so I have found using a Dictogloss an effective way of developing the self-confidence of my students when they encounter a new genre of writing. It normally takes a bit of preparation, but these are the main steps. Firstly, I group my students into differentiated pairs and discuss the topic of the text such as recycling generally with the group and ask questions to prompt them to draw on their prior knowledge of the subject. I make sure that we discuss any problematic terms or new subject specialist vocabulary from the text and get them to note them down in their books. Then I select a text that is related to the discussed content and read it aloud at a normal speaking pace. At first, they just listen carefully and then I re-read the text at a much slower speed. I advise them now to jot down key words and phrases. Students now need to work in pairs to re-create as much of the text as possible using the notes taken by each of the partners. I tell the students to write their text as closely as possible to the original as read by me and to write in complete sentences and not in bullet points. I then like to have two differentiated pairs meet and pool their re-creations of the text to reconstruct it more completely on a piece of flip chart paper. The group of four are encouraged to work together to write down as much of the text as possible as their aim is to re-create it as closely as possible to the original. One by one each group then has to read their re-creation of the text and the other groups have to feedback and comment on how closely it matches their versions. I then display the groups' flip chart papers on the wall and, collectively, we compare and discuss them with the original text, noting the sections in the text that were difficult to re-create. As an alternative, I ask them to summarise the original text rather than reconstruct it. Sometimes I ask them to represent the ideas visually using a graphic such as a mind map or a table or a bar chart which supports those students who struggle with literacy.

(Simeon, English Teacher)

Some other assessment activities using Dictogloss

Dictogloss negotiation

Students are given the opportunity to discuss the key points after each section of text has been read. Sections can be one sentence long or longer, depending on the difficulty of the text relative to students' proficiency level. This will help develop the understanding of those texts in those learners who struggle with language.

Student–student dictation

In pairs, students read out sections of the text, or different texts, to each other and then go through the reconstruction process and finally cross-compare the reconstructed versions with the original texts.

Self-selected Dictogloss

Students bring in their own text and divide them into sections which are then given out to small groups to discuss and take notes.

Scrambled structure Dictogloss

The teacher will read out a text that has been deliberately scrambled in structure, so it lacks coherence. The onus is on students to reorganise the information in their written notes and then to summarise it collectively.

Exam model answer Dictogloss

Use Dictogloss to help students prepare for examinations by using model answers as reconstruction texts. This also helps students to practice the structure of exam answers and to revise some of the exam content by reconfiguring it.

Genre Dictogloss

For students who are studying literature Dictogloss can be an effective way of introducing the stylistic conventions of genre and can enable them to develop an understanding of the differences between genres.

Elaboration Dictogloss

Students summarise the text in groups and then are asked to research specific areas of the text and elaborate or rebut some of its key arguments and then to feed back to the group.

Dictogloss debate

Students are given the opportunity to discuss some of the central ideas of the text by inserting these comments in the text, proving a running commentary on the original text. Alternatively, these remarks can be footnotes at the end of the text (Jacobs and Small, 2003).

Cued Spelling

Cued Spelling is a well-researched example of peer teaching and assessment (Dunlosky et al. 2013). It is an especially effective way to develop spelling ability in students who struggle with literacy. Cued Spelling encourages the use of mnemonic strategies to help students remember the structure of words. These may include phonic sounds, letter names, syllables, chunks of words, or wholly idiosyncratic strategies such as drawings (Topping, 1995). In pairs, students practice spellings regularly and are assessed by frequent 'Speed Reviews'.

There are many benefits of Cued Spelling. It can help develop knowledge of subject specialist terminology and may develop a greater awareness of the mnemonic strategies they are using by developing their own cues. It is individualised learning which is student-driven and individually paced and therefore students can develop their ability to self-monitor their own learning and evaluate the effectiveness of their own strategies (Brierley et al. 1989).

Assessment and feedback 79

This can also help students develop their skills in metacognition. EAL students can develop their own cues for spelling drawn from their first language in order to make recall less problematic and can support less confident spellers who might be anxious about making spelling mistakes in front of the whole class. Because it encourages students to choose their own problematic spellings and their own cues, it allows them to take greater ownership of their learning and to support students to self-regulate and to become more autonomous learners which can help improve their own confidence as spellers (Cordewener et al., 2016). It can also facilitate collaborative learning opportunities and social interactions with peers.

What to do

Box 4.5 10 steps to Cued Spelling

Teaching strategies

1 The speller selects the words they wish to learn to spell
2 The speller checks the spellings and writes them in a glossary along with a definition.
3 Pair read word together and alone
4 Speller designs cues for each word
5 Pairs say agreed cue together
6 Speller says cues. Helped writes down the word
7 Helper says cues. Helper writes down the word
8 Speller says cues and writes word
9 Speller writes down words quickly
10 Speller reads words fluently

Box 4.6 Using the Cued Spelling approach on a Hair and Beauty course

Student feedback

Mary: When I first started on my Hair and Beauty course, I was drowning in long words which I had to learn as part of the Anatomy and Physiology unit. I had always struggled with spelling and was really anxious about how I was going to cope. The teacher showed me the Cued Spelling technique and how I could practice it with my friend on the course. Every week the teacher gave us new words to learn and spell for the examination. We worked on 10 new words a week and by the end of the term I could spell them confidently and was not worried at all by the examination.

Some tips on how to use Cued Spelling effectively

Encourage your students to decide upon own which spellings they struggle with using a Cover, Checks, Mistakes, Praise, cycle, and a Speed Review every session in which all the subject specialist words of the day are written down quickly and the spelling is compared with the original list. Incorrect spellings should be corrected by going through the 10-stage process.

Use as Mastery Review every week to reinforce learning. All the words should be written down as fast as possible and spellings should be checked with the master copy.

When there is continuing mistakes, the student should be encouraged to devise alternative cues and to begin the 10-stage process again. Don't expect immediate improvements in spelling and improvements in accuracy and speed initially.

Using rubrics

A rubric is an assessment tool that clearly presents the learning outcomes across all the components of any kind of student work, from written to oral to visual. Rubrics can be used by the teacher for marking assignments summative and also as a means of assessing formative performance such as class presentations, role plays (Rhodes, 2009). They can be used by students as a form of formative peer assessment and self-assessment in order to check they have met all the learning outcomes before they submit their summative work and to support revision for examinations. It can also facilitate collaborative learning opportunities and social interactions with peers. They can used to develop learner autonomy in less confident students, and they can support students who struggle with language as they help to break down the assignment (Wollenschlager et al., 2016).

There are two types of rubrics: Holistic and Analytical.

Holistic rubrics are used to group several different assessment criteria and classify them together under grade headings or achievement levels. The teacher should decide what are the central criteria, components, or elements that must be present in your students work. It can be useful to draw on your marking schemes to provide guidance and also criteria or elements used in other courses. You should describe in detail what the performance at each level of achievement should look like for every criterion, component, or element. Try and make these as explicit as possible. When they are being given to the students, it can be useful to provide them with exemplar work to illustrate the different levels of achievement (Dawson, 2017).

Analytical rubrics separate different assessment criteria and explain to students how they can meet the criteria. Ideally, they should explain *exactly* what the student needs to do. Analytic rubrics can either by written by the teacher or written by the teacher and students. When they are written by the teacher, the teacher draws upon the assessment criteria of the assignment and then unpacks them for the students who are then scaffolded to meet their criteria (Stevens and Levi, 2013). When they are written by both, this can be an effective way of empowering the students and giving them a greater understanding of the processes of assessment and enables them to begin to understand the rudiments of self-assessment.

Box 4.7 An example of how an analytical rubric can be used in a business class

Teaching example

I normally use this approach when I am introducing a new unit to my students as I find that it encourages them to think more deeply about how to pass the assignment. It works especially well with those students who struggle with reading assignment briefs as they benefit from the group discussions. It normally works best by taking the following steps. Firstly, I provide the students with the assessment criteria for a module or a programme and then I break them into small groups and ask them to discuss how they will meet each one of the criteria and draw this out on a sheet of flip chart paper. Once all the groups have finished, I tell the students to go around from one table to another and to annotate all of the other groups' rubrics adding their own suggestions. Then I take in all the annotated rubrics and design a master rubric containing all the students' ideas. We then meet as a whole group so the students can discuss this collectively and decide collectively on the final contents of the rubric.

(Caron, Business Studies Teacher)

How to use rubrics effectively

Try to ensure inter-rater reliability

Whether the teacher develops their own or uses an existing rubric, it can help if they show it to another teacher on the programme and other similar programmes and gain their feedback as they can help its inter-rater reliability.

Be transparent

Discuss it with students when you first give them the assignment brief and give them a copy of it. These are not meant to be surprise criteria. Hand the rubric back with the assignment. Ask your students to provide feedback about the rubric after they have used it. Always be prepared to revise the rubric and to make changes accordingly to fit their needs and preferences

Integrate the rubrics into assignments

Require students to attach the rubric to the assignment when they submit it. Students could also be asked to self-assess or give peer feedback using the rubric prior to handing in their work.

Mark the rubrics

Ensure that when the rubric is returned the rubric is also marked and show how each one has been criterion has been achieved. This can then be cross-mapped against comments in the assignment and the grade itself and also always allow teacher feedback space to include any additional specific or overall comments that do not fit within the rubric's criteria.

Peer assessment

Why is it useful? It develops autonomy in students and empowers the learner to take control of their own assessment. It develops students' confidence in assessing/marking peers work and their abilities to self-evaluate and reflect, gaining an ability to 'stand back' from own work for assessment purposes and to reflect more clearly on recently completed assessments and improve their understanding of their strengths and weaknesses (Petty, 2002). It provides the student with a stronger understanding of what is required by their teachers for assessments and hence can create more interactive classes and more transparent open marking systems (seeing what is required and improving work). Ultimately, it can allow students to learn from each other's successes (Boud and Falchikov 1989).

According to Wiliam (2011) one of the underlying conditions of its success is:

> … a classroom culture or ethos where errors are valued as learning opportunities and admitting to not understanding something is acceptable. Pupils act as critical friends, critiquing the work of others in a way that both supports and challenges them and facilitates their future success. In order for such a culture to thrive teachers must be able to show that they too can make mistakes.

Many types of student work lend itself to peer assessment. Some suggestions, according to Race (1999), include the following: student presentations, reports, essay plans, mathematical calculations, role plays, annotated bibliographies, practical work, poster displays, portfolios, exhibitions, artefacts, and performances.

Some peer assessment methods (Petty, 2002)

Basic two medals and a mission

Students identify two positive aspects of the work of a peer and then express a wish about what the peer might do next to improve another aspect of the work. Teachers model this strategy several times, using samples of student work, before asking the students to use the strategy in pairs on their own. They check the process and ask pairs who have implemented the strategy successfully to demonstrate it to the whole group.

Advanced two medals and a mission

Peers comment on what was done well in relation to the success criteria, and also on what could be done better. This strategy may be better used after the students have become adept at using medals and a mission. This strategy can also be used as part of self-assessment, where students use 'What's next?' to set a personal learning target. This strategy could also be delivered in the learners who have EAL home languages, and it can especially be effective at developing self-confidence in learners who are struggling and who respond well to peer support.

Warm and cool feedback

When students comment on the positive aspects of a peer's work, they are said to be giving warm feedback, and when they identify areas that need improvement, they are providing cool feedback. They provide hints on 'How to raise the temperature' when they give advice about how their peer could improve their work. Alternatively, using the strategy known as find it and fix it, peers check work quickly but do not mark the work. They only identify the number of mistakes. They then return the work to the student to find and fix the mistakes.

Traffic lights

Students 'green-light' (using a green highlighter on the margin of the work) the work of their peer to indicate where the success criteria have been achieved, or 'amber-light' where improvement is needed. This strategy is best used on a draft before they submit the assignment although it could also be used, with coloured sticky notes, to provide feedback on a final piece of work. The suggestions for improvement would then relate to the next occasion on which the students undertook work which required similar skills. They could also be encouraged to develop assignment rubrics based on the assessment criteria which they would then use to assess their peers' work.

De Bono's thinking hats (De Bono, 1985)

Teachers need to model the use of the Thinking hats and to train students in their use before asking them to use the hats as one of the peer feedback strategies. The Thinking hats encourage thinking from different perspectives and can be used to focus students' feedback to their peers. For example, the White Hat encourages students to focus objectively on the facts of the criteria, whereas the Red Hat prompts students to rely on their intuition and hunches. This can be used more effectively when students are given a case study in a Child Care lesson to analyse or a practical problem to solve as in a Construction lesson.

One question, one comment

Students are given a text to read from which they are asked to provide one question and one comment. This process passes from student to student, who can either answer the question posed to them or make their own comment. This can also be used as a successful plenary activity for those learners who have struggled to keep up with the class because of learning or language barriers.

Sixty seconds

Organise the group into two teams. Ask for three volunteer speakers from each team. The speakers must speak on a teacher-specified topic for one minute without hesitation, repetition, or deviation. Their performances will be assessed by the opposing team according to criteria which have been agreed with the students. If the speaker fails, the topic passes over to the other team. Alternatively, your students could be asked to write a one-minute essay about one of the topics discussed in the class for peer feedback.

Peer-created questions

Students in pairs/groups pose a question for the class to answer at the beginning of the session and write it on mini whiteboards or post-its. At the end of the lesson take the questions and ask other groups to answer them. Students in groups then work on answers. Groups feedback to the class with answers. If necessary, the teacher expands on the answers. The teacher could finish off by providing a question for the whole group to discuss and answer.

Box 4.8 I, you and we table

Teaching resource

One	Two	Review	Review…
I learned this …	You thought/ explained/added	I now know	I didn't know/think of this because

---

The process starts with the students' individual learning experiences, progresses towards the prior experience, and ends up on individual deeper refection on learning.

Five bullet point summary

Students are given a key quote that encapsulates all or part of the lesson and are asked to summarise it in five bullet points.

Box 4.9 An example quote

Here is an example quote which I gave to a group of mainly students who had EAL or literacy issues studying Level 3 Access to Education class to summarise in five bullet points:

The strongest argument for differentiation to me is looking at the kids sitting in the classroom. It's rare to go into a classroom where kids are all from the same language group, the same culture, the same socioeconomic status, the same background experience, the same wiring in terms of abilities, areas of weakness, that sort of thing. Realizing how seldom you go into a classroom and find virtually everyone fully engaged and participating in an optimistic way signals a need for instruction that addresses individual variance as well as common content requirements. We have way too many students who bring to school with them needs and differences that we just don't take into account in our thinking and planning. And we fail many learners when we do that (Curry magazine, 2011).

The group worked in pairs for 10 minutes on the task. They were then asked to feedback their responses which were recorded by a student scribe on a flip chart and then discussed by the group as a whole. The group managed to mention all the key ideas, diversity, individual learning needs, language barriers, and socio-economic barriers. The students then took pictures of the flip chart on their phones and also posted it on their social media groups for those students who were absent.

Conclusion

In this chapter we have discussed different methods of teaching, learning and formative assessment specifically designed to meet the needs of EAL students with literacy needs. We have analysed a variety of collaborative methods, including comprehension tasks, questioning approaches, and peer assessment, which can create opportunities for your students to become more confident and more engaged and better able to achieve. The next chapter will develop these themes and will focus more on approaches to self-assessment and the role of feedback.

Box 4.10 Over to you!

Peer assessment – The killer pass

This peer assessment method is best used at the end of the teaching day. At the end of the session the teacher starts the plenary with a question directed to the whole class. Whoever answers it correctly gets the right to go home and to direct another question at a student. This process continues throughout the group until everyone has left the room. This strategy can work very well in groups that thrive on friendly competition too, such as those on Public Service or Sports courses.

Box 4.11 Take away self-reflective questions

How do you ensure that your students take your formative assessments of learning seriously?
How do you record and track students' progress from formative assessment?
How do you plan for a range of questions in your classes?

References

Boud and Falchikov (1989) in Falchikov, N. (2005) *Improving Assessment Through Student Involvement*. Oxon: Routledge Falmer.
Brierley, M., Hutchinson, P., Topping, K., and Walker, C. (1989). Reciprocal peer-tutored cued spelling with ten year olds. *Paired Learning*, 5, 136–140.
Cordewener, K. A. H., Verhoeven, L., and Bosman, A. M. T. (2016). Improving spelling performance and spelling consciousness. *The Journal of Experimental Education*, 84(1), 48–74. DOI: 10.1080/00220973.2014.963213
Curry Magazine (2011). Faculty conversation: Carol Tomlinson on differentiation. Available from https://education.virginia.edu/news/faculty-conversation-carol-tomlinson-differentiation.
Dawson, P. (2017). Assessment rubrics: Towards clearer and more replicable design, research and practice. *Assessment & Evaluation in Higher Education*, 42(3), 347–360.
De Bono, E. (1985). *Six Thinking Hats: An Essential Approach to Business Management*. Boston, Massachusetts, United States: Little, Brown, & Company.
Dunlosky, J., Rawson, K. A., Marsh, E. J., Nathan, M. J., and Willingham, D. T. (2013). Improving students' learning with effective learning techniques: Promising directions from cognitive and educational psychology. *Psychological Science in the Public Interest*, 14, 4–58. DOI: 10.1177/1529100612453266
Ellis, Rod (2003). *Task-based Language Learning and Teaching*. Oxford, New York: Oxford University Press.

Gibbons, Pauline (2009). *English Learners, Academic Literacy, and Thinking*. Portsmouth, NH: Heinemann.

Jacobs, G., and Small, J. (2003). Combining Dictogloss and cooperative learning to promote language learning. *The Reading Matrix*, 3(1). Available from http://www.readingmatrix.com/articles/jacobs_small/article.pdf

Lewis, G., Jones, B., and Baker, C. (2012). Translanguaging: Developing its conceptualisation and contextualisation. *Educational Research and Evaluation*, 18, 1–16. DOI: 10.1080/13803611.2012.718490.

Petty, G. (2002). *Teaching Today*. Oxford: Oxford University Press.

Race, P. (1999). *The Lecturer's Toolkit* (5th ed.). London: Routledge.

Rhodes, T. (2009). *Assessing outcomes and improving achievement: Tips and tools for using the rubrics*. Washington, DC: Association of American Colleges and Universities.

Richards, Jack C., and Schmidt, Richard, eds. (2009). "Dictogloss". *Longman Dictionary of Language Teaching and Applied Linguistics*. New York: Longman.

Stevens, D. and Levi, A. (2013). *Introduction to rubrics: An assessment tool to save grading time, convey effective feedback, and promote student learning* (2nd ed.). Virginia: Sylus.

Topping, K. (1995). Cued spelling: A powerful technique for parent and peer tutoring. *The Reading Teacher*, 48(5), 374–383. Available at: http://www.jstor.org/stable/20201450. Accessed: 30 August 2021.

Wajnryb, R. (1990). *Grammar Dictation. Resource Book for Teachers*. Series Editor: A. Maley. Oxford: Oxford University Press.

Wiliam, D. (March 2011). What is assessment for learning? *Studies in Educational Evaluation*, 37(1), 3–14.

Wollenschlager, M., Hattie, J., Machts, N., and Harms, U. (2016). What makes rubrics effective in teacher feedback? Transparency of learning goals is not enough. *Contemporary Educational Psychology*, 44–45, 1–11.

5 Self-assessment and feedback

Self-assessment

According to Boud (1995), self-assessment is about students developing their learning skills. It is not primarily about individuals giving themselves marks or grades. And it is not about supplanting the role of teachers.

Self-assessment has many benefits. It enhances learning, including deep and lifelong learning, and can develop better understanding of content and increased quality and thoughtfulness on assignments because students are learning from giving and receiving feedback. It provides better understanding of the assessment process and can alleviate student anxiety and ease student–teacher conflict by making the grading process more transparent (McDonald and Boud, 2003). It promotes active engagement with learning and can develop learner self-reflection and autonomy, cognitive abilities, and metacognitive engagement, and build self-confidence and motivation for learning.

Some of the most effective approaches to self-assessment

Peer then self-assessment

Help students cut their teeth on peer assessment before they self-assess as it is often easier for students to make judgements about their own work when they have looked critically at what others have done. This can also be developed into Vygotskian self-assessment, where you scaffold learners at the outset, then progressively let them take a greater degree of responsibility for their assessment as their understanding of the process matures and they are able to evaluate their own strengths and weaknesses (Panadero et al., 2019).

Unpacking the assessment criteria

Provide opportunities for students to discuss what the criteria will mean in practice and get them to describe exactly what sorts of performance or evidence will demonstrate achievement of the criteria. This could also be done in combination with a self-produced rubric.

Use self-assessment as part of group assessment

Include self-assessment when assessing group process. Give students the opportunity to assess the contributions of their peers and then assess their own contribution using the same criteria. This could be developed on an individual basis by encouraging students to film their own group contributions, presentations, routines, etc. as this can allow them to reflect very deeply on their skills within the privacy of their own home. His method is very commonly used in performing arts assessment.

Self-assessment as goal setting

At the end of a task, topic, or lesson, students are reminded of the goals, objectives, or assessment criteria. Students can then be asked to take several minutes to look over their work and self-assess what they have learned, know, and can do and what they still need to learn or practice to achieve the goal or objectives. Students use this to set themselves an individual action plan. The action plan is implemented in the next lesson. For example, students studying English might set tasks to improve their spelling.

Self-assessment with integrated peer/tutor feedback

Students carry out self-assessment based on marking sheets provided along with criteria and standards required; and give themselves a grade. The teacher provides feedback using the grading criteria, but without providing a mark or grade. Students then also receive peer feedback and, finally, taking all feedback received into account, they revise and re-grade their own work.

Box 5.1 An example of self-assessment in biology using the traffic light system

Teaching example

I use this technique because it gives me instant feedback from the learners and enables me to personalise learning quite quickly. I give each student three cards: A Green, a Yellow and a Red card. I then ask them to raise these cards accordingly during the session whilst the outcomes are being reviewed. Raising the Green card would mean that the student believes they have achieved the outcome. Showing the Yellow card would mean they need some further support, and the Red card would mean they need a lot more scaffolding. This would then be followed up by using differentiation so that students with Green cards would receive slightly more advanced tasks. Those with Yellow cards would receive extra scaffolding from the teacher or from another peer. The students

> with Red cards would require the teacher to use more intensive reinforcement. This can also be combined with self-marking with mock papers. I provide them with a list of topics and subtopics that appeared in the test, and are ask them to mark each as: Green if they can understand how to do them (ignoring careless slips)/Red if they do not understand how to do them. Amber if they are not sure.
>
> (Fiona, Science Teacher)

Using technology

Use flexible learning materials. Most such materials include a lot of self-assessment exercises in one way or another. Usually, the primary benefit of these is not strictly self-assessment, but the delivery of feedback to students who have had a try at the exercises. However, flexible learning continuously develops students' own picture of their progress. Teachers can also provide self-assessment opportunities as diagnostic aids. Open learning or computer-based packages can include sets of questions designed to help students identify which sections of their work may need particular attention (Andrade, 2018). The packages can also include remedial 'loops' that students experiencing particular difficulties can be routed through.

Self-assessment can also be done by learners using applications on their phones. For instance, at the end of the session give the students a code to scan which contains questions about the session and let them test their knowledge and feedback the answers as part of the plenary or as part of a recap starter next session. You could also ask your learners to mark each as: Green if they can understand how to do them (ignoring careless slips)/Red if they do not understand how to do them. Amber if they are not sure. You might also consider asking your students to use their phone to create short narratives about the session explaining what the highlights were, which bits they did not understand.

Or they could use Twitter to expand their knowledge. Encourage your students to summarise the session in 140 characters and send it as a Tweet. If they haven't got Twitter, they could use a large Post – it note and attach it to the wall as they leave the class. This can also be achieved by encouraging learners to complete entries on a blog or an online learning journal. If you encourage students to review their own performance regularly through keeping journals, so they can build up a picture of their own so work over a period.

Today's targets

Students set three targets for themselves at the beginning of the session. They secure them to the underside of the desk and review them at the end of the session, feeding back the results to the rest of the class. These targets could also be peer-reviewed by classmates who could vote on each student's success at meeting their own targets. In sports science classes, learners can use this to record and then review their personal best practical performance targets for circuit training etc.

Ongoing annotated bibliographies

Students assess their understanding of the texts have read by providing short evaluations as part of an annotated bibliography. They can also refer back to these when they are doing assignments in future to ascertain which sources are worth using again.

Outcomes self-assessment

Individually or in pairs students are given the Learning Outcomes at the beginning of the unit and told to map the assignment tasks against the individual Learning Outcomes and develop a plan on how they are going to meet each Learning Outcome. They feed them back to the whole group and the group is given the opportunity to develop a master plan of action for the assignment. This could also be extended into a planning task by organising your students into small groups and encourage them to break down the process of completing the assignment into a set of stages with mini deadlines. Once they have done this, they can feed them back to the rest of the group in order to gain a general consensus. Each student will then be able to monitor their own progress against a timetable to which they have all contributed. This strategy is especially effective in planning project work, as in public service courses.

Reflective questions

Race (1999) suggests using a series of prompted questions to get students thinking about their performance. This might include the following:

> *What do you think is a fair grade for the work you have handed in?*
> *What did you do best in this assessment task?*
> *What did you do least well in this assessment task?*
> *What did you find was the hardest part?*
> *What was the most important thing you learned in doing this assessment task?*
> *If you had more time to complete the task, would you change anything?*
> *What would you change, and why?*

Positive evaluation

Give students practice at positively evaluating themselves. For example, give them nine Post-it™ notes and ask them to list nine qualities or skills they have, and get them to prioritise them in a ranking order of 1 to 9. Once they have listed their nine qualities or skills, they should select the bottom three in the first instance and set them as performance targets to achieve in each session. Then they should move onto the next three and so on until they have achieved all their original skills targets. It is important to consider what only students can really assess. For example, students alone can give a rating to how much effort they put into a task, how strong their motivation is in a particular subject, or how much they believe they have improved over a period.

Using self-assessment to determine students' prior knowledge

Use self-assessment to establish existing competence. Self-assessment exercises and tests can be a quick way of enabling students to establish how much of their prior learning is relevant to the prerequisite knowledge for their next course or module.

Self-assessment before formal submission

Use self-assessment sometimes in lectures and tutorials. For example, when students have brought along coursework expecting to hand it in for tutor marking, it can be useful to lead the whole group through self-assessment against clear marking guidelines. The work can still be handed in, and it is usually much faster and easier to moderate students' own assessments than to mark the work from scratch. This will help students to learn to make balanced judgements about themselves that relate directly to the assessment criteria by providing clear evidence of what has been achieved by highlighting sections of their assignment, for example.

Self-assessment as part of learning contracts

When students are producing evidence specifically relating to their own learning contracts, it can be useful to ask them to self-assess how well they have demonstrated their achievement of some of their intended outcomes. One way of firming this up is to allocate some tutor-assessed marks for the quality of their own self-assessment; students can be given feedback on this too.

Self-assessment as workshop review

The objectives are stated at the beginning of each lesson by every teacher in the team and are written by students in an exercise book specifically for this purpose. Students review their learning against the objectives at the end of each session. The workshop teacher deals with any objectives with which the whole class has had trouble. Students are also supported in personal work towards their learning objectives. They can also draw on peer support if need be and receive support in their own language.

Box 5.2 An example of video self-assessment in a dance class

Teaching example

I find that using video self-assessment is a strong technique and very engaging for the learners who like using their phones all the time! I encourage them to film their routines video to informally self-assess using applications like TikTok. Watching films of their own performances in the comfort of privacy can allow them to reflect very deeply on their skills. In fact, it is sometimes useful to suggest that students view each other's videos informally after self-assessing, to put the self-critical evaluations some students may have made of themselves into more comfortable perspective. I find that this also boost their self-confidence and makes them better at critical evaluation in general.

(Claire, Dance Lecturer)

Using model answers to self-assess in an English class

Box 5.3 Using self-assessment in an English class

Teaching example

I use this method extensively in the run-up to examinations as it provides learners with a clear opportunity to reflect on where their learning is and how they can move on from this. Firstly, I explain to them that they will mark their own work on this exercise, and that I will not be marking it. (However, I reserve the right to check whether or not students have self-assessed.) My students complete the exercise, which might be a series of questions or a short composition to write. When they have finished, they proof-read their own work before the next stage. Students are then given model answers or exemplars. These might have a mark scheme on them. They mark their own work against these model answers. If they do not understand an answer, or why their answer is wrong, they try to work this out for themselves rather than asking immediately for help. I give them help where it is needed but I do not mark the work or check the students own marking usually. Students can then do the next few questions and so on. I think this process also develops confidence in students that lack literacy skills and helps build motivation.

(Marcus, English Teacher)

Three-minute pause

Ask students to complete one of the following phrases:

> I have changed my attitude about…
> I became more aware about…
> I was surprised about…
> I felt…
> I related to…
> I empathised with…

Box 5.4 A RAG rating table for self-assessment

Teaching resource

Vocational skills

Complete the table by writing down the skills you need to complete this unit and RAG rate them according to the key below:

Red: needs improving
Amber: average/okay
Green: good

Skill	Red	Amber	Green	Teacher assessment
For example. Critical analysis	*			

Which of these skills do you need to improve most?
Learning Target for next piece of work.

Ipsative assessment

The term 'ipsative' derives from the Latin word *ipse*, meaning 'of the self'. Ipsative assessment was originally used in psychology for intelligence testing of children in the 1940s as an alternative to norm referencing. An ipsative assessment is a comparison with a previous performance. It is a self-comparison. The ultimate goal in an ipsative assessment is a personal best performance (Malecka and Boud, 2021). Ipsative assessment is non-competitive because the performance of others is irrelevant; the goals are internal and individual.

There are many benefits of Ipsative assessment. It provides credit as to how far the student has advanced since the previous assessment. It is non-competitive, since it is irrelevant where the learner started off. It is longitudinal and cumulative in that it takes place over significant timescales and identifies lack of progress as well as progress. It can provide opportunities for all students to achieve at different levels of performance and it can raise students' future expectations, enhance levels of self-reflection and critical thinking, and support the development of Self-Regulatory Learning as it empowers and motivates through the setting of self-targets (Nishizuka, 2022). Because it focuses on development over time, it can develop self-belief and the confidence to achieve and be adaptable, flexible, and responsive to changing contexts. It thereby acts as a bridge between one learning task and the next (Hughes et al., 2017).

How this can be used

League table grading

> **Box 5.5 An example of league table Ipsative assessment used in a sports class**
>
> **Teaching example**
>
> My students used to struggle with consistency of effort across the course. Many of them had issues with literacy and tended to be less motivated in the less practical units. I decided to build on their competitive instincts and their love of football by introducing a league table system into the sessions. Each student designed an individual league table containing their subjects. They ranked them according to the grades the student had received in each subject. Each grade was equivalent to points. For example, a Pass was one point, a Merit was two points, and a Distinction was three points. The subject in which the student was most successful was top of the league and the one they are most struggling with was bottom. I encouraged my students to compete against themselves in a race to improve overall points across all subjects. Every few weeks, they were asked to bring their league tables to class to be discussed with peers or in individual tutorial sessions. Over the academic year their grades started to become more consistent as they worked hard to bring the subjects in the 'relegation zone' towards the top of the table.
>
> (Mark, Sports Lecturer)

Using online software

Using online software like Grammarly you could encourage your students to check their draft work for mistakes section by section and try to reduce the number of errors until they finish on Zero at the end of the draft. They could also use closed online blogging space such as on Google Classroom or VLEs students could be encouraged to comment on their own learning progress on an assignment on a weekly basis. The teacher's role would be to feedback on these and provide further targets of development for the coming week.

Online quizzes and tests

Students can be given an online quiz from Kahoot, for example, to complete after a lecture from which they receive an instant score and instant feedback. The following session they are given a similar test to see if they can beat their previous one. This could be combined with performance posters which they could design for their bedrooms containing targets for each assignment and encourage them to give themselves medals for each target they hit. Each medal will represent a treat they will give themselves (McDonald and Boud, 2003).

Feedforward, reflection, response and feedback, feedforward (FRRFF) (taken from Hughes, 2017)

There is a three-stage feedback process which consists of the following:

In stage one, the student submits a draft of their assignment along with an assignment cover sheet consisting of the following questions:

> *Please indicate what feedback you were given, for your last assignment, in terms of how you could improve.*
> *Please indicate what feedback you were given for your draft of this assignment in terms of how you could improve (if applicable).*
> *Please comment on the extent to which you feel you have responded to feedback.*

The draft is then formatively assessed by the teacher who also provides feedforward on how the assignment could be improved for the final submission. In stage two, the student reflects upon the feedforward given and implements it whilst making amendments to their final submission. The teacher marks the work in stage three and feeds back on to what extent previous feedback has been utilised by the student. They also provide feedforward for the next assignment.

Reflecting on and comparing feedback

Similarly, before undertaking a new assignment encourage your students to complete reflection on their progress in implementing past feedback and the obstacles they may have encountered. The teacher will need to provide an evaluative response to the reflection and then feedforward some developmental targets for the new assignment. You could also encourage learners to compare feedback and feedforward from previous assignments before they start new ones in a tutorial. Ask them to reflect on the most recurring issues. Feed back to them on their responses and ask them to develop a plan to build upon this in their coming assignment.

Feedback

Feedback is information that is communicated to a learner based upon their performance on a particular task. It aims to develop students' conceptual understanding of the topic and their problem-solving skills. It is especially important for EAL students as it can contribute to the creation of a collaborative, inclusive, and constructive learning environment.

Feedback can be in a number of forms: Formative, Summative, Informal, Peer Feedback, and Self-feedback. Formative feedback is ongoing feedback and helps teachers to focus on student learning and students to better understand the limits of their own knowledge and how to improve. Summative feedback occurs at the end of a learning process and functions to provide students with an overall judgement of their learning. It is normally focussed directly on the student's performance against the marking criteria, strengths, weaknesses, and opportunities for improvement.

Informal feedback normally occurs spontaneously a teaching session. It can be done either face to face or online. Its success is highly dependent upon the rapport between teacher and student. Peer feedback is defined by Topping (1998) as 'all task-related information that a learner communicates to a peer of similar status which can be used to improve his or her academic performance'. It can be either formative or summative but tends to be associated more with the former than the latter (Huisman et al., 2019). Self-feedback is given by the student to themselves to generate the understanding and the skills to close the gap between their current performance and their desired level. It can improve a student's knowledge of their own capabilities, develop their understanding of the way that they strategise their learning and enhance their ability to self-regulate their studying patterns (Panadero et al., 2019). Feedback can be given individually, or group-based.

Individual feedback

Individual feedback is personalised and specific to the individual's performance. It can be given as oral feedback, written feedback, or online feedback. It can be given on an ad hoc basis during the session to respond to a student's question or answer, used to orally scaffold individual students whilst the lesson is progressing or given orally or in a written form during individual tutorials. It can also be provided when a summative assignment is being returned and the teacher needs to discuss how the student is progressing and how they can use their developing knowledge and skills acquired in the next assignment. Research suggests that EAL students prefer this form of feedback and argue that it has the strongest impact on their motivation and self-efficacy (Topping, 1998).

Group-based feedback

Group-based feedback is more generic and is normally given when a group of students could benefit from the same information and guidance. It can be given as oral feedback, written feedback, or online feedback. It can be used in combination with individual feedback to particularise. Group-based feedback could be used in different situations. For example, it could be given at the start of a session in to evaluate the group's performance in the previous session. Or, when it is necessary to review a lesson or to re-teach because the group is struggling to meet the learning outcomes. It can also be effective when a summative assignment is being returned and the teacher needs to highlight patterns of results, the collective strengths and weaknesses shown by the group and how the group can use the knowledge and skills acquired in the next assignment.

Hattie and Timperley (2007) argue that feedback should provide answers to three key questions for the learner: Where am I going? How am I going? Where to next? It should be underpinned by five central ethical principles (McNair, 1996): learner centredness, as feedback should aim to support the progress of the individual student; confidentiality, as it should be transparent and available only to those that need to have access to it such as the individual student and relevant programme staff; impartiality, as it should be fair and objective; accessibility, as, ideally, it should be jargon-free and clearly explained; and equality of opportunity, as it should be given in a way that no student is discriminated against.

Four levels of feedback

There are four levels of feedback (Hattie and Timperley, 2007): Feedback About the Task (FT); Feedback About the Processing of the Task (FP); Feedback at the Self-Regulation Level (FR); and Feedback About the Self as a Person (FS).

Feedback About the Task (FT)

This relates primarily to whether work is correct or incorrect but may include directions as to where the student needs to expand in their assignment. The main characteristics of FT are that it is specific and can often only build surface knowledge, and it is most effective when it targets faulty information or when feeding back on simple tasks when expressed as written comments or annotations rather than numerical grades alone. For example, it can be used when correcting spelling errors or errors in calculations. One of its major shortcomings is that too much feedback at this level can result in students focussing too much on correcting errors rather than understanding the strategies behind the corrections; it can lead to more random trial-and-error learning strategies.

Feedback About the Processing of the Task (FP)

This feedback is aimed at the processing of information used to complete a task. It is concerned with deeper understanding of learning and the construction of meaning and provides information about the processes of the task and can often provide directions for improvement. It is aimed at supporting student in finding strategies for the detection of errors in their work and it helps to provide cues to students, resulting in more effective information search. It can improve motivation and self-efficacy in students and it can be especially powerful when linked with FT. For example, when teachers feedback on spelling and calculation errors, they should advise students on how to spot errors in their own work rather than show them what they have done wrong in their work. Research suggests that immediate feedback is better for FT and delayed feedback for FP (Hattie and Timperley, 2007).

Feedback at the Self-regulation Level (FR)

FR focusses on the way that students monitor, direct, and regulate their actions to achieve their learning goals. It implies the development of autonomy, self-control, self-direction, and self-discipline in students.

There are many factors that can mediate its effectiveness on students. For example, the ability in students to self-appraise, which implies the ability to evaluate ability and understanding and to self-manage, which implies the ability to develop plans and strategies to complete the task effectively. Students' attitudes and self-belief towards past failures and successes can also impact on the extent to which the student is motivated to act on the feedback (Deci and Ryan, 2008). At the FR level, the impact of praise can be dependent on whether the student desires to complete the task or is compelled to do so. In the latter case, negative feedback is more effective and in the former, positive. Ultimately, positive feedback has a stronger impact on students who receive FR feedback (Hattie and Timperley, 2007).

Box 5.6 An example of how FR is used in an access to sociology class

Teaching strategy

I prefer to do this on an individual level and to balance of praise against achievable goals and targets. I also have a mental list of self-prompts that I use to help me keep on track and to allow me to focus on how I can move my students forward. Here are some of my examples. I ask myself:

> How can the student monitor their own work?
> How can they carry out self-checking?
> How can they reflect on his/her own learning?
> What learning goals they achieved?
> How have their ideas changed?
> Can they now teach another student how to …?
> (Richard, Sociology Teacher)

Feedback About the Self as a Person (FS)

In this feedback there are positive and negative evaluations made about the student and less focus on the work. It tends to have little impact on effort, engagement, or feelings of self-efficacy in students as little information is provided in the feedback about the task itself. It can only be effective if it is directed to the effort, self-reflection or the processes, strategies, or engagement of the student. This can develop self-efficacy, but its effects are influenced by students' own self-concepts as students as student bias and the way they select feedback information is often based on their self-identity as a learner (Deci and Ryan, 2008). Overall, the impact of praise can be unpredictable often due to the representational lens and biases of individual students (Townsend, 2014).

Some of the central principles of feedback practice (Juwah et al., 2004)

This facilitates the development of reflection/self-assessment in learning. Students should be able to use feedback given to monitor the gap between the tasks set and their own personal goals and outcomes that are being produced. To do so, students need to understand more about the processes and the products of learning. Some examples of how this can be achieved include:

Self-selection of feedback

The student will highlight the sections of their assignment which they found most problematic and ask the teacher to focus upon those in their formative feedback. This will also develop autonomy and independence in the student.

Self-designed feedback checklists

The student will use the feedback provided by the teacher to design a checklist consisting of the areas to be improved upon which will be used in future assignments to self-monitor their progress and achievements and bolster self-efficacy and self-belief.

Feedback can encourage dialogues between the student and the teacher, and the student and their peers. Studies recommend that giving feedback should be part of a democratic dialogue between teacher and student and student and student and not a one-way top-down process by the teacher (Forsythe and Johnson, 2016, Townsend, 2014). Some examples of how this can be achieved include:

Peers swopping feedback

Students could exchange feedback given by the teacher with a peer and discuss with them how they can improve their work. Research has suggested that peer feedback is often more powerful than that given by the teacher and more acted upon (Wiliam, 2007).

Using one-minute papers (Weaver and Cottrell, 1988).

Box 5.7 Using minute papers in a drama class plenary

Teaching reflection

I have used one-minute papers continuously in my plenaries as it seems to suit both me and my students. I give them one minute to answer a question posed by me about something we have discussed in class or one of the learning objectives. They seem to like the challenge of writing under pressure, and it provides for me a real snapshot of learning. I find that it can indicate to me how much they have understood important concepts presented during a class and it provides me with an insight into future teaching improvements.

(Kirsty, Drama Teacher)

Student evaluation of feedback

After a student has received formative feedback on an assignment, they could highlight those comments which they found most helpful and how they have used them to improve their work and feed this back to the teacher.

Feedback can help clarify for students what constitutes good performance though identifying their goals, the assessment criteria, and expected standards. Some studies indicate that students will only be able to achieve their goals, if they understand what they are, take ownership of them and know how to achieve them (Wiliam, 2011). Some examples of how this can be achieved include:

Make assessment criteria more transparent

Make assignment briefs more detailed and user-friendly by breaking down the criteria/standards into plain English and walking through them with your students when you launch the assignment.

Use exemplars

Provide students with marked exemplars of previous students' work and let them map the feedback given against the learning outcomes. This could also be done using model answers to mark against the learning outcomes to develop their understanding of the outcomes and how to meet them effectively.

Feedback as a way of closing the gap

Feedback should also provide opportunities for closing the gap. Students need to understand where they are and where they need to be to be able to close the gap. Without this support from their teacher, their efforts will be misdirected and wasted. Some examples of how this can be achieved include:

Modelling answers

Teachers could model the strategies that students need to close the performance gap in class. For example, this could be done by breaking down an essay into sections and talking through the content in each section.

Providing work-in-progress feedback

Research suggests that detailed and frequent formative feedback during the production of work is most effective at closing the gap. This could be a combination of teacher and peer feedback (Juwah et al., 2004).

Reviewing action plans

Students could be encouraged to draw up their own action plans based on formative feedback which could then be reviewed frequently by the teacher to ensure that the student is meeting their own targets.

Feedback should deliver high-quality information to students about their learning. It should be detailed, concise and easy to act upon by students. It should focus on those areas that are of the most significance in their work and should offer corrective advice mapped against the assessment criteria. Some examples of how this can be achieved include:

Feedforward

Teachers should ensure that the tone of their feedback is non-authoritative and encouraging and motivating rather than terse and judgmental. To do this more effectively they might focus less in their feedback on the strengths and weaknesses of their students' work and more on how they can develop their work in future assignments. This could also be done by prioritising areas for improvement. Teachers could cut down the length of their lists of areas of improvement and focus on the most significant areas so as to make the student feel that these are more achievable.

Feedback provides information that can be used to help shape future teaching. Effective feedback can help teachers as it can provide data about the effectiveness of the teaching and enable them to review and amend their future accordingly. Some examples of how this can be achieved include:

Online pop quizzes

These can provide an instant snapshot of how much learning is taking place and provide a breakdown of student responses that can be used to target students in subsequent lesson plans. Applications like Kahoot! *Who Wants to be a Millionaire?* tend to be enjoyed by all students, but especially those who struggle with written answers. When these are staged in MS Teams students also benefit from collaborative support and they can also confer in their home languages.

Using student voice

Students could be asked in groups which areas they would like the teacher to focus on in teaching sessions and may even become involved in the design of schemes of work. Or they could identify where they are having problems when they submit their work which would enable the teacher to build this within their lesson planning.

Feedback can be given in different ways: oral, written or online.

Oral feedback

Arguably, this is one of the most powerful forms of feedback because it allows teachers to clarify students' misconceptions immediately. It can do the following: appraise and praise, distil and summarise learning on the spot, re-direct learning if the learner is drifting from the point, correct errors and seek clarification and encourage exploration, elaboration, or experiment which can develop reflection-in-action (Clarke and Mayer, 2016).

Two examples of how oral feedback can be used in practice are ipsative tutorial feedback and self-reflective feedback.

Ipsative tutorial feedback

> **Box 5.8 Using structured questions designed to stimulate self-reflection**
>
> **Teaching strategy**
>
> This form of feedback identifies concrete areas for improvement by using structured questions designed to stimulate self-reflection and to move students towards their next assignment. These could include the following:
>
> 1. How do you think you did on this paper?
> 2. With which parts of your work were you happiest?
> 3. Which comments on the text make the most sense to you?
> 4. Have you had these kinds of comments on previous work? What have you done to address them?
> 5. Which comments don't really make sense, or are surprising to you?
> 6. Let's look at the first section – see what is said here… how could you avoid getting that comment on your next paper?

Self-reflective feedback

In this exercise students need to reflect on the feedback questions and explain the relevance of the questions and how they responded to them.

> **Box 5.9 A self-assessment checklist for students**
>
> **Teaching resource**
>
> | *Questions to students* | *Why could these questions prove useful to you? How did you answer them?* |
> |---|---|
> | What do you honestly consider will be a fair grade for the work you are handing in? | |
> | What do you think was the thing you did best in this assignment? | |
> | What did you find the hardest part of this assignment? | |
> | If you had the chance to do this assignment again from scratch, how (if at all) might you decide to go about it differently? | |
> | How difficult (or easy) did you find this assignment? | |
>
> *(Continued)*

(Continued)	
Questions to students	Why could these questions prove useful to you? How did you answer them?
What was the most important thing that you learned about the subject through doing this assignment? What was the most important thing that you learned about *yourself* while doing this assignment? What do you think are the most important things I am looking for in this assignment? To what extent has doing this assignment changed your opinions? What's the worst paragraph, and why?	

Written feedback

According to Hillier (2005), this should be specific, detailed, direct and concise and at the right language level (which is particularly important when it is being given to students who struggle with reading). It should refer to examples in the assignment and avoid woolly generalisations as less is more and accompanied by action points which are linked directly to the learning outcomes or grading criteria.

This makes it clearer and more specific to the student, highlighting which areas they have met and to what degree and which they have not yet met. Ensure this is not over-emphasised, however, as it can encourage students to see their assignment work as a box-ticking exercise. It can also be supported by individual oral feedback as feedback should be dialogic, allowing students to ask questions and to discuss areas of their work (Wiliam, 2011).

A follow-up tutorial after the student has been given the opportunity to digest the written feedback can enable them to be directed to specific teaching sessions or resources which might help them when they submit summatively or for future reference, and to encourage the student to own their feedback and use it to close the gap between their current performance and their desired one, which can help to support the student in developing an action plan in conjunction with the teacher for future development and skills. The tutorial session should be recordable by both teacher and student so both students and teachers need to keep copies of the written feedback for future reference. Students could also be encouraged to develop the comments into SMART targets which could form action plans.

Online feedback

Online feedback can replicate all the ways in which a student could receive face-to-face teaching. This may be done, for example, via written feedback on assignments, oral feedback in class and tutorials and peer feedback. Some research also suggests that using online media, beyond text comments, positively impacts the students' perception of the quality of feedback (Burgstahler, 2015). These can include some of the following:

Audio feedback

One study suggested that audio feedback was found by students to be clear, detailed, and personal. It left the students more satisfied and provided more explanatory as well as motivational comments than written feedback. It concluded that audio feedback is better feedback in terms of the student experience than other forms of feedback, but that it did not necessarily impact more in terms of achievement (Voelkel and Mello, 2014).

Video feedback

A study suggested that most of its respondents preferred video feedback to text-based forms. Students reported that it was more individualised and specific and personalised (praising individual efforts), more honest and authentic, supportive, caring and motivating; clear, detailed, and unambiguous; prompting reflection; and constructive, which helped them progress them onto further achievement (Henderson and Phillips, 2015).

Real-time feedback tutorials

During online workshop sessions teachers can schedule 10-minute feedback sessions with students in which they share their work with the teacher and receive formative feedback on the section of the work they are currently writing. This gives students the opportunity to ask questions and to clarify any areas of confusion they may have. They can also help online teachers develop a stronger relationship with their students.

Multi-media feedback podcasts

Podcasts which combine audio, video and text elements can often combine the best of all possible online worlds for students as they can appeal to the widest range of learning preferences.

Box 5.10 An example of a feedback podcast in a catering class

Teaching example

The majority of my students struggle with note taking because of language difficulties so I started to design podcasts. I trialled them during the lockdown and found that using an online programme like MS

> Teams or Zoom can help me to produce a multi-purpose podcast that contains a PowerPoint, video material, an audio commentary and supplementary reading notes as text which is portable and easily accessible on their PCs or laptops or their mobile phones. They became very popular with my students because they could access them on their phones. Even after we went back to face to face learning I still use them as my class keep asking me to produce them.
>
> (Evelyn, Catering Lecturer)

Online portfolio peer feedback

One study found that designing an online academic writing portfolio, consisting of a writing exercise, a peer feedback task and a re-writing task based on peer and tutor feedback, did improve student learning outcomes. They suggest that by breaking down the learning outcomes into smaller tasks students were able to meet them more successfully and develop their generic writing skills (Poyatos Matas and Allan, 2005).

Forum-based group feedback

The same study devised a group feedback task which involved placing anonymised assignments with a mixture of generic and individual feedback and asking students to write peer feedback for other class members. Students responded positively to this arguing that it enabled them to access a much wider range of feedback and that it helped them to understand the different ways there were to answer a question. The feedback prompted them into asking questions about why certain aspects of the assignment were valued more than others. It also provided them with an opportunity to learn directly from their peers (Poyatos Matas and Allan, 2005).

Feedback and motivation

Feedback can have a variety of different effects on students which may or may not be directly related to their achievement in a task. Research suggests some students respond immediately to feedback and others take longer (Henderson et al., 2019). Effects may be delayed or have ripples. They can be cognitive. Students may now have a better understanding of a concept or skill. it is possible that students may shift not only in what they think, but also in how they think. For example, it could impact on their ability to regulate their thinking processes and learning or to enhance their evaluative judgement.

They could be affective or motivational and the feedback can impact positively or negatively on self-esteem and self-efficacy. They could also be relational as the relationship between the teacher and the student can influence the impact of the feedback. According to (Henderson et al., 2019), students' perceptions as to credibility, trust and safety can influence the way in which students engage with the feedback process, and may change values, beliefs, and identity and that engaging with the feedback process can develop academic self-identity and professional socialisation.

Feedback should encourage positive motivational beliefs and self-esteem. Research has suggested that feedback has an impact on how students feel about themselves and therefore how they feel about their own learning (Townsend, 2014).

Feedback enables students to evaluate their own work and to develop their own skills in autonomous learning (Hyland and Hyland, 2006). When they become actively involved in the process, they can become more motivated to respond positively to the feedback and to achieve. This can also help to develop their self-confidence and help them become more independent students.

- There are many debates about the various merits of corrective feedback, direct versus indirect feedback, praise versus criticism, product, and process feedback (Townsend, 2014), but the key to increasing motivation seems to be unlocking feelings of competence and autonomy (Deci and Ryan, 2008). According to some research, feedback is most motivational when:
- It is immediate,
- It is related to specific achievement,
- It is task-orientated,
- It provides examples,
- It builds from previous targets,
- It provides challenges that are individualised and can be achieved and
- When it is given in a positive environment that helps to develop confidence and welcomes intrinsic motivation (Deci and Ryan, 1985; Forsyth and Johnson, 2016).

Using teachers' feedback effectively

One of the biggest problems that teachers face post-assessment is encouraging students to understand the importance of using feedback effectively. This can be because of a number of reasons. For example, sometimes they only focus on the grade and do not really read the feedback comments. They are so disappointed/elated by the grade that the feedback is irrelevant to them. Sometimes the feedback given is so brief that it does not help them move forward or sometimes the feedback is poorly written or poorly explained and if the student has literacy and language issues, they may fail to understand how to improve their work. Focussing the feedback on behaviour that can improve competence can also help to create a sense of belongingness and connectedness (Hyland and Hyland, 2006).

It could also be that the feedback given by the teacher is ego-centred, i.e. that it compares the learning which has taken place relative to other class members and not task-focussed, i.e. it looks at the mastery achieved by the individual student (Wiliam and Swaffield, 2008).

What to do

Encourage your student to use your feedback strategically to help them improve their work and get better grades in their next assignment. They could re-read the teacher's feedback and, if need be, discuss it again with the teacher to make sure that they understand fully what they need to next time and the reasons behind the details of the feedback. They should make notes of all the comments or annotate the feedback and ensure that it is recordable. They might also use the assessment criteria and the course marking scheme and categorise the comments into 'Major' and 'Minor' issues on a list. The former being those that lose a lot of marks like not answering the question or meeting the assessment criteria. And the latter matters such as intermittent Spelling, Punctuation and Grammar (SPaG) errors and referencing.

They could compare this list with a previous one and note down which comments appear most frequently. This will enable them to draw up a table of feedback comments and prioritise them. Box 5.11 is an example of a feedback priorities list.

Box 5.11 A feedback priorities checklist table

Teaching resource

Major issues	Order of priority	Minor issues	Order of priority
Too much description	4	SPaG	1
Too much personal opinion	2	Poor presentation	3
Limited discussion of evidence	5	Lack of writing fluency	2
Inaccurate knowledge	7	Referencing errors	4
Reading not integrated into the structure of the assignment	6		
Lack of practical examples	3		
Poor essay structure	1		

They might select the top three major issues of the list and one minor issue and convert them into SMART targets, deciding how they are going to deal with these issues and meet their targets for the next assignment submission. They could then discuss the targets with their peers and then with their teacher to check if they are valid. Finally, they could draw up an action plan like the one below based on the four action targets and agree them with the teacher. This would help them to develop feelings of competence, autonomy, and locus of control:

Box 5.12 A completed student self-evaluated action plan

Student feedback

A student self-evaluated action plan

Issues	Solution	Target
Poor structure	Write an essay plan before I begin to write my essay	Allow enough time to write an essay plan and show it to my teacher before I start writing
Too much personal opinion rather than argument	Read the recommended texts and take notes of as much sources as possible	Make sure that every comment that I make in the assignment is backed up by a reference
Lack of practical examples in my work	Take a diary with me to work and note down anything interesting that happens there and use it in my future assignments	To make sure that I support my ideas and my analysis by applying more examples drawn from my personal experience
Improve my spelling	Proof-read more carefully. Ask one my friends to help me to check my spelling before I submit my assignment	To reduce the number of spelling errors in my work to below 10

Some tips on effective feedback (Wiliam, 2011)

Ask four questions

Providing answers to the following four questions on a regular basis will help provide quality feedback. These four questions are also helpful when providing feedback to parents:

> *What can the student do?*
> *What can't the student do?*
> *How does the student's work compare with that of others?*
> *How can the student do better?*
> *Concentrate on one ability.*

It makes a far greater impact on the student when only one skill is critiqued versus the entire paper being the focus of everything that is wrong. Feedback should reference a skill or specific knowledge. This is when rubrics become a useful tool because they allow you and the student to focus discussion on a particular learning outcome or criteria.

Try to notice a student's behaviour or effort at a task. For example, "I noticed when you consulted the Harvard guide more consistently, your referencing was much stronger." "I noticed you arrived on time to class this entire week." Acknowledging a student and the efforts they are making goes a long way to positively influence academic performance.

Provide a model or an example

Communicate with your students the purpose for an assessment and/or feedback. Demonstrate to students what you are looking for by giving them an example of what a grade nine assignment looks like. Provide a contrast of what a grade four assignment looks like. This is especially important at the upper learning levels.

Use medals and missions

Using medals and missions is arguably a way of ensuring that feedback is forward-looking, positive and constructive and centred on the task, rather than on the ego (Petty, 2004).

Medals

Grades and marks are measurements, not medals. Medals are information about what exactly was done well. The feedback should aim to clarify the criteria, providing examples where necessary, in that the student can understand. It should encourage the learner to self-assess against the criteria before the teacher provides feedback and provide information about what a student has done well e.g. *Your paragraphs and punctuation are good 'That's good evidence'*. It should accept the student's present standard and not belittle it; and should provide competition with the task and their own previous work, rather than that of other students.

Missions

This is information about what the student needs to improve, correct, or work on. The medals and missions need to be given in relation to clear goals, which are usually best given in advance. Goals might include assessment criteria such as 'Use paragraphing to show the structure of your writing' or give evidence, provide illustrations and examples for the points of view you express. It is best when it is forward-looking and positive e.g. *'Try to give more evidence for your views'*, *'Use more paragraphs to show the structure of your writing'*.

Conclusion

In this chapter we have examined how different methods of self-assessment can enhance deep and lifelong learning and promote student motivation. We have also seen how different approaches to feedback, including peer feedback, can help students with EAL and dyslexia to enhance their abilities to self-regulate their emotions and to manage their learning more efficiently. In the next chapter we will investigate in more depth different approaches to differentiated teaching.

Box 5.13 Over to you!

Feedback on feedback

In tutorials, ask students to examine your feedback comments and get them to: explain what was/was not useful and why; and how they would like you to feedback in future in order to improve their performance (Nicol and MacFarlane-Dick, 2006). This will help them take more responsibility for their learning and make them feel more empowered within the assessment and feedback process.

Box 5.14 Take away self-reflective questions

How can you develop in your students the capacity to assess their own work?
How do you encourage your own students to track their own progress using self-assessment?
How do you ensure that your students take your feedback on board?

References

Andrade, H. (2018). "Feedback in the context of self-assessment," in *Cambridge Handbook of Instructional Feedback*, eds A. Lipnevich and J. Smith (Cambridge: Cambridge University Press), 376–408.
Boud, D. (1995). *Enhancing Learning through Self-Assessment*. London: Kogan Page.
Burgstahler, S. (2015). *Universal Design in Education: Principles and Applications*. Washington, DC: Project, DO-IT & Publications.
Clark, R. C., and Mayer, R. E. (2016). *E-Learning and the Science of Instruction: Proven Guidelines for Consumers and Designers of Multimedia Learning* (4th ed.). London: Wiley.
Deci, E. L., and Ryan, R. M. (1985). *Intrinsic Motivation and Self-Determination in Human Behavior*. New York: Plenum.

Deci, E. L., and Ryan, R. M. (2008). Self-determination theory: A macrotheory of human motivation, development, and health. *Canadian Psychology/Psychologie Canadienne*, 49(3), 182–185. DOI: 10.1037/a0012801.

Forsythe, A. and Johnson, S. (2016). Thanks, but no-thanks for the feedback. Assessment & Evaluation in Higher Education. 42. 1–10. 10.1080/02602938.2016.1202190.

Hattie, J., and Timperley, H. (2007). The power of feedback. *Review of Educational Research*, 77(1), 81–112.

Hillier, Yvonne. (2005). *Reflective Teaching in Further Adult and Vocational Education*. London: Bloomsbury.

Henderson, M., and Phillips, M. (2015). Video-based feedback on student assessment: scarily personal. *Australasian Journal of Educational Technology*, 31(1). https://doi.org/10.14742/ajet.1878

Henderson, M., Ryan, T., and Phillips, M. (2019). The challenges of feedback in higher education. *Assessment and Evaluation in Higher Education*. Epub ahead of print 5 April 2019. DOI: 10.1080/02602938.2019.1599815.

Hughes, G. (2017). *Ipsative Assessment and Personal Learning Gain. Exploring International Case Studies*. London: Palgrave Macmillan.

Huisman, B., Saab, N., van den Broek, P., and van Driel, J. (2019). The impact of formative peer feedback on higher education students' academic writing: A meta-analysis. *Assessment & Evaluation in Higher Education*, 44(6), 863–880. DOI: 10.1080/02602938.2018.1545896.

Hyland, K., and Hyland, F. (2006). Feedback on second language students' writing. *Language Teaching*, 29(2), 83–101.

Juwah, C. Macfarlane, D. Nicol, D. and Ross, D. (2004). Enhancing Student Learning Through Effective Formative Feedback. Available from https://www.researchgate.net/publication/238720929_Enhancing_Student_Learning_Through_Effective_Formative_Feedback/citation/download

Malecka, B., & Boud, D. (2021). Fostering student motivation and engagement with feedback through ipsative processes. *Teaching in Higher Education*. 1–16. DOI: 10.1080/13562517.2021.1928061

McDonald, B., and Boud, D. (2003). The impact of self-assessment on achievement: The effects of self-assessment training on performance in external examinations. *Assessment in Education: Principles, Policy & Practice*, 10(2), 209–220. DOI: 10.1080/0969594032000121289.

McNair, S. (1996). Putting learners at the centre: Reflections from the guidance and learner autonomy in higher education programme. Higher Education and Employment Division, Department for Education and Employment.

Nicol, D. and MacFarlane-Dick, D. (2006). Formative assessment and self-regulated learning: A model and seven principles of good feedback practice. *Studies in Higher Education*, 31(2), 199–218.

Nishizuka, Kohei. (2022). Significance and Challenges of Formative Ipsative Assessment in Inquiry Learning: A Case Study of Writing Activities in a "Contemporary Society" Course in a Japanese High School. *SAGE Open*, 12. DOI: 10.1177/21582440221094599.

Panadero, E., Lipnevich, A., and Broadbent, J. (2019). Turning self-assessment into self-feedback. DOI: 10.1007/978-3-030-25112-3_9.

Petty, G. (2004). *Teaching Today*. Oxford: Oxford University Press.

Poyatos Matas, F., and Allan, C. (2005). Providing feedback to online students: A new approach. Conference paper. *Higher Education in a Changing World: Research and Development in Higher Education*. Available at: http://hdl.handle.net/10072/2459.

Race, P. (1999). *The Lecturer's Toolkit* (5th ed.). London: Routledge.

Topping, K. J. (1998). Peer Assessment Between Students in Colleges and Universities. *Review of Educational Research*, 68, 249–276.

Townsend, M. (2014). *How Can Feedback Increase Self-Determined Motivation to Keep Writing?* Western Tributaries. Available from https://journals.sfu.ca/wt/index.php/westerntributaries/article/view/10

Voelkel, S., and Mello, L. V. (July 2014). Audio feedback – Better feedback? *Bioscience Education e-Journal*. DOI: 10.11120/beej.2014.00022.

Weaver, R. L., and Cottrell, H. W. (1988). Motivating students: Stimulating and sustaining student effort. *College Student Journal*, 22(1), 22–32.

Wiliam, D. (2007). Keeping learning on track: classroom assessment and the regulation of learning. In Lester, F. K. (Ed.) *Second Handbook of Research on Mathematics Teaching and Learning* (pp. 1053–1098). Greenwich, Connecticut, USA: Information Age Publishing.

Wiliam, D., in Swaffield, S. and Williams, M. (Eds.) (2008). *Unlocking Assessment: Understanding for Reflection and Application* (pp. 123–137). London: David Fulton.

Wiliam, D. (2011). Formative assessment: Definitions and relationships. *Studies in Educational Evaluation*, 37(1), 3–14.

6 Differentiated teaching and learning

Differentiation is a multi-faceted programme of activities aimed at meeting the individual needs of students and the way they learn in a pluralised classroom. Studies indicate that successful differentiation can impact on the motivation and achievement of all students but that it is particularly important as a framework to support the needs of students who struggle to access the curriculum because of language or literacy difficulties (Hertberg-Dawes, 2009).

Differentiation involves the development of teaching practices, assessment resources and an innovative approach to the curriculum. It situates the student in the centre of the classroom and the teacher's role becomes one of facilitator. Students are encouraged, therefore, to develop the skills to take responsibility for their own learning.

There are no definitive approaches to differentiation, however; in reality, it is up to individual teachers to decide on what they consider to be effective strategies in their own different learning environments which can also be impacted upon by other non-classroom factors such as social class, socio-economic circumstances, gender, age and cultural background. In this chapter, I intend to highlight some of the main strategies which I have either used or experienced or which have been suggested to me by staff members. These include the following: Scaffolding, peer and pair teaching and assessment, experiential, and Self-Regulated Teaching, gamification and metalinguistic awareness and translanguaging.

Scaffolding

The concept originated in an article by Wood et al. (1976) and was intended to mean guided support given to students which is systematically removed as they learn. It is an especially effective method when supporting students who might struggle in class because of language or literacy barriers (Frey and Fisher, 2010). Wood et al. argued that successful scaffolding required six components:

DOI: 10.4324/9781003181583-6

Recruitment

The teacher needs to gain the interest of the student in the task and the steps needed to be taken to solve the problem, and that, therefore, an understanding of the solution must precede its production.

Reduction in degrees of freedom

The teacher must break down the task into small, restricted steps so as not to overwhelm the student.

Direction maintenance

The teacher must keep the student 'on task' and be aware of potential distractions of the learning.

Marking critical features

The teacher should signpost the task and emphasise the key milestones in the problem-solving process for the student, mapping out where they need to go next.

Frustration control

The teacher needs to be mindful of the need not to over-scaffold when the student is struggling and becoming frustrated with their efforts to complete the task as this could led to learner dependence.

Demonstration

The teacher needs to perform the task as clearly as possible so that the student can imitate the steps to solve the problem efficiently.

There are three types of scaffolding: sensory, social interactive and graphical. Sensory scaffolds allow students to use their senses to understand abstract concepts or learn new ideas. For most students, using visuals and manipulatives are effective forms of sensory scaffolding because images and gestures contain meaning without any dependence on language. Social interactive scaffolding creates opportunities to use language for meaningful purposes such as to discuss ideas, offer observations, and form opinions. Graphical scaffolding incorporates the use of charts, tables, and graphic organisers that present numbers and data into visual representations. They are particularly effective when teachers want to communicate highly abstract concepts or show the relationships between things in a phenomenon.

There are several factors to be aware of when thinking about how to use scaffolding in teaching. You need to be mindful that different students need different kinds of scaffolding so be prepared to use all three methods. You also need to have two mental models in mind. Your own mental model, which is of the overall problem to be solved, and the students' models of their own individual obstacles to be overcome to solve the problem. Thus, you should differentiate your support and support students to see the differences between the two models and how to reach solutions. In the first instance, you should verbalise the task, especially your own thought processes to guide the students through the task and allow students the time and the room to experiment and aid at the appropriate level which, according to Vygotsky (1978), is just above their current level.

It is important to know when to give support and also when to reduce it and to be empathetic and patient when you are supporting your students in order to prompt and encourage them either verbally, in writing, or using visual representations such as diagrams to master lower-level skills before they can move onto higher-level skills. Keep the task short, provide clear feedforward and keep checking the students' solutions to the problems until they can work autonomously.

Box 6.1 An example of scaffolding used to support a student who is learning how to paint a door

Teaching example

Many of my learners have issues with reading the PowerPoint so I find it is a lot more effective to break down the task individually to them. If I was explaining to them how to paint a door, for instance, I would discuss what they needed to have. I would talk them through the order of preparation, then I would point out to them the areas to paint first. Then I would paint a section slowly so they could study my techniques, how I was handling the roller, etc. and while I was doing this, I would explain why I was doing it this way. Then I would step back and let them paint and only step in if they were struggling. I would watch them for a bit and offer advice if I though they needed it. When I felt they were painting confidently I would leave them to complete the door and only return to them if they asked for my help. I find this method builds their self-confidence and makes them independent learners.

(Dave, Construction Lecturer)

Small group work and differentiation

Small group work enables teachers to target specific individual needs in terms of knowledge and skills. It has been shown to be effective at most levels and in most subjects and is both motivating and popular with students Although there is no consensus about the optimum group size, research seems to suggest a group size of between three and five works well (Mills and Alexander, 2013).

In general, it has several main qualities that make it ideal as a differentiation strategy. It promotes learning through social interaction and develops a sense of community amongst students. It is therefore inclusive and develops cultural understanding. It creates opportunities for individualised support and assessment for learning and provides opportunities for peer support and peer teaching pre-class, in class and post-class (Hall and Burns, 2018). It can be facilitated flexibly either face to face or online and provides space for the development of language. There are many small group activities, including: project-based learning, seminars, role plays, buzz groups, micro debates, and information gap/exchange activities.

Information gap activities are especially effective for differentiation amongst students who have EAL as they develop accurate spoken and written language use and strong listening skills and they also promote language development through interaction, effective questioning, and note taking (Hall and Burns, 2018). Among the many varieties of information gap/exchange activities are the following:

Barrier activities

In these types of activities, a physical barrier is placed between two learners, so they are looking at different texts, images, or objects. Barrier games can encourage learners to develop speaking and listening skills within the context of a curriculum topic.

There are a variety of ways they could be staged. The students might have a partially completed version of a map, diagram, chart, timeline etc. with different information missing. Students are then given identical sets of photographs, picture cards, and real objects to arrange or sequence in an identical way. Alternatively, students instruct each other to draw or complete a picture or diagram, and vice versa, or students describe an idea/concept to each other and have to name it. Barrier activities can support learners in developing strategies for a variety of communication skills, including rewording, requesting clarification, questioning, and giving and following simple clear instructions (explaining), clarifying, or describing. If the students require assistance, the teacher can either model the language orally or provide a written model.

Jigsaw activities

Jigsaw activities involve the pooling of information between groups and finally the coming together and completion of a task. It has several stages. Students are put into groups and given specific information on a topic which they then become experts in by discussing and researching extra information. Word banks and dictionaries (bilingual or English) may be useful at this stage. Then they are reorganised into jigsaw groups so that each group consists of a student from a different group, and they are able to pool their expertise to complete a joint task such as completing a table, designing a leaflet or poster, and preparing a group presentation. Students who have EAL can be grouped with students who have English as their first language and given extra support by the teacher if they struggle.

Split texts

In this activity a text is divided into sections and each student in the group has to paraphrase their section of the text either orally or in writing. Then the group had to reconstruct the text in sequence and compare their group paraphrase with the original text.

Resource-based tasks

Students are provided with a range of resources (these could be articles, quotations, X-rays, tables of data, test results, photographs, printouts etc.). They are asked by the teacher to solve a problem or address a question using the provided resources.

Simulations

The teacher provides the students with a set of 'briefs' that provide information and background to the simulation. The students often work in small teams to adopt different roles within the simulation.

Peer teaching and learning

Collaborative learning, peer tutoring and scaffolding are important elements of cognitive learning theories. Much of the contemporary research on this area derives from the work of Vygotsky in the early 20th century. According to Vygotsky (1986), the best way of teaching and learning is direct instruction in which a More Knowledgeable Other (MKO) or peer helps another student to learn effectively by supporting them in their particular Zone of Proximal Development. Student peers are supported by their MKO using questioning, suggesting, displaying, narrating, boosting, and recapping. As a result of this, students will ultimately be able to independently solve the problems that they were unable to solve previously.

There are many benefits of peer learning. These include: peer and MKO academic development; improved motivation; enhanced participation in learning; improved self-confidence; and greater sense of self efficacy in learning and developed thinking skills (Topping and Bryce, 2004).

Box 6.2 An example of using a fishbowl activity in a childcare class

Teaching example

I like using fishbowl activities because it means that I can get everyone in the class involved and they develop a variety of confidence building and communication skills. Sometimes I give the group a scenario to debate so I divide the group into a series of subgroups of 2–3 students

> arranged in a small circle of chairs. Each sub-group of students is observed (in the 'fishbowl') by the rest of the students. I ask the students in the bowl to argue a case, debate, or role play a situation. The students who are observing are then called upon to feed back, summarise the discussion, or take their places in the fishbowl. All the students seems to enjoy this approach and those students who have EAL seem to benefit from the opportunity of developing their spoken English.
>
> (Alicia, Childcare Teacher)

Reciprocal Teaching (RT)

Reciprocal Teaching (RT) is a prominent technique that comes under the umbrella of peer teaching and learning. It is a scaffolded, or supported, discussion technique that can help enhance the thinking and problem-solving skills of students with dyslexia. RT is a small group discussing technique which begins with the teacher modelling the techniques and then allows the students to take over (Doolittle et al., 2006).

According to Hattie's research (2008), it is the ninth most effective teaching technique in raising achievement. Research has also suggested that RT is effective at a variety of different levels of learning and that it is especially effective for EAL students and students who have dyslexia. When EAL students combine RT with translanguaging in small groups it is particularly beneficial and can be inclusive as students may have the opportunity to bring their own social and cultural experiences to the discussions.

The technique teaches cognitive strategies for reading and comprehension through reading as co-operation and develops reading skills in context so it tends to be regarded as more relevant and motivating by students who struggle with reading. It improves retention as well as reading and comprehension and can also develop Self-Regulated Learning and also metacognition (Zimmerman, 2002). It can be used effectively in conjunction with flipped learning if a text is provided for initial viewing before the class begins.

RT can be differentiated by using mixed-ability groupings, texts of differing complexity and varying amounts of scaffolding provided by the teacher. It incorporates four main strategies within its talking framework: Predicting, Questioning, Clarifying, and Summarising (Koch and Spörer, 2017).

Predicting

When studying a text, students should preview it, searching for initial clues by examining: the text's title, subheadings, bold print, visuals such as maps, tables, and diagrams. the author's purpose and the topic of the text.

Questioning

Questioning the text helps students develop critical thinking skills. The students will monitor and assess their understanding of the text by asking themselves key questions. They will seek to identify the key information and the central themes of the text and use these to generate questions as self-tests to explore the text. They should be seeking to find connections to their prior learning, controversial arguments, personal connections to their own work practices or their own culture and areas of argument that they agree or disagree with.

Clarifying

During this stage students should be trying to make transparent areas of the text that need more clarity. For example, they could be discussing unfamiliar words or difficult expressions, complex ideas that need unpacking, contradictions and holes in arguments, inferences of meaning. Crucially, they need to be mindful of what they need to re-read from the text to get a better understanding of it, what information they need to check by looking it up on the internet and which new words they could use to update their glossaries

Summarising

Students will finally evidence their understanding of the text by providing an oral summary. Teachers should provide start them off by providing summarising prompts to the students such as: What were the most important themes in the text? What were the main ideas being expressed? How convincing were the arguments in the text? How do the ideas expressed compare with those of other authors they have read? How can they apply these ideas to the own work context or within their assignment?

Box 6.3 An example of using reciprocal teaching in an Economics class

Teaching example

The students in my class have a variety of reading difficulties and work much better as pairs. Peer teaching seems to work very well with them. I organise my students into mixed-ability pairs and then I distribute the text to the group. In their pairs, they have to preview it and work out the general content and stance of the text. If we have already discussed the subject, I ask directed questions to remind them of what they already have learned. We all read a section of the text silently. Then I model some questions about the text generally to the group and point out some of the key arguments. The group are given the opportunity to

> pose their own questions generally. Collectively, we also discuss unfamiliar terms and any contradictions of flaws in the arguments. I then allow them to read the rest of the text in their groups. After that, I go from group to group and scaffold them into becoming teachers by asking them questions and prompting their discussions of the text until they are deliberating independently amongst themselves. When I have been around to all the groups. I used directed questions to prompt them to feedback to the whole their summaries and analysis of the text.
>
> (Simone, Economics Teacher)

Paired thinking

Paired thinking is another prominent method of peer collaboration and as a classroom technique combines a variety of different cognitive skills via the medium of collaborative learning. These can include problem solving, questioning, reflection, summarising, analysing, and explaining (Thurston and Cockerill, 2016).

Think, Pair and Share

One of the most well researched subcategories of paired thinking is Think, Pair and Share (TPS). There are many variations of TPS but in its most basic model it has three simple stages:

Think

The teacher provides the class with a single question and asks them to think about the answer individually in silence. Be aware that open-ended questions are more likely to generate more discussion and higher-order thinking. A think–pair–share can take as little as three minutes or can be longer, depending on the question or task and the class size.

Pair

Each student is then asked to share their answer with a peer and work together on a collective answer.

Share

Each pair is asked to share their answer with the rest of the class and take feedback or questions from their peers (Kaddoura, 2013).

There are many benefits of Think, Pair, and Share. It can warm up the class and prime them for learning, especially if it is used as a starter, for instance. It can develop students' skills in discussion on an individual and on a group level and develop skills in reflection and develop understanding and independent thinking. For EAL students in particular, it can build self-confidence and self-assurance in speaking because it allows them to clarify their answers and check for mistakes in understanding or vocabulary in a non-threatening discussion before communicating their ideas in front of the whole class which can also develop interaction between students and help to break down cross-cultural barriers (Kaddoura, 2013). It can also develop their abilities to use subject specialist vocabulary more fluently and generate more in-depth explanations and responses to questions and improve problem-solving skills.

Since the origination of TPS in 1981, it has evolved into a variety of different formations. These have been summarised by (Gerrard et al., 2005) as

Write–Pair–Share

Students write down their individual responses to the question before they swop notes with their pair and confer.

Think, Pair, Square

After the pairs have discussed their answers collaboratively, the pairs form groups of four and work on a group response to the question which is then fed back to the rest of the group.

Think, Pair, Jigsaw, and Share

In this variation after students have discussed the question as a pair and then as a square, they form a group of eight and then 16 and so on until the entire class has collaborated and agreed on an answer which is addressed to the teacher.

Pair and Compare

Students discuss answers in their pairs and evaluate their individual responses. They then discuss the strengths and weaknesses of their responses with the rest of the class.

Think, Pair, Write and Share

Students think and discuss ideas in pairs and write them down as notes or as a short preparation before they share with the rest of the group.

Think, Pair, Broadcast and Share

After discussing their ideas, students broadcast their using Twitter or WhatsApp and then discuss it as part of the group.

Think, Pair, Broadcast and Vote

As in the previous scenario, students broadcast their answer and then the rest of the group is given the opportunity to vote on which answer is the strongest.

When using any of the variations of TPS as a technique it is worth considering some of the main dos and don'ts. For example, remember to provide questions challenging enough to meet the time that has been allotted for the activity and allow the students enough time to reach a consensus on their area they are discussing. In addition, differentiate the pairs to ensure that both students contribute to the discussion, providing scaffolding for those pairs which may need extra support such as learning aids for those who struggle with literacy or language (Kaddoura, 2014). Be mindful of allowing one student to dominate the discussion and to foist their conclusions on their partner. Similarly, be careful that the discussions do not drift off the topic.

In spite of its effectiveness many questions have been raised about the conditions that can impact on the effectiveness of peer teaching and also of learning in general (Topping and Bryce, 2004). Here are some of the central ones. For example, *Age*. Could an age gap make a difference in the way the support is given or received? *Gender*. Does mixing the genders make a difference in the way feedback is given or received? *Competency levels between peers*. Does it matter whether one of the peers is more advanced in knowledge in this subject area or not? *Relationships between peers*. How does friendship impact on a working relationship in class? *Interaction styles*. Are some students better at supporting learning than others? *Levels of motivation between peers*. What could be the potential impact if one student is more motivated to learn than their peer? *Type of feedback provided*. Teacher feedback? Peer feedback? Feedback from resources? Or a combination of them.

Clarity of modelling. How much modelling needs to be provided by the teacher to ensure that students have the skills to support effectively? *Selection of tasks to be undertaken as peer learning*. Should the peer teaching only serve to support areas in which the students have struggled? Or should it be used in teaching new materials as well?

Experiential learning

Experiential learning is a form of learning that is particularly effective for adult learners which has also been beneficial for EAL students and those who have dyslexia because it blends practical and written skills. It draws upon the work of a variety of different reflective theorists, including Dewey, Schon and Kolb (Kolb and Kolb, 2011). Experiential learning seeks to mobilise students' prior knowledge and their past and present practical experiences to develop their understanding of new material.

There are many benefits of experiential learning. It encourages students to integrate theory into practice and their past and present skills into the learning of new skills. It can create opportunities for peer learning and group collaboration through the sharing of experiences and skills and can develop different ways of kinaesthetic learning via the opportunities for differentiated group work and therefore a cross-fertilisation of real-world skills. It can help to replace text-based activities with non-text-based practical activities and function as a form of intrinsic motivation and increase learning effectiveness during the process of 'inside out' learning (Kolb and Kolb, 2011). It can develop the ability to self-reflect and self-evaluate and to learn in more depth and also help to develop self-regulated learning and autonomy and improve commitment to learning. Ultimately, it can prompt a 'big picture' perspective and help to develop deeper thinking via the linking of past and present experiences.

Here are some ways experiential learning can be used in the classroom:

Provide the students with subject-specific case studies to analyse and give them the chance to compare their own personal and professional experiences with those described in the case study.

Role play scenarios can be an effective way of creating space for students to use their real-life expertise and to promote self-reflection and evaluation and project-based activities to help challenge students' previous knowledge and skills and to allow them to reappraise their knowledge and skills. When using group work select the groups so that they represent a range of skills and experiences in each and then set them a problem or a research task that requires a combination of skills to compete.

Teachers could also use the flexibility of online learning to increase the effectiveness of experiential learning by giving students a practical research task to do before the class and then asking them to feed back the results online. Or using synchronous or asynchronous tools like web conferencing or social media to build collaboration and skill exchange. Or promoting learning via online simulations using subject-specific virtual environment platforms and using games to replicate real-life experiences or YouTube videos and follow them up with reflective exercises to develop deeper understanding.

Work skills can also be brought into the classroom by field work and laboratory work, or you could ask your students to produce learning logs or blogs based on their work experiences to develop their practical skills. Alternatively, you could organise joint projects with local businesses to enable students to see the relevancy of what they are learning and how they can apply their classroom skills in real-life contexts.

Or ask local businesses to come into the classroom and become part of the assessment process by, for instance, judging assignment presentations. Or provide opportunities for students to research their own workplace and use the results as the basis of case study work. For instance, Health and Social Care students could conduct a policy analysis based on the care homes where they work.

> **Box 6.4 An example of experiential learning used in a marketing course**
>
> **Teaching example**
>
> Many of my students struggle with learning marketing theory because of literacy issues so I try to set them as many practical problems as I can. Sometimes I use case studies and sometimes we use real clients. Recently, the college was revising its marketing strategy, so I decided to use the students' expertise to benefit the college directly. I organised them into mixed-ability groups and they were all briefed by the marketing team to come up with new marketing strategies. Working independently in their own groups, they were given several sessions to come up with their plans. Finally, they were asked to present their ideas to Senior Management Team and the marketing team in the college.
>
> (Angela, Marketing Teacher)

Differentiation and Self-Regulated Learning (SRL)

Self-regulation refers to self-generated thoughts, feelings, and behaviours that are oriented to attaining goals (Zimmerman, 2002). Becoming a Self-Regulated Learner means becoming aware of their strengths and limitations and being guided by personally set goals and task-related strategies. Self-Regulated Learners tend to be goal-driven, self-satisfied and motivated. They also have a clear perception of own self-efficacy and are more likely to achieve academically and to be optimistic about their futures.

According to Zimmerman, (2002), the central component skills of an SRL include: setting specific proximal goals for oneself and adopting detailed and powerful strategies for attaining the goals; monitoring one's performance selectively for signs of progress; managing one's time use efficiently; and self-evaluating one's methods. There are three cyclical phases in effective Self-Regulated Learning: Forethought, Performance, and Self-reflection (Panadero et al., 2019).

Forethought

This relates to processes and beliefs that precede the task. This can consist of two micro phases. Firstly, goal setting and strategic planning, where the student decides to break down the task into manageable chunks and works out how to achieve them. Secondly, self-motivation, which reflects own past successful experience in a particular learning area and self-confidence in own abilities to learn underpinned by intrinsic interest in the subject.

Performance

During the performance of the task the learner will evidence two strategies: self-control and self-observation. Self-control refers to the use of strategies or methods that the learner has decided upon during the forethought phase. Self-observation is essential to keep the learning on track and could be formal, in terms of a reflective journal, or informal, as in self-monitoring.

Self-reflection (Self-Reflected Learning) (SRL)

Research has suggested that this is central to the success of SRL and can take many forms such as self-evaluation against a student's prior performance, self-reaction which involves feelings of self-satisfaction regarding meeting one's own specific proximal goals (Quigley et al., 2013).

There are many ways in which SRL can be developed through differentiation. For example: individualised targeted support from the teacher and personalised extension tasks designed to stretch, and challenge can help students reach their full potential and provide opportunities for students to self-evaluate through reflective writing, or Vlogs if they struggle with literacy. For EAL students, SRL can be enhanced by encouraging the use of translanguaging and the use of specific technology designed to support their individual needs e.g., for grammar, spelling, translation. Or encouraging the use of peer teaching and reciprocal teaching and reading, whether online or in class, and providing differentiated forms of feedback and feedforward.

Teachers also need to be mindful of the cultural and gender barriers faced by some students in developing student autonomy and using scaffolding to build self-confidence and increase notions of self-efficacy, especially for students who struggle with literacy (Helyer, 2015).

Box 6.5 An example of building SRL in a Science class

Teaching example

When I am teaching topics that can be discussed in a wider international context like the environment, I try to use my learners as resources. Many of them have recently arrived in this country and struggle with spoken English so I provide opportunities for them to use their own rich life experiences and home examples to enrich the learning of the group and also to develop their confidence in speaking. Then I ask them to research mini projects as homework comparing their own experiences of things like flooding with similar occurrences in the UK. This helps to motivate them and develop them as independent learners.

(Henrietta, Science Teacher)

Gamification

Gamification has become a much-discussed topic in education at all levels over the past twenty years. It is first thought to have been used by computer scientist Nick Pelling in 2002, having appeared on his company's website in late 2002 or early 2003 (Pelling, 2011). Gamification in learning involves incorporating game elements to motivate learners. Gamification activities work very well with students who struggle with literacy and language because they are more of a 'hands-on' method of teaching (Dichev and Dicheva, 2017).

There are many potential benefits to the usage of gamification in teaching. It can develop a stronger sense of ownership over students learning and help to create a more relaxed learning environment with regard to failure, since students can simply try again if they don't succeed. It can provide a more student-centred learning experience and develop more creative and imaginative independent learning through the exploration of different identities via different avatars/characters. It can develop group cohesion and a more collaborative approach to learning and problem-solving skills though group work. If student progress is recorded and reported, learning can become more visible and measurable.

There are three main ways that gamification can be broadly applied to a learning environment. For example, adapting grades so that students are offered points, or rewards which can be used to motivate or set targets or changing the classroom language so that subject specialist terminology is embedded into tasks and assignments became briefs, students become trainees. Or modifying the structure of the class. This can be done on a temporary or permanent basis as student groups become teams or squads.

Some of the key game elements that also apply in education include the following: Narratives can be used to create a storyline or work withing a real-life scenario to improve motivation and make learning more exciting(Biro, 2014). Immediate feedback can be provided mainly online but could also come from peers or teacher, depending on the type of game selected such as role playing. Scaffolded learning can be used with challenges that increase in complexity and mastery as students improve knowledge and skills by completing the tasks.

Progress indicators (for example, through points/badges/leaderboards, also called PBLs) can help to develop self-assessment and facilitate assessment for learning openings and gamification can improve inclusion building on all students' strengths and weaknesses and can become more responsible for their own learning and more autonomous (Tulloch, 2014).

Some of the main concepts used in education drawn from commercial games include the following

Quizzes and puzzles

Quizzes are the most common form of games used in classes. They are particularly effective as a form of assessment for learning as they provide an instant snapshot of progress. For example, using a game show format like

Who Wants to be a Millionaire? Puzzles are another commonly used class-based activity which helps to expand students' problem-solving skills and their interpersonal skills. For example, students have to search for internet answers to a scenario-based legal case study.

Strategy

These activities are normally multi-layered and are built upon critical thinking and forward planning. They work particular well within Project-Based Learning (PBL). These games are often complex, and students struggle to complete them; in doing so they learn via feedback and trial and error. For example, providing students with long-term creative design projects with tight micro deadlines. Or, researching a menu for a chain of hotels that serve only vegan food.

Highly replayable scenarios

These types of activities have enough complexity to them and so many different outcomes that they can be staged several times in the class without becoming tedious to the students. They can be stretched out across an entire academic year and often involve several stages of complexity of information or task which have to be mastered by the students before they can move to the next level. They encourage experimentation and adaptability as students are given the chance to solve to solve often real-life scenario-based dilemmas through critical thinking and problem solving in a safe environment. For example, students form companies and become involved in designing a new application for language learning. Or giving leaderboard points for supporting other peers.

Multiplayer – competitive

This is a popular option used in class because it can build motivation though competition, whether competition against others or against own performance. For example, preparing for a mock interview for a job in competition with peers. There is also Multiplayer – collaborative. This activity helps to develop group cohesion and peer teaching and learning. For example, designing an Early Years playroom. Or Multiplayer – competitive and collaborative, which combines both of the above categories and promotes team against team and enhances deep interpersonal sense-making experiences and social learning. For example, pitching a product in a Dragon's Den scenario.

Box 6.6 An example of gamification used in formative assessment in media theory

Teaching example

I created a league table idea to encourage competition in the class between the different seminar groups. I knew that this had been used in other HE classes but never in a Media class. Every week the students were given one or more journal articles or book chapters to read and discuss. One of their groups of two or three also to produce a short video on one of the set readings for that week. Each group of students would typically make two to three videos over the course of the module. Those students who were not presenting that week had to peer assess the video, discuss their conclusions and grade it out of 10. All the scores were recorded on a leaderboard so that each group could see how well they were doing compared to their peers. At the end of the module the scores were averaged, and a winner was declared.

(Lucy, Media Studies Teacher)

Metalinguistic awareness

The term was coined in the 1970s when researchers used it to describe the process of learning multiple languages; however, it applies to many facets of language and there is no single definition of it. Metalinguistic awareness is the ability to look at language as an entity and a process and a system. It is a focus on the forms of language and analyses language as a system with patterns (rules) and exceptions. Many researchers argue that it can enable EAL students to develop comprehension and metacognition and that metalinguistic ability can help new language development (Sinar, 2018; Carlisle, 2003; Gombert, 1992). Some researchers have also pointed out how it is directly linked to the act of writing because as a process it involves selecting, shaping, reflecting, and revising (Schoonmaker, 2015; Myhill, 2011).

Metalinguistic awareness was defined by Gombert (1992) as comprising: (1) activities of reflection on language and its uses, and (2) subjects' ability intentionally to monitor and plan their own methods of linguistic processing (in both comprehension and production).

It has five subdomains which consist of: Metaphonological, which is developing understanding of the sounds that build words. Metalexical/ Metasemantic, which is developing understanding of word structures and word meanings. Metasyntactic, which involves developing the ability to reason consciously about syntax and intentionally control it. Metapragmatic, which is developing understanding of how to use language appropriately in social contexts; and Metatextual, the understanding of text structure including cohesion and coherence (Schoonmaker, 2015).

Some tasks to develop metalinguistic awareness include the following: Self-talk, which is like a running commentary inside the head. It is silent thinking, making sense of the external environment and reflecting upon actions. Self-questioning, which is really part of self-talk. Both methods help the learner develop their metalinguistic awareness as self-questioning uses the thinking out loud strategy. By thinking out loud, students communicate with themselves and tries to make sense of what they think.

Predicting uses prior knowledge and is an excellent way of improving metalinguistic awareness as it encourages the student to make particular predictions before and during speaking and listening. It involves predicting the meaning of unknown words from surrounding text or the meaning of a sentence whose structure is unknown or complex. Students could predict an opinion based on for and against arguments in a text or predict a conclusion, based on previous parts of the text. When teachers target the development of metalinguistic awareness, these activities need to be followed by a justification to make sure students make their thoughts explicit (Sinar (2018).

Paraphrasing can be used to rearrange an original text in a more condensed form in writing or verbally. During the restructuring of the content students can develop their Metasemantic, Metasyntactic, Metapragmatic Metatextual and metaphonological skills and knowledge.

Box 6.7 The checklist approach

Teaching resource

1. Read the article through quickly
2. Write down the reference in full and the library location so you can find it again.
3. Summarise the contents in two sentences
   1
   2
4. Summarise the conclusion in a single sentence
   1
5. What are the main strong points of the article?
   1
   2
   3
   4
   5
6. What are the main weak points of the article?
   1
   2
   3
   4
7. Do I agree/disagree with the argument?
   Yes – Why?
   No – Why not?
8. Read it again more slowly
9. Expand the summary of the article's content by adding detail
10. Expand the summary of the article's conclusion by adding detail
11. Add examples to your discussion of the strong and the weak points of the article
12. Explain why you agree/disagree with the argument
13. How does this information fit in with my current understanding of the topic?

14 How can I use this information as a launch pad to a greater understanding of the topic
15 Read the bibliography very carefully and note the most important and most relevant sources cited in the article and then read them yourself

---

Box 6.8 The triple section approach

Teaching resource

Signposting	*Notes*	*Learning outcomes of the assignment*
Main points of the text Central ideas Central theories New definitions New vocabulary	Expanded versions of the Signposting notes Main points of the text expressed as: • Bullet points • Diagrams/charts • Abbreviations • Paraphrases • Outlines	The LOs could either be represented in full or as numbers. The main points of the Note section should be mapped directly against the LOs in this section.
This section summarises all the central information from the text	Summary It should be written after the Notes section has been completed It highlights the most relevant material It can be expanded by adding extra information to it It can be used by the student to expand upon how the content meets the LOs of the assignment	

(Schoonmaker, 2015)

Reverse comprehension

This has a variety of stages and can be applied in most subjects as a precursor to a comprehension exercise for students with literacy issues. The teacher introduces a new topic and discusses the context of the topic. Students are then given the opportunity to discuss it in class in small groups and come up with real-life examples of this drawn from personal and professional experience. They then feed this back to the whole class and the teacher presents the questions to answer on the text to the whole group. The group are then given the text to read, analyse in their groups and provide feedback on the answers. (Alternatively, one member from each group could scribe the answers on a white board.)

Multiple meanings

This is a task that allows the students to explore meaning and learn how to use the concept in different ways which is very effective for students who struggle with literacy. It has several stages. Students are provided with a new word and then encouraged to explore different definitions of the word. In groups of two or three, students are told to discuss and provide different contexts for the use of the word and then they are encouraged to extend its use by using it in different sentences in a variety of different contexts and, finally, they will attempt to find figurative uses of the word.

Box 6.9 An example of using metalinguistic awareness in an engineering class

Teaching reflection

Many of my students have newly arrived in this country and I have to be mindful that many of the subject language and concepts are difficult to get their heads around, so I find different ways to break them down. For instance, if there is a group of students doing Level One Electrical I could introduce them to the notion of Conduction.

They might define it as one of the following:

- the transmission of heat or electricity or sound
- the transmission of impulses along nerves.
- the transfer of heat through matter by communication of kinetic energy from particle to particle with no net displacement of the particle

They might discuss it in the following different contexts:

- if you are cold and someone holds you to warm you up, the heat is being conducted from their body to yours.
- chocolate in your hand will eventually melt as heat is conducted from your hand to the chocolate.
- when ironing a piece of clothing, the iron is hot and the heat is conducted to the clothing.
- they might use the word in different sentences like these:
    - a poker will become very hot if it is left in a fire because it conducts heat.
    - silver is the best conductor of electricity.
    - glass, porcelain, and plastic are examples of good non-conductors.

134 *Differentiated teaching and learning*

They might use it figuratively as in:

- a conductor directs the performance of musicians or a piece of music
- a conductor used to collect fares on public transport
- a lightning conductor is used to protect a building from being struck by lightning

(James, Construction Lecturer)

Meaning triangles

This is a task which allows students to explore the relationships of concepts to each other. Draw a series of triangles for students and provide them with a list of words. Ask them to complete the triangles by writing between three and six single concept words along each edge and one underpinning concept in the middle. You could also provide an underpinning word in the middle and find support for it.

Box 6.10 A meaning triangle for a catering class showing the stages of making bread

Teaching resource

A meaning triangle for a catering class showing the stages of making bread.

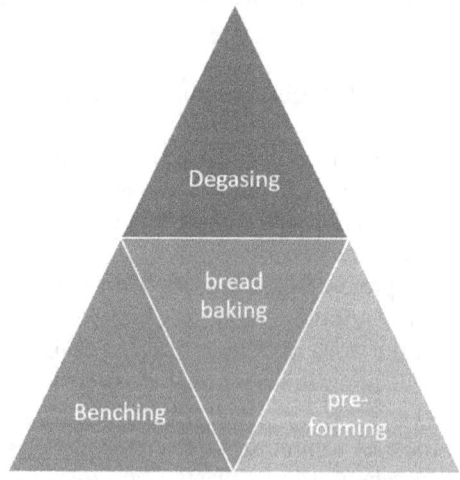

Other ideas

Students can also be encouraged to:

- underline/identify difficult words and concepts and compare them other known words which are similar to the difficult words.
- identify and correct grammatical errors from passages that have been altered
- break the words down to try to recognise bits of morphology/identify word formation techniques and discuss whether there are other possible meanings of that word.
- compare the similarities and differences of forms and structures in texts
- transfer information and literacy across languages investigating the root words of new terminology
- use word banks and sentence starters to develop vocabulary and improve self-confidence
- analyse parts of speech from oral text

Differentiating teaching of terminology

The correct usage of terminology is important because of several reasons. It enables students to express subject-specific concepts more precisely and helps them to understand subject-specific texts more easily and, ultimately, it can help improve fluency in writing assignments and examinations. It is particularly problematic for students who struggle with literacy. In order to meet their needs, teachers need to develop structured vocabulary programmes.

According to Graves (2000), there are four components of an effective vocabulary program:

- Wide or extensive independent reading to expand specialist knowledge.
- Instruction in specific words to enhance comprehension of texts containing those words,
- Instruction in independent word-learning strategies and
- Word consciousness and word-play activities to motivate and enhance learning.

Wide or extensive independent reading to expand specialist knowledge

Teachers need to encourage students to use reading lists as springboards for independent research during flipped learning exercises. This could be reinforced by annotated bibliography exercises in order to encourage them to read widely.

Instruction in specific words to enhance comprehension of texts containing those words

There are many ways in which this can be done effectively. For instance, teachers should provide students with multiple exposures of subject-specific terminology in multiple contexts, e.g., textbooks, newspaper articles, YouTube videos, and TV programmes. They could also place the terminology within specific scenarios for which they must answer verbal and written questions. Or use context cues by providing texts with new vocabulary words embedded in them. Students should then attempt to guess the definitions. This will help them develop critical thinking skills and to apply the words in the correct contexts.

Give the students the opportunity to use the terms in sentence form by asking them to design leaflets based on the words or ask students to prepare five-minute PowerPoint presentations based on individual words and their meanings and then ask the group to update their glossaries using the new words.

Select a variety of sources using the same terminology and ask students to paraphrase them and present them to the group for feedback. Alternatively, encourage students to peer teach words and definitions to each other and then test each other.

Instruction in independent word-learning strategies

Break words down into prefixes, suffixes, and roots. This can help students make links with previous words of which they understand the meaning. You could also pre-select key terms every lesson and ensure that each student has noted and is able to define them and use them in the lesson. You could also provide them with a self-diagnostic grid at the start of the class. You might even encourage your students to design their own subject glossary which they can add to each lesson with definitions, images, analogies, synonyms, antonyms, and example sentences. They could also create word-based graphic organisers showing their antonyms, synonyms, definitions, and example sentences. Or they could develop their Word-learning strategies using dictionary search games based on etymology/morphemic analysis and contextual analysis.

Box 6.11 An example of breaking down terminology in a Business Studies class

Teaching reflection

I have found using this approach as a starter a good way of introducing new vocabulary and of recapping old vocabulary. I get them to draw the table in their books so they always have a hard copy of the vocabulary to work from and use in their assignments and for examination revision.

Term	No idea	Seen it before	Understand it – sort of	Fully explain	Definition
Assets					
Capital					
Liabilities					
Revenue					
Equity					

(Jaz, Business Studies Teacher)

Word consciousness and word-play activities to motivate and enhance learning

Some examples of these include the following ideas:

Justified lists

Make justified lists in which students must justify why something is or isn't from a written definition.

Charades

Students take it in turns to act out each word from a list for the rest of their team to guess.

Taboo

Students must describe a new term to their team to help them guess the word without using five taboo words.

Word Bingo

Give students Bingo cards with new terms written on them. You then give them clues as to the words and the students strike them off if they have the word on their card.

Jeopardy

To play this game, the teacher gives the definition, and the students have to provide the correct word.

Alphabet games

Ask students to provide A to Z lists of new terms complete with definitions and with a visual image when they begin a new topic.

Fill in the blanks

Provide worksheets with missing terminology and ask students to fill in the blanks. Or worksheets with terminology and missing definitions.

Flashcards

Students could test each other on terminology using flashcards.

Wordle

Using the software ask students to design Wordles based on specific terminology using antonyms, synonyms, word roots, prefixes, suffixes, etc.

Alien invasion

Students have one minute to explain to an alien the meaning of a particular word. They can explain the concept verbally or using pictures or both.

Box 6.12 An example of terminology teaching from an Anatomy class

Teaching reflection

I find my students who have literacy and language issues can become overloaded with physiological terms at times and need to have them reinforced by imagery. So I have designed terminology matching cards for things like the regions of the brain and provided terminology and a visual on one set of cards and a definition on the other set of cards. This can be used as team game or individual activity as a starter or plenary. I think it also helps their word consciousness which impacts on their spelling too.

(Martins, Science Teacher)

Translanguaging

Translanguaging is another effective method of differentiating teaching. The term is used to describe teaching practices that give EAL students the opportunity to use their full linguistic repertoire in order to empower them and help them to realise their full potential. According to Garcia (2009, p. 45), it is a range of "multiple discursive practices in which bilinguals engage in order to make sense of their bilingual worlds".

In practice, this can mean encouraging students to speak, write and/or translate to and from their first language or any language they speak and English, to support their learning.

In order to encourage translanguaging teachers need to develop positive attitudes and pride in their students towards their multilingualism and encourage them to us it to their advantage by allowing them to choose which language to use at any time (Hungwe, 2019). It is essential that EAL students in the class are clear that they are encouraged to use their first language in lessons (unless asked to use English for a specific task) and that this will help them to develop both/all their languages. Translanguaging as a strategy can be used with students of all ages and across all levels of the curriculum.

Here are some examples of how translanguaging can be used in class

Bilingual and multilingual glossaries

These are useful to help students draw from their prior knowledge. Teachers should encourage their students to develop their own based on specific subject concepts and terms. Teachers could also develop academic word walls to enhance understanding of subject-specific terminology by designing in conjunction with students' displays of key words in different first languages.

First drafts/research in first language

Teachers could suggest that students write the first draft of an assignment in their own language to build up their confidence in writing academically and to focus on content and structure of argument. Then they could translate it into English and focus on grammar and spelling. Online research could be done in their own first language and then the notes could be written up in English.

Encourage metasemantical analysis

When introducing new subject specialist vocabulary teachers could provide opportunities for EAL students to examine the root structures of similar words in their first languages and compare them with the English equivalent. This could help develop understanding of meaning and recall of the meaning and the spelling of the word.

Note making and note taking

Teachers should get students to write these in their first language or in a combination of both first and second languages. Subject-specific books or textbooks in their first language could also be provided.

Use of translanguaging in academic skills development

In Hungwe's (2019) research, students in groups were given a text to paraphrase in their first language and then in English and told to merge the two. This helped to develop their understanding of the text and to improve their ability to paraphrase with more precision.

Group discussion

Teachers could ensure that EAL students are always paired with students who speak their own language in group or paired work. This will develop their confidence in discussion and provide mutual support when encountering issues over comprehension. Teachers can also try to use mixed-language ability pairings to reinforce peer scaffolding.

Conclusion

In this chapter we have discussed the importance of differentiation and focussed on some of the main concepts, such as scaffolding and the significance of peer collaboration. We have also analysed different ways to diversify teaching, such as the use of gamification and translanguaging. The following chapter will focus on the application of technology, and, in particular, mobile technology, as a specific approach to differentiation.

Box 6.13 Over to you!

Wheel of fortune

Write new subject specialist terms on a series of cards and give each student one card. Create a wheel of fortune from an internet site like https://wheeldecide.com/ and fill it with a series of commands like define the term, compare, and contrast the term with something similar, write the word as a topic sentence in a paragraph. Then ask each student to spin the wheel and obey the commands. This will develop their familiarity with new terminology very quickly.

Box 6.14 Take away self-reflective questions

How do you ensure that your differentiation approaches benefit all your students?
When you plan for differentiation how do you also plan for external barriers to learning like social class and gender?
How do you manage some of the key problems associated with collaborative learning like free-riding and group conflicts?

References

Biro, G. I. (2014). Didactics 2.0: a pedagogical analysis of gamification theory from a comparative perspective with special view to the components of learning. *Procedia – Social and Behavioral Sciences*, 141, 148–151.

Carlisle, J. (2003). Morphology matters in learning to read: A commentary. *Reading Psychology*, 24, 291–322.

Dichev, C., and Dicheva, D. (2017). Gamifying education: What is known, what is believed and what remains uncertain: A critical review. *International Journal of Educational Technology in Higher Education*, 14. DOI: 10.1186/s41239-017-0042-5.

Doolittle, P., Hicks, D., Triplett, C., Tech, V., Nichols, W., and Young, C. (2006). Reciprocal teaching for reading comprehension in higher education: A strategy for fostering the deeper understanding of texts. *International Journal of Teaching and Learning in Higher Education*, 17, 106–118.

Frey, Nancy, and Fisher, Douglas. (2010). Identifying instructional moves during guided learning. *The Reading Teacher*, 64, 84–95. DOI: 10.1598/RT.64.2.1

García, O. (2009). Education, multilingualism and translanguaging in the 21st century. In A. M. P. Mohanty, R. Phillipson, and T. Skutnabb-Kangas (Eds.), *Multilingual Education for Social Justice: Globalising the Local* (pp. 128–145). New Delhi: Orient Blackswan.

Gerrard, J., Collette, D., and Elowson, S. (2005). Using cooperative learning techniques with adults. Presented at *NW Regional ASTD Conference*, November 2005 Orlando, Florida, USA.

Gombert, J. E. (1992). *Metalinguistic Development*. London: Harvester Wheatsheaf.

Graves, K. (2000). *Designing Language Courses: A Guide for Teachers*. Boston, MA: Heinle & Heinle.

Hall, M., and Burns, M. K. (February 2018). Meta-analysis of targeted small-group reading interventions. *Journal of School Psychology*, 66, 54–66.

Hattie, J. (2008). *Visible Learning a Synthesis of Over 800 Meta-Analyses Relating to Achievement*. London: Routledge.

Helyer, R. (2015). Learning through reflection: the critical role of reflection in work-based learning (WBL). *Journal of Work-Applied Management*, 7(1), 15–27. DOI: 10.1108/JWAM-10-2015-003

Hertberg-Davis, H. (2009). Myth 7: Differentiation in the regular classroom is equivalent to gifted programs and is sufficient classroom teachers have the time, the skill, and the will to differentiate adequately. *Gifted Child Quarterly*, 53(4), 251–253.

Hungwe, V. (January 1, 2019). Using a translanguaging approach in teaching paraphrasing to enhance reading comprehension in first-year students [online]. DOI: 10.4102/rw.v10i1.216. Available at: https://hdl.handle.net/10520/EJC-17203aed1bs.

Kaddoura, M. A. (2013). Think pair share: A teaching learning strategy to enhance students' critical thinking. *Educational Research Quarterly*, 36, 3–24.

Koch, H., and Spörer, N. (2017). Students improve in reading comprehension by learning how to teach reading strategies. An evidence-based approach for teacher education. *Psychology Learning and Teaching*, 16(2), 197–211.

Kolb, A, and Kolb, D. (2011). Experiential learning theory as a guide for experiential educators in higher education. *ELTHE: A Journal for Engaged Educators*, 1(1), 7–4400.

Mills, D., and Alexander, P. (2013). *Small Group Teaching: A Toolkit for Learning*. Higher Education Academy Publications. Available from https://www.advance-he.ac.uk/knowledge-hub/small-group-teaching-toolkit-learning

Myhill, D. A. (2011). 'The ordeal of deliberate choice': Metalinguistic development in secondary writers. In V. Berninger (Ed.), *Past, Present, and Future Contributions of Cognitive Writing Research to Cognitive Psychology* (pp. 247–274). New York: Psychology Press/Taylor Francis Group.

Panadero, E., Lipnevich, A., and Broadbent, J. (2019). Turning self-assessment into self-feedback. DOI: 10.1007/978-3-030-25112-3_9.

Pelling, N. (2011). The (short) prehistory of "gamification". Available at: https://nanodome.wordpress.com/2011/08/09/the-short-prehistory-of-gamification/.

Quigley, A., Muijs, D., and Stringer, E. (2013). Metacognition and Self-regulated Learning Guidance Report. Education Endowment Foundation (EEF). Available from https://educationendowmentfoundation.org.uk/public/files/Publications/Metacognition/EEF_Metacognition_and_self-regulated_learning.pdf

Schoonmaker, A. (2015). Increasing metalinguistics awareness as a necessary precursor for preservice teachers. Electronic Theses and Dissertations, 2004–2019, 1470. Available at: https://stars.library.ucf.edu/etd/1470.

Sinar, B. (2018). Promoting metalinguistic awareness in a classroom to improve reading comprehension: Examples from Roald Dahl's novel The BFG. *Acta Didactica Norge*, 12(2), Article 11.

Thurston, A., and Cockerill, M. (2016). *Peer Tutoring: Cross-age Paired Reading* (4th ed.). Belfast: Queen's University.

Topping, K. J., and Bryce, A. (2004). Cross-age peer tutoring of reading and thinking: Influence on thinking skills. *Educational Psychology*, 24, 595–621.

Tulloch, R. (2014). Reconceptualising gamification: play and pedagogy. *Digital Culture & Education*, 6(4), 317–333.

Vygotsky, L. S. (1978). *The Mind in Society*. Cambridge, MA: Haravrd University Press.

Vygotsky, L. S.(1986). *Thought and Language*. (A. Kozoulin, trans). Cambridge, MA: MIT Press.

Wood, D., Bruner, J. S., and Ross, G. (1976). The role of tutoring in problem solving. *Journal of Child Psychology, Psychiatry, & Applied Disciplines*, 17, 89–100.

Zimmerman, B. (2002). Becoming a self-regulated learner: An overview. *Theory Into Practice*, 41, 64–70. DOI: 10.1207/s15430421tip4102_2

7 Assistive Technology

According to Doyle and Robson (2002), Assistive Technology is 'equipment and software that are used to maintain or improve the functional capabilities of a person with a disability' (p. 44). Its main purpose is to make learning more accessible and inclusive. Assistive Technology can come in many forms and can be designed to meet many different needs. One of the most common types of Assistive Technology is designed to support students with literacy and general academic skills issues.

The following are some of its broad characteristics: it can be user-friendly and accessible and portable on a range of devices. It has the potential to build confidence in students and it can decrease anxiety. It can also develop literacy and communication skills in students and raise achievement (Diallo, 2014).

Here are some examples of Assistive Technology that is available for EAL students who have dyslexia: speech recognition software, text-to-speech software, translation applications, spellcheck software, Grammar checking software, online dictionaries and thesaurus, mind mapping software, scanning of handwriting pens, SMART pens, PC-based learning programmes, online word bank, note-taking software, citation applications, electronic calendars, audio books in different languages, subtitling software, video and audio recording software, digital enhancement tools used to adjust screen colour or magnify text and in-built assistive tools on web browsers such as caret browsing or key word finding.

Using technology to differentiate

Blended learning

Blended Learning is arguably the most effective way of differentiating and meeting the needs of students who have literacy difficulties using technology because it has the potential and the flexibility to meet a variety of individual needs, interests and learning preferences. Blended Learning has the capacity to be used within the five main differentiation strategies suggested by Tomlinson et al. (2003).

DOI: 10.4324/9781003181583-7

Differentiation by content

Differentiating content includes using a variety of different delivery formats such as video, readings, lectures, or audio and internet to meet the various learning needs of a diverse group of learners. Class content may be delivered as bite-sized chunks, developed through online mind maps, discussed on a Facebook page.

By dialogue

In differentiation by dialogue the relationship between student and teacher is central and the focus is on spoken communication between them. There are various aspects to differentiation by dialogue; in essence, it involves varying the vocabulary and complexity of language for different students. This is especially important for students who have EAL. It can also involve the differentiation of the context of dialogue such as offering a face-to-face tutorial or an online tutorial.

By task

When differentiating by task the onus is on the teacher to provide a range of learning opportunities to meet the differing preferences of the group. For example, a teacher could ask the group to research the roles of the Speaker of the House of Commons in a Politics class and the activity could be given to the group to do as options, as a short essay, an oral filmed presentation, or as a series of tweets depending on their literacy skills.

By outcome

In this situation all of the students in the group are asked to complete the same open-ended task but with different outcomes depending upon their ability and interest. This also helps to develop their self-confidence as they are empowered though this process to set their own targets. Students could be encouraged to use a variety of online, M-learning and offline tools to meet their own differentiated outcomes.

By learning environment

In this case, the teacher adapts the physical and the virtual learning environment to meet the learning preferences of the group. For instance, the teacher might create islets of seating in the physical classroom if the group contains students who have EAL who prefer to work in language groups or use the breakout rooms in Microsoft Teams for online group work.

Types of blended learning

Although there are many varieties of Blended Learning along a continuum of strategies, according to O'Connell (2016) there are seven main types:

Blended face to face

The class is delivered mainly based in the classroom, but with online activities used to supplement teaching such as online quizzes, wordsearches and other forms of Assessment for Learning activities to be done online as homework. Blended Face to Face learning is designed to meet the needs of students who benefit from the direct support given face to face but who may also struggle with traditional written tasks.

Blended online

The content is delivered mainly online but with some face-to-face content. One long-established example of this form of study are Open University courses.

Flipped classroom

This is a very common method of Blended Learning and is designed to promote individualised and autonomous student-centred learning. Students are given texts to read or videos to watch before a class by the teacher and then have to complete a series of activities based on what they have done as homework.

Rotation model

This is a model that seems to be popular in the US and allows students to rotate between various modalities of learning which include online, such as Individual and Laboratory, to meet a diverse range of learning preferences.

Self-blended

In this type of Blended Learning students can mix and match online and offline modules or units depending on their individual preferences.

Blended Massive Open Online Course (MOOC)

Some MOOCs provide face-to-face discussion groups to supplement the online learning, which forms the bulk of the teaching.

Flexible model enriched virtual

In many Higher Education Institutions (HEIs) courses can be taken either fully online or fully offline. Enriched Virtual delivery is mainly online, but has also contains compulsory face-to-face sessions.

Substitute, Augmentation, Modification, Redefinition (SAMR) model

Brubaker (2013) has suggested that Blended Learning classrooms tend to fall into one of four categories as part of a SAMR model: **S**ubstitute, which is where technology is used as an alternative to the non-digital completion of a task. For example, an online worksheet, **A**ugmentation, where technology adds a new dimension to traditional teaching such as asking students to complete an online quiz as a start activity, **M**odification, where technology is used by the teacher to change the traditional methods of teaching. For instance, a teacher could ask students to produce an interactive PowerPoint presentation rather than an essay; and **R**edefinition, as, in this case, the teacher uses the genres of online technology to replace traditional teaching methods. For example, they might ask a group studying GCSE English to produce a vlog of a text rather than write a book review.

Active Blended Learning (ABL)

Globally, ABL is becoming an increasingly researched area of online learning yielding broadly positive results (Rodriguez and Armellini, 2020). It was originally developed by the University of Northampton and was initially implemented in 2013. Supporters of the approach claim that, in contrast to Blended Learning, it does not run on two separate tracks, one in the classroom and one online via a VLE. ABL is truly integrated and takes place both online and in class.

This method attempts to combine the benefits of online learning with a stronger emphasis on interactivity and digital community. In ABL, students work in conjunction with peers and lecturers in learning. They discuss ideas, work in teams, and experiment and research and receive tutor support and feedback online and from the comfort of their own homes.

Active Blended Learning (ABL) can provide flexibility of time and place alongside community of practice and teacher and student participation. It tries to offer both learner-centred and interactions-based teaching: a suitable balance between learner–tutor, learner–learner, and learner–content interactions. The benefits of ABL for students can include the following possibilities. It can provide personalised learning that encourages independence and develops autonomy. It can also offer flexible learning tailored to individual circumstances and strong online and offline pastoral and academic support underpinned by a supportive online community of practice including peers and teaching staff.

Its key components include Blended Learning Environments (BLEs), offline and online platform/peer collaboration facilities, remote and virtual learning, podcasts, M learning and social media learning.

Blended learning environments

Blended Learning environments fuse face-to-face teaching with a combination of modes which can include using social media, to problem-solving gamification, to videoconferencing, to role-playing activities, to online interactive quizzes or challenges.

Students learn when they engage, connect, collaborate, and communicate with each other through purposeful and planned group work. Group work in BLEs can be used in a variety of learning strategies, including team-based learning, problem-based learning, collaborative learning, and cooperative learning and assessment. They can also be used to promote peer teaching and feedback through online discussions. Online peer assessment provides opportunities for students to rethink and receive critique, correct themselves, and provide feedback to peers. Assessment tools like discussion forums, wiki, true/false tests, and multiple-choice tests can also encourage more interactive learning.

In Blended Learning the teacher can become a facilitator of learning through face-to-face encounters such as lectures, tutorials and seminars and online supplementary resources such as webinars and computer-based instruction which could encourage independent learning and learner autonomy.

How BLEs could support the learning of EAL and SEN students

BLEs can offer many learning opportunities for learners who struggle with literacy. For example: students can work at their own pace and be given more time to complete work and they can be supported by their own online communities. They can express their own individuality in their work without feeling embarrassed or being disrupted by their peers. They can also develop their literacy skills and use online correction tools to perfect their work. Its flexibility means that it can provide students with individual face-to-face support and online reinforcement within the classroom. One design model of interactive eLearning was developed by Churchill (2006) and is called RASE (Resources–Activity–Support–Evaluation).

Resources, Activity, Support and Evaluation (RASE)

The RASE model brings together units of interactivity (where students engage with each other and course material, learning objects, and other tools), with educational technology and applications of Web 2.0 and other social media.

According to Churchill (2006), the central principles for RASE include some of the following. The curriculum is designed so that learning opportunities span the digital and physical environment, inside and outside the classroom. This results in increased interaction between lecturers and students, among students, and students with course materials and inclusive digital and physical environments.

Resources

The resources used should be a combination of traditional and digital and include: (a) content, e.g., lectures, textbooks, journal articles, digital media;

(b) materials, e.g., chemicals for an experiment, paint, and canvas; and (c) tools that students use when working on their activity, e.g., laboratory tools, brushes, calculators, rulers, statistical analysis software, word processing software.

Activity

An activity should provide your students with an opportunity to show their knowledge and skills in a learning context.

The following are two key characteristics of an effective activity: An activity must be student-centred and authentic, – involving real-life scenarios and Problem-Based Learning (PBL).

Support

Scaffolding is vital for students to develop learning skills and independence. There are three categories of support: pedagogical, administrative, and technical. All three should work in conjunction to help students manage problems and to anticipate student problems. It can take place in a classroom and in online environments such as through forums, wikis, blogs, and social networking spaces.

Evaluation

Formative assessment and evaluation are central to the success of learning in the model. Opportunities should be provided for online feedback and peer and self-assessment to triangulate learning (Churchill, 2006).

Box 7.1 An example of using RASE in a hotel management class

Teaching example

I have found that using a mixture of online and hard copy resources is really effective in meeting the needs of my students who struggle with literacy. This was particularly apparent during the lockdowns. I set the group a project to produce a set of different menus for a set of restaurants in a five-star hotel. I organised them into a series of breakout rooms and they were given time to search different style of food online and draw up their menus. Then they displayed them via the chat facility and were asked to peer assess each menu. All the group seemed to enjoy the interactivity of the activity and even those students who had writing barriers felt they could contribute too.

(Mariq, Hotel Management Lecturer)

Assistive Technology 149

Using interactive online facilities

If used with imagination the internet can provide many different options for interactive teaching which can be differentiated to meet a variety of different learning needs. For example, online communication platforms such as MS Teams or Google classroom, or online forums and Moodle tools.

Differentiation using an online communication platform

MS Teams

During the lockdowns of 2020–2021 Microsoft Teams (MS Teams) came into its own as a versatile teaching package. One of its most effective educational facilities was its interactive Chat facility. Chat is the central messaging functionality of MS Teams. During a conversation it allows the caller to message, call, screen share, and add other people all from a single interface. In the Chat bar, the conversations are presented linearly and flow into each other so everyone who is part the Chat can see what was previously written and respond.

Box 7.2 Some reflections of using the chat facility in MS Teams

Teaching reflections

I asked several teachers how they used the Chat facility during this period, and they came up with the following suggestions:

- Through writing on it your students could develop their writing skills and their confidence in writing
- It can help develop effective Think, Pair, Share activities (along with Breakout rooms)
- Students can receive instant feedback from teachers
- Teachers can provide both individual and whole-group written feedback
- It can create opportunities for learners who have EAL to answer and pose questions in front of the whole class
- It can facilitate peer teaching and peer assessment
- It can create a written forum for self•assessment
- It can encourage students to have more reflective responses to questions or tasks because they can be given time to think before they respond
- It can be less embarrassing and less pressurised to respond to a question on the Chat than a verbal question
- It can promote reading skills for students who have dyslexia

- Questions can be posed orally and in writing to help those students with slower processing speeds
- Used in conjunction with breakout rooms it can further differentiation
- The discussion can be recorded so that students can take notes from it after the session
- It can promote discussions between students
- It can allow the teacher to control the pace of online teaching more effectively
- Students can also be supported individually silently while the rest of the group is engaged in an activity
- Students can share links and documents amongst themselves and develop their abilities to work in groups
- Students can discuss amongst themselves without interventions from the teacher
- It can also develop students' abilities to work autonomously
- Feedback can be given to learners graphically using emojis for those that struggle with literacy
- Task can completed in the Chat facility and the results could be shared amongst the rest of the group for a group critique.
- Discussions through Chat can give students time to research their responses and provide more in-depth discussions
- The teacher can provide literacy support for those students who struggle with literacy
- It can be linked with a DARTS activity in which the students could be asked to provide written responses to a passage via Chat.
- Using the survey facility teachers can obtain instant feedback from the group about how the lesson is going and make change in situ
- Students who have EAL can discuss things in their own language in the chatrooms before feeding back to the whole class

Differentiation using online forums

Online forums

These are online discussion sites where conversations and information exchange can take place via posted messages. They can function effectively in combination with peer assessment and peer feedback, since, at any point in time, it is possible to have a look at the "work in progress" – i.e. a more or less developed draft of what groups already have written in the wiki environment.

Online forums give students the opportunity themselves to take responsibility for assessing their own and their peers' work. Learners become responsible for their own learning and as active participants in instructional activities (Boud, 1995; Falchikov, 2001; McDonald and Boud, 2003).

One of the main benefits of peer feedback is that it can be more immediate and individualised than teacher feedback (Boud, 1995). Feedback can also be more honest and motivating than teacher feedback as it comes from a peer. It can also lead to increased levels of time on task and practice and a greater sense of accountability. (Topping, 2009).

Online peer feedback can be differentiated in the following ways: It can be done by pairing more advanced students with ones that are struggling in this area and giving each student the opportunity to teach and learn from each other and to share their ideas and experiences. Alternatively, it could be done by providing differentiated assessment criteria for the students to assess the work against. Differentiation could be done by encouraging students that struggle with writing to use emojis or gifs as visual feedback or by creating the opportunity for EAL students who share a similar language to feed back in their first language

---

Box 7.3 Using Moodle Forum in a child care class

Case study

Here is an example of how one Childcare Teacher used this approach with a group of Level One learners

> After a session about Craft activities on MS Teams I set them some homework to do over half term. They were to select a craft activity that we have discussed in class and to do it with their young children at home. Then they were asked to digitally photograph the end results and to post the end results on Moodle Forum. In order to develop their writing skills, under the pictures they were asked to describe the resources they used and which areas of learning such as Physical, Intellectual, Cognitive, and so on, the activity was intended to develop.
>
> The students were also asked to provide peer feedback on each other's work using a rubric that they had designed themselves during the class. I had tried using peer feedback before in face-to-face sessions but some of the learners seemed to lack the confidence to feed back in detail. Using the online forum, however, seemed to encourage seemed of them to write more because they could. see the comments of some of their peers.
>
> (Olu, Childcare Teacher)

Online resources

Most Moodle packages also contain many interactive tasks for your students. Examples include the following: Dialogue Cards, Drag and Drop activities, Find Multiple Hotspots, Wordsearch, Flashcards. Image sequencing, Interactive video, 360 virtual tours and Mark the Words.

> **Box 7.4 Using Mark the Words in a Functional Skills session**
>
> Here is an example used by a Functional Skills teacher for a Level One EAL class
>
> **Mark the words**
>
> I used Mark the Words because they enjoy working online and because they like doing this in pairs, I can differentiate this relatively easily. My students were given a letter to proof-read and told to find and mark the 12 incorrect spellings online with an asterisk. This helped to show them the importance of proof-reading and enabled them to practice it. The software provided them with instant feedback and allowed them to make as many changes as possible until they got it right.
>
> (Rebecca, Functional Skills Teacher)

Content Acquisition Podcasts(CAPs)

CAPs are multimedia-based instructional modules consisting of images, texts and sounds that pack learning into a small package. It has been suggested that they combine the best features of a podcast, for instance ease of use and creation, with validated design principles such as paring words with images (Kennedy et al., 2014). Some of the characteristics of a CAP include brevity (ranging in length from one to three minutes), and that they combine images, text and audio. Their main role is to develop background knowledge and vocabulary by providing only the key content for a topic written at the right level of the learners.

When designing a CAP, it has been suggested that the following guidelines should be followed: Prior to teaching, teachers should provide an advance organiser that highlights and reviews key content and signals the beginning of major sections or elements of the material being covered should be given. Screen text and pictures should be in close proximity to one another to limit eye shifting during presentations. Concrete images and words should be placed together in conjunction and key vocabulary should be repeated several times in the Podcast and recapped at the end (Mayer, 2008b).

Some of the impacts that a CAP can have upon learning

- They could support students who have difficulties learning content-specific words via reading, or during a lecture and provide evidence-based vocabulary instruction during class.
- They could offer a multi-media supplement to learning and be re-watched by students at various times/places to gain multiple exposures and support students who have oral and visual learning preferences.

- Ultimately, they could give a focussed introduction to specific words and their meanings to be used during examinations or assignments and constitute a portable revision tool for examinations.
- Be mindful that they can also be motivational and empowering if learners can be encouraged to produce their own CAPs.

According to research by Kennedy et al. (2014), they are particularly effective at developing vocabulary because of the ways in which they develop the processing of information. There are six specific instructional practices within The Vocabulary Planning Framework which underpin the use of CAPS (Kennedy et al., 2014). These include the following: promoting word consciousness (e.g., pronunciation, spelling, syllables, prefix, suffix, root words; providing direct instruction of word meanings (Archer and Hughes, 2011); providing guided practice and scaffolding instruction that promotes awareness of closely related terms (Graves, 2006; Dexter and Hughes, 2011); using a keyword mnemonic strategy (Mastropieri et al., 1987); and providing a statement of purpose/rationale for why the student needs to learn a given term or concept.

Box 7.5 An example of a CAP session for some students with dyslexia on a Level 3 Sport and Exercise Science class

Case study

I explained the Clark and Mayer's (2016) guidelines for producing a multi-media product to the whole group:

> Use words and graphics rather than words alone.
> Line up the words to the corresponding graphics.
> Present words as audio narration rather than on-screen text.
> Explain visuals with words in audio or text but not both.
> Less is more.
> Use a conversational informal style on your voice-over.
> Break the CAP into parts.

I then showed them an example of a CAP which I had made and talked them through every stage of the process. I selected ten new terms from a new unit specification on Sport and Exercise Physiology on the Endocrine System and allocate them to five paired groups. I explained that they would need to know these terms both for homework and for their examination. I gave them 30 minutes to produce a one-to-three-minute CAP explaining the term using images and audio on their laptops using webcams and the internet for information. I differentiated the pairings according to differing levels of literacy and

> competence with technology and spent more time supporting some of the groups more than others. When they completed them, they displayed them on the SMART board and received feedback from the rest of the group. I helped to clarify terms on occasion and also suggested where they might have used a better graphic or a mnemonic. For homework, they were asked to complete two four-mark and one eight-mark examination questions using the new terms they had learned from their CAPs.
>
> (Jaz, Sports Lecturer)

Remote teaching

There is some debate about what defines Remote Teaching. It is often argued to be synonymous with e-learning, although remote teaching can be offline, as occurred during COVID-19 (Diallo, 2014). Many primary and secondary schools in the UK opted to send out homework to students' homes and then collected them physically when they had been completed rather than teach online. It is also sometimes deemed to an emergency form of teaching in a time when face-to-face classes have been interrupted. Its flexibility makes it an ideal tool for differentiation, however.

- Many writers agree that its main characteristics are:
- It takes place outside of a physical classroom with no teacher present and it can be either live or recorded.
- It can be accessed via a variety of different digital devices, including PCs, tablets, and phones, and take place through a variety of different digital platforms, including MS Teams, Zoom, and Google classroom.
- It can also be provided either asynchronously or synchronously (Stanford et al., 2010; Mayer, 2008a, 2008b; Doyle and Robson, 2002).

Asynchronous teaching

Asynchronous learning is student-centred pre-packaged learning. It is normally delivered digitally online but can also be offline, as in courses on CD-ROMS. It can be differentiated in the following ways:

Its learning can be easily accessed at any time of the day or night because it has been pre-recorded or pre-designed as in recorded classroom sessions, or uploaded handouts or worksheets or is available online as in an online quiz, YouTube video or blog. It can support those students who struggle with literacy because it is reviewable, and students can work at their own pace with it. Learning can take place over any time duration which can be individualised because resources on a VLE can be personalised to meet the individual needs of the students who access it and also to provide opportunities for individualised assessment for learning via the use of personalised activities. It can be supported by individual online or face-to-face tutorials and it can build student self-confidence and autonomy in students with a low sense of self-efficacy (Doyle and Robson, 2002).

Synchronous Teaching

Synchronous Teaching is delivered in real time and both online and offline. It can be delivered via a series of methods, including webinars, online group discussions, and virtual learning environments (VLEs). It can be differentiated in a large number of different ways. It can prompt on-the-spot interactivity from the students and create opportunities for impromptu assessment for learning. For example, using deep and surface-level questioning. The teacher can provide individual support to students in situ, and it can help to develop a community of learning and group interaction through the provision of breakout rooms and chat facilities and, thus, struggling students can receive support from their peers (Stanford et al., 2010).

If it has taken place using an online communication platform like MS Teams or Zoom, and it can be recorded and reviewable. It is increasingly common in education to blend the two methods in varying degrees to provide a hybrid version or a notion of Active Blended Learning.

Virtual learning

Virtual Learning has become very popular in education over the past decade as it is deemed to provide unique opportunities for problem-based collaboration and the individualisation of learning (Jestice and Kahai, 2010). With regard to the latter, it can be especially effective for teaching students who are EAL or who have dyslexia. Virtual Learning is effective when students can interact with the course content, their peers, and their instructors (Johnson and Marsh, 2014). This is enhanced when the virtual and the real-world learning spaces develop a sense of community and belonging in the learners. Although there are many definitions of it, there are two main types:

Virtual worlds

These are a non-immersive form of virtual learning in which users view images limited to a computer screen. Virtual worlds (VWs) provide digital environments which are replicas of the real world and which can be interacted with and manipulated by the use of avatars. There are many versions of VWs, including social VWs, role-playing VWs, content creation VWs and educational VWs (Duncan et al., 2012). Second Life is probably the most well-known educational VW.

Virtual Reality (VR) (which is now also known as extended reality (XR)

This is a fully immersive system in which the user is surrounded by a 360 degrees simulated environment accessed by a helmet and glasses. These systems are becoming more popular in classrooms now because of their portability and their linked mobile phone applications. There are many educational VR/XR applications on the market now, which cover a range of subjects from History, English, Science to Construction and Geology. Among Virtual Reality's main characteristics are: Its physicality as students can move around in the virtual environment; its interactivity and not only with objects but with other users; and its developmental nature as students can review, analyse, evaluate, and create (Pantelidis, 2010).

There are many ways in which Virtual Reality learning can be used as a form of differentiation. It can personalise and individualise a learning experience and use a student's own experiences and perceptions to help to construct knowledge. It visualises information and allows it to be manipulated. It can also help support the students who struggle with oral explanation and note taking and can make comprehension easier for EAL students because it presents content in 3D using audio and video.

Students that struggle with literacy can benefit because it can illustrate physical processes more effectively than description. It can transcend language barriers because the text or commentary can be instantly translated into different languages and develop cross-cultural understanding because some applications allow students to take on different cultural roles.

It can also bring unavailable experiences or situations into the classroom and to students and help to deepen their individual understanding of different contexts providing cross-cultural experiences and to develop group cohesion. It can help to enhance the benefits of Remote Learning and make it more collaborative and analytical via group Problem-Based Learning (PBL).

Mobile learning (aka M-learning)

A bland definition of M-learning would be 'using portable computing devices like IPADs, laptops, tablet PCs, tablets and Smartphones with wireless networking as a teaching and learning tool' (Stanford et al., 2010). It is also regarded as a fusion between e-learning and online learning through the use of mobile devices. Its strengths include flexibility, mobility, varied resources, personalised learning, and availability of access. It is regarded as especially useful for meeting the needs of students who struggle with written forms of language including those with dyslexia and those who have EAL.

M-learning and differentiation

Mobile learning means different things to different people, and this is reflected in the many ways it can be used in differentiation. Students can collaborate in mixed-ability groups using mobile devices given different learning resources, such as e-books via tablets or IPADs. It can supplement face-to-face classes with differentiated activities provided through mobile phone applications and assessment for learning activities can be differentiated, made more creative and varied using video and audio recording, for instance.

It can help teachers to differentiate teaching based on individual and specific goals for each learner using rubrics and rubric development websites like Rubistar (Stanford et al., 2010) and help provide different levels of options and activities both on- and offline to meet the different interests of students. M-learning creates opportunities for peer assessment and peer teaching using online collaboration tools. Differentiated feedback can be also provided directly to students via mobile devices. The pace of learning can be varied according to the learning needs of the students by breaking up the sessions into interactive tasks and using time as a flexible resource (Tomlinson et al., 2003).

Students who struggle with language can access online translators, directories and thesaurus and can also access more diverse material from the internet or the VLE to use in their classroom activities and students who struggle to attend classes can access the sessions thorough the use of Zoom and MS Teams.

It can provide different ways for students to express what they have learned during a class such as through designing a PowerPoint, making a video, a wiki or a digital poster, help students communicate using non-text-based representations like digital images, and videos, and develop abstract thinking. Students who prefer to learn from videos can benefit from short online quizzes and interactive exercises using applications like TikTok (Escamilla-Fajardo et al., 2021).

Students who struggle with literacy can develop cognitive, technical, and behavioural skills via access to simulation games which develop their understanding of real-life issues. Students who have problems writing assignment can complete them on their mobile technology using talk-to-text applications and when students struggle with note taking at speed, they can be encouraged to photograph resources on their phones and access them at leisure.

Alternatively, students who struggle with note taking can record peer-tutoring or peer-teaching sessions using note-taking applications like Evernote and review the sessions afterwards. Material can also be broken down and presented in smaller sections, as in Micro Learning for those students who struggle with note taking. There is also the option for case-based learning for students who struggle with writing to be facilitated using M-blended learning case discussion and resolution.

Mobile learning can also help to create a more diversified learner-centred environment in which students can work autonomously on their learning and see the personal relevance and utility of it (Vygotsky, 1986). It can encourage students to reflect more fully on what they have learned via mobile applications like Edmondo and Padlet and, therefore, it can help to develop Self-Regulated Learning and motivation amongst students – who struggle with whole-class teaching because of language and literacy issues by providing individual web-searching tasks (Hanif et al., 2018).

Skills can be captured and taught to groups by the teacher and reviewed by students by students outside class using applications like Screencast-O-Matic and students that need extra reinforcement in an area of learning like spelling could use Quick Response (QR) codes.

Social media and differentiation

A common form of M learning is social media applications. On one level these can be seen as a series of websites on which people can interact. Beyond this it is increasingly being used in both FE and HE as an effective way to promote learning across a wide range of abilities and as a powerful differentiation strategy. Social media platforms include social networking like Twitter or Facebook, media-sharing sites like YouTube or Instagram Creation and production sites like wikis and blogs and collection and reproduction sites like Pinterest and TikTok.

Many of its characteristics lend themselves directly to differentiation. For example, it is flexible, accessible, and intuitive to use, and it can support formal and informal teaching. It can be used pre-class, in class and post-class, can be accessible from any online connected device and can facilitate connections and communications irrespective of time and space. It can support communication in varied ways using pictures, videos, and text-based information and thus is ideal for those students that struggle with language or literacy.

It can be used to reach small groups in tutorials and seminars and provide niche, topic-specific information, developing communities of practice and support inclusion by building group cohesion and collaborated learning both within the institution and outside. It can empower more confident students to take control of their own learning and provide focussed support for those students who struggle in class (Diallo, 2014).

It is not without its critics, however, and some researchers have suggested that it can have negative effects on learning if not properly managed. For example, it can distract students from learning and provide them with unreliable information. It can also potentially create divisions between those who can afford access and those who cannot and can also widen the skills division between those who are technologically literature and those who are not. There are also concerns about social media's privacy practices (Schroeder and Lundgren, 2019; Fenn and Reilly, 2020). The five most popular Social Media websites in the globe at present are: Instagram, TikTok, Pinterest, Snapchat and Twitter (Statista.com, 2021).

Instagram

Instagram is a video- and photo-sharing site that is used widely in education. According to research, it is particularly useful for teaching students who have

EAL (Douglas et al., 2019; Erarslan, 2019; Carpenter et al., 2020). It can be used to differentiate in several different ways. For example, teachers can provide customised and targeted images or links to provide individual support and teachers can post reminders and projects to individual students; even tutorials can be photographed and send to students as a series of pictures. Teachers can prepare collages of images and use visual storytelling to support students with reading issues. Teachers can provide quick, personalised formative feedback to students about their work which is delivered to their phones and also provide individual pastoral support whilst commenting on their posts.

Teachers can also assess the range of students' subject knowledge by posting multiple-choice tests online. Teachers can develop literacy skills in struggling students, for example, by setting passages to paraphrase as homework on Instagram or they can also provide short video-based content to reinforce class content for those students who struggle to take notes. Teachers can also differentiate so that case study work meets different levels of understanding by posting on Instagram (Douglas et al., 2019).

Teachers can use it to promote a community of practice amongst the class which shares solutions to common problems, and which supports individual needs. They could also use it to develop new friendship groups in the class which could be especially useful for those students who many have recently arrived in the UK or who are being marginalized because of their learning needs. Teachers can also use the application to network with other teachers to develop their understanding of how to differentiate for their own student groups. (According to research by Carpenter et al. (2020), this was the second most popular reason why they used Instagram.)

Students who have EAL can learn new English structures when they communicate online via Instagram outside of formal classes and also do not feel so stressed when they make mistakes. (According to research by Erarslan (2019), this was a very common practice amongst non-English-speaking students.) They can also take photographs of their own work and feedback and review it later and illustrate their work by using pictures which can help students who have recall issues, providing visual solutions to their tasks. Students who have language difficulties and who sometimes struggle with the pace of the session can benefit from Instagram postings which precede the class and help them to become more familiar with the content. They can use these to develop their speaking and listening via the recording and replaying of the sessions.

It can support the application of theory to real-world practice by the use of pre-filmed role plays. This can be especially effective for students which have EAL (Erarslan, 2019). Beyond the classroom, Instagram can help to enable students who have EAL to become members of a wider digital community (an affinity space) which shares their languages and their culture and may have similar educational issues (Carpenter et al., 2020).

Students who struggle with academic writing can express themselves visually using pictures to represent their ideas; alternatively, they can develop their skills through writing short captions to accompany the pictures on their posts. Students can support each other through peer assessment of posts in class. This can also be an aid to spelling as students who struggle with the spelling of subject-specific words can produce short video prompts for revision purposes.

> **Box 7.6 An example of using Instagram in a performing arts class**
>
> **Teaching reflection**
>
> I use Instagram as a means of promoting reflection amongst my students. At the beginning of every session, they review the targets they set on Instagram during the end of the previous class and they read them out to the rest of class. At the end of the class, they review the targets, reflect on whether they have met them or not and set new ones and send them. They say they feel more confident about writing short reflections and targets on the application rather than in their notebooks.
>
> (Clarisse, Singing Coach)

TikTok

TikTok is a video-creation platform which blends social networking and media sharing (Hurst, 2018). Its popularity as an application grew during the Covid-19 pandemic. Its benefits as an educational tool for students that struggle with literacy are becoming more evident to researchers. TikTok builds essential 21st-century skills such as collaboration, communication, critical thinking and creativity, which are often difficult to develop because of language and literacy barriers (Solomon, 2021).

Teachers can use it to produce short, differentiated content videos that are pitched at different levels of complexity and produce short videos of their sessions that can be viewed after the sessions so that those students who struggle to keep up with the session can review it afterwards. They can also provide bite-sized verbal feedback to individual students to supplement their written feedback.

They can produce differentiated formative video assessments using the application in which students that struggle with writing could, for example, produce short oral definitions of concepts and differentiate content by giving students different videos of varying difficulty to watch and learn from. (I have observed this technique used a lot during Performing Arts sessions where students are asked to learn differentiated dance routines.) They can produce videos differentiated by complexity or by Bloom's Taxonomy content videos to ensure that all students are taught at the appropriate level. This can also allow them to progress independently.

> **Box 7.7 Grading TikTok videos**
>
> **Teaching example**
>
> According to Sanaz, a Lecturer in Sports Science:
>
> > My TikTok videos are labelled Pass, Merit and Distinction and the content in each one is mapped against the appropriate Learning Outcome so that every student knows what they need to learn to achieve at every grade. This also gives them targets to aspire to and they can also self-check their knowledge before they move onto the next grade of video.

Teachers can use the differentiable hashtag challenge facility to support students who struggle with written language and to build their confidence. For instance, teachers could ask students to summarise a piece of text verbally in different durations such as 10 seconds, 20 seconds, etc. and can motivate students who lack confidence by showing them examples of previous students' videos archived on TikTok. Teachers can support students who struggle with literacy by recording their sessions and embedding them as links on web pages stored on VLE systems so that students can access them along with their classroom handouts.

Those students who struggle with critical analysis in writing could be encouraged to use videos to compare and contrast ideas, such as between Fascism and Communism in a Politics class, and students that struggle with writing assignment plans can use the application as a form of self-teaching by filming their talking through and planning of a task and then playing it back whilst they are actually doing it. According to research by Literati (2021), this was highly effective during the Covid-19 lockdown in Spain.

TikTok can increase engagement and support social and emotional well-being by enhancing social relationships and building a more connected classroom which is particularly important for these potentially marginalised (Solomon, 2021). Students can use TikTok's learn area for research into a variety of educational subjects such as English, Maths, Science, and Cooking. For students that struggle with reading, teachers could provide 30–60-second summaries of key texts to reinforce their classroom knowledge. Students could also contribute ideas on the comment sections of the video; if students struggle with presentations because of oral language problems they can produce their own short videos instead.

In mixed-ability pairs students can support each other's learning by producing How-to guides which can also be peer-assessed – and using the split-screen function in TikTok enables students to compare their ideas against another video and to develop skills in self-assessment. Students who lack confidence in their creativity can be given the option to draw inspiration from other videos or create their own using audio clips, sound bites and visual content from other TikTok videos. Students with dyslexia can benefit from the interactive study sets provided by Quizlet which can be linked directly to TikTok (Escamilla-Fajardo et al., 2021).

Pinterest

Pinterest is a visual platform for archiving images on boards. It is an electronic pinboard and publishing website in which contributors 'pin' items to their board which they can collect from within and without the website. It is well known as a teaching resource and many teachers use it to find inspiration and resources for their sessions (Schroeder and Lundgren, 2019). It can be of benefit to differentiate teaching in several ways.

For example, students who struggle with reading and who lack the confidence to develop ideas without scaffolding can be encouraged to search the site for creative ideas and topics and can also 'pin' the work they would like to emulate and use it for their own inspiration later, and students that have difficulties with writing can use Pinterest as an updatable digital portfolio that they can access via portable media. Pinterest can help being marginalised students together in group pin projects and matching students of different abilities for peer feedback can be easily facilitated via the site.

For students with EAL who lack confidence in their ability to speak English in a discussion, Pinterest could be used to conduct debates using pictures, extracts of information and YouTube links as pins or present their work in progress to the group as a Pinterest storyboard using a set of images. Those students with dyslexia who struggle with organising their ideas could be encouraged to use Pinterest as a repository. Students who struggle with reading could develop understanding of vocabulary, for example, by finding images of subject-specific terms and defining them with captions – or teachers could design a game involving subject-specific terms with pins and captions. Students with literacy issues can also use Pinterest boards for writing assignment plans and can produce their own individualised assignment project boards by pinning research, pictures from Pinterest and YouTube links and use them as sources for their assignments.

Students could also convert a written bibliography into a pinboard if they have difficulties with writing. Students who struggle with producing PowerPoints for classroom demonstrations could use Pinterest boards to present their work instead. Pinterest could also be used to develop self-reflection in less confident students by allowing them to create their own online journals. Pinterest can also be used to provide classroom tasks using Bloom's Taxonomy.

Assistive Technology 163

Box 7.8 An example of how Pinterest can be used in GCSE Film Studies

Teaching resource

Here is an example of how Pinterest can be used in GCSE Film Studies. Students could complete differentiated tasks on the same or different boards:

Create	Students could storyboard a sequence from a Film Noir using some of its visual conventions
Evaluate	Students could write a checklist on the strengths and weaknesses of the genre and ask peers to help complete it
Analyse	Students could write and pin a short review of a famous Film Noir and receive peer feedback
Apply	Students could provide photograph examples from Films Noir to illustrate its main generic conventions
Understand	Students could provide a short YouTube video link explanation of the main conventions of Film Noir
Remember	Students could research, select, and pin the movie posters of several Films Noir on a board

---

Teachers could encourage reflective practice in those students who struggle with writing by asking them to develop visual reflective journal projects and teachers can motivate struggling students by creating achievement boards or boards that provide exemplars for students to follow. Teachers could also ask students to summarise texts using visual images only, which would also develop their critical thinking.

Teachers can also differentiate resources by using Pinterest as a mini-resource inventory allowing students to access personalised resources and links to resources and also contribute their own ideas. Differentiated assignment subjects can be provided to students via individual boards. Differentiated group work can also benefit from students using Pinterest boards. Groups could research topics and present them as compare-and-contrast boards to the rest of the class.

Box 7.9 An example of using Pinterest in a Politics class

Teaching reflection

Many of my students have reading issues and sometimes feel overwhelmed when they have research projects and end up trying to compile lists of online research sources. Sometimes they lose them or muddle them up and have to spend a lot of time trying to make sense

> of them again. I encourage them to set Boards for their sources so they can use the site as a virtual bibliography of links they can update and access when they need them. This helps them to organise them more efficiently and encourages them to peer-support each other with ideas for reading too.
>
> (Emma, Politics Lecturer)

Snapchat

Snapchat is a photo-sharing application used in a private space. It has been argued to have high potential as a tool for pedagogy (Fenn and Reilly, 2020). According to research by Freyn (2017), although it has been relatively under-researched compared with Facebook or YouTube, Snapchat is being used increasingly by teachers to transfer more learning from outside the classroom onto their students' smartphones and to facilitate dialogue between teachers and students in a variety of different ways:

Snapchat tutorials can feel less formal than face-to-face tutorials and hence those students who struggle with spoken English can feel more confident writing on the application. Students who struggle with spoken English might also feel more comfortable to pose multiple questions to their teacher and get a quick response over the application rather than use emails.

Students who struggle to write reflectively can provide self-evaluations of presentations using Snapchat photographs and receive formative feedback from their teachers. Students who struggle with reading may benefit from videos and images which enable concepts to be introduced to them in a more direct, realistic, and practical way. Students who struggle with writing can also use the application to narrativize their learning using the Story feature by sending sequences of images, texts, and videos to each other for discussion and to feedback to the teacher (Freyn, 2017).

Students who have EAL can be encouraged to use Snapchat as a research source for real-life experiences which can help them to understand their vocational subjects more clearly and also enable them to connect with other people to receive support, and advice and those that struggle with learning new vocabulary can benefit from using the application to develop their retention of words. For example, students can take pictures of items, teachers label them in Snapchat and then post a video of themselves testing their knowledge. Then they can receive instant feedback from their teacher.

Teachers can use it to support those students who struggle with note taking in class. For instance, a homework discussion question for students to research for the next session could be posed via the application. To help those students who struggle with examination revision because of literacy issues, teachers could encourage the use of Geofilters on the application. These could be used in a variety of ways, including customising scanned revision notes to make them more memorable, and making demonstrations of a skill more memorable by using the augmented reality filters to add humour. Bitmojis can also be used to provide instant assessment for learning feedback from students who lack the language or literacy to respond using text on a mini-whiteboard or orally in front of the whole class.

To support students with slower processing speeds, teachers could model and record the skills they want to teach on Snapchat to reinforce learning. For example, how to paint a door. Students can also do the same, which enables them to personalise the knowledge and attach it to their prior understanding and receive instant feedback. Teachers can use the feedback feature on Snapchat for reciprocal teaching and peer assessment both inside and outside class sessions.

Teachers can use Snapchat Question and Answer to provide individualised answers to students' questions rather than responding by email. It can also facilitate synchronous follow-up discussions and a more online face-to-face approach to tutorial support. Summaries of class content using pictures and short videos could also be used to reinforce learning after the class for those students with literacy difficulties.

If teachers bring in outside speakers to address the class and students who have EAL lack the oral ability or the confidence to pose direct questions, it can be useful to encourage them to write them down and send them to the speaker via Snapchat. The answers can then be shared and responded to by the class. Subject specialist vocabulary can also be developed via the use of flashcards or by using images and captions to explain subject specialist language. This can also help to develop greater language fluency and metalinguistic awareness.

Box 7.10 An example of how Snapchat was used in a Health Care class

Teaching example

Many of my students struggle with writing so I find using a phone application a good way of building confidence and developing their subject specialist vocabulary. Recently, I gave them a series of pictures of different people working in a care home and asked them in pairs to research online and define their roles by adding speech bubbles to each picture. I was then able to ask them to peer-assess and feed back on the work produced and also to use the examples as part of their assignment.

(Abbi, Health Care Lecturer)

Twitter

Twitter is a micro-blogging portal which has been widely used in education. It has been one of the most researched social media applications since 2010.

According to Tang and Hew (2017), research has suggested that it is most effective as a 'push' technology and as a platform for peer assessment and collaboration in many different ways. For example.

Twitter can be argued to be a strong platform for peer collaboration because it can offer continuous conversations between students which help develop reciprocal learning sessions as information and feedback can be built upon to develop new ideas and potentially deeper thinking (Tang and Hew, 2017). This can also help to develop a more open and inclusive form of cross-communication and, in doing so, break down barriers between students and develop a sense of belonging to community of the class.

Twitter can be used to increase post-class discussion of content and extend class discussions beyond the session which can benefit those students who struggle using oral English, for example. This can also provide opportunities for students to pose questions which they might have lacked the confidence or the fluency in language to pose in an open class. Twitter can promote active participation, encouraging more reserved students to participate in class discussions, engaging their learning, and helping students who are introverted or who lack self-confidence (Raes et al., 2016).

Students who struggle with writing can learn the structures and the disciplines of writing more concisely as a result of the word limit of tweets and it can also allow students who struggle to write at length opportunities to express themselves in fewer words using gifs, videos links, etc. (Purvis et al., 2016). Students who struggle with language could be encouraged to use the application's advanced search functions and find specific phrases and words, names of people, locations, and specific hashtags for their research. Students who struggle with literacy can use the application to reflect upon what they have learned, their own progress and to offer advice to their own peers.

Using Twitter Chat can be a tool that bonds and connects individuals on a specific topic. Discussion takes place in real time at a pre-arranged time on a pre-arranged subject. Twitter allows students to connect, engage, learn, and engager and others in real time on a global scale. Students who lack self-confidence or fluency in spoken English could be encouraged to use Twitter to develop contacts with professional contacts and find interesting and useful people to follow to help them in the future and they may also be happier to bring their own real-life experiences into the class as a result of this. Students who have EAL can also use Twitter to network though hashtag chats which can be useful for those students who want support from their own communities.

Using Twitter can also help Inclusion in the class as some research shows that it can help build a stronger and more trusting relationship between student and teacher and that some students perceive their tutors as more approachable both in person and online as a result of the application (Junco et al., 2011). Research has suggested that Twitter can help students who struggle with writing to learn the skills of paraphrasing more directly than teaching it in isolation. This can also develop their meta-cognition (Raes et al., 2016).

Teachers can send out whole class and differentiated individual reminders and prompts relating to assignments, extra reading, and special events and provide individualised encouragement and support to students outside of class time. Teachers can also use Twitter to support students that struggle with reading in class by sending subject related content on a regular basis to update students. This can be integrated with a cloud storage system like Dropbox or a VLE so that resources can also be shared. Differentiated tweets could provide a strong scaffold to develop reading and comprehension skills and entry points in new more complex areas of content.

Teachers can reinforce learning activities by using Twitter to set course-related differentiated research tasks in which the discover function on Twitter can use connections to display shared stories and provides updates on new content and to differentiate formative assessment in and out of class, using quizzes, big questions, discussions, research tasks to fit all kinds of needs. To support those students who may be struggling with language to follow the lesson, promote knowledge sharing and understanding by getting students to tweet about what they learn while the course is continuing and can ensure that they are meeting all the individual needs of students by collating the views of the students via Twitter and provide instant group and individual feedback. Teachers can also use the 'Direct Questions' function on Twitter to individualise questions and direct feedback.

Teachers can use live feeds to make participation by students who struggle with language more dynamic and simultaneous and enhance classroom interaction virtually. They could be encouraged to post ideas or supplementary materials (links, pictures, articles, videos, etc.) without the pressure of speaking aloud or writing reams in class.

Box 7.11 How using Twitter has made students with dyslexia more autonomous and self-directed as learners

Teaching reflection

A Business Studies teacher explains how using Twitter has also made her students with dyslexia more autonomous and self-directed as learners:

> When I first met my new group of students, I encouraged them to set up their own outside study groups. Since we were using Twitter in class exercises so effectively, they began to use Twitter to organise themselves. They became a lot more independent and self-motivated about their learning and began to do things like finding and swopping relevant Open Education Resources amongst themselves. Some of the groups even started to communicate with other Twitter users on similar courses outside the college with whom they exchange ideas and experiences.
>
> (Angela, Business Studies Teacher)

Conclusion

In this chapter we have analysed some of the key areas of e-innovation such as Remote Teaching and Active Blended Learning and explored some of the central teaching interventions, such as social media, in the growing use of mobile technology to develop academic skills both in and outside the classroom. The final two chapters build upon this discussion and will highlight approaches to the development of these in more depth.

Box 7.12 Over to you!

Using social media

Support the academic writing skills of EAL students who have dyslexia by asking them to write paraphrases of articles as captions on Pinterest to accompany appropriate images. This can help to develop their ability to summarise information and to develop recall by linking images with text.

Box 7.13 Take away self-reflective questions

How do you manage when there is unequal access to technology in your classroom?
How do you ensure you have the right balance between e-learning and face-to-face lessons in your teaching?
How will you develop your own technological skills to keep up with those of your students?

References

Archer, A., and Hughes, C. (2011). *Explicit Instruction: Effective and Efficient Teaching*. New York: Guilford Publications.
Boud, D. (1995). *Enhancing Learning through Self-assessment*. London: Kogan Page.
Brubaker, J. (2013). SAMR: Model, metaphor, mistakes. Available at: http://techtipsedu.blogspot.com/2013/11/samr-model-metaphor-mistakes.htm.
Carpenter, P., Morrison, S. A., Craft, M., and Lee, M. (2020). How and why are educators using Instagram? pp 1–14 *Teacher and Teacher Education*, 96.
Churchill, D. (2006). Student-centered learning design: Key components, technology role and frameworks for integration. *Synergy*, 4(1), 18–28.
Clark, R. C., and Mayer, R. E. (2016). *E-Learning and the Science of Instruction: Proven Guidelines for Consumers and Designers of Multimedia Learning* (4th ed.). London: Wiley.
Dexter, D. D., and Hughes, C. A. (2011). Graphic organizers and students with learning disabilities: A meta-analysis. *Learning Disabilities Quarterly*, 34, 51–72.

Diallo, A. (2014). The use of technology to enhance the learning experience of ESL students. Unpublished MA Thesis, Concordia University. Available at: https://files.eric.ed.gov/fulltext/ED545461.pdf. Accessed 13 October 2021.

Douglas, N. K. M., Scholz, M., Myers, M. A., Rae, S. M., Elmansouri, A., Hall, S., and Border, S. (2019). Reviewing the role of instagram in education: Can a photo sharing application deliver benefits to medical and dental anatomy education? *Medical Science Educator*, 29, 1117–1128. DOI: 10.1007/s40670-019-00767-5.

Doyle, C., and Robson, K. (2002). *Accessible Curricula: Good Practice for All* [online]. Cardiff: University of Wales Institute. Previously available at http://www.jisctechdis.ac.uk/techdis/resources/detail/investinyou/Accessible_Curricula. No longer available but archived by the Wayback Machine at https://web.archive.org/web/20070418114542/; http://www.techdis.ac.uk/resources/files/curricula.pdf. Accessed 16 November 2019.

Duncan, I., Miller, A., and Jang, S. A. (January 2012). Taxonomy of virtual world usage in education. *British Journal of Educational Technology*, 43, 949–964.

Erarslan, A. (July 2019). Instagram as an education platform for EFL learners. *TOJET: The Turkish Online Journal of Educational Technology*, 18(3), 54–69.

Escamilla-Fajardo, P., Alguacil, M., and Carril, S. L. (2021). Incorporating TikTok in higher education: Pedagogical perspectives from a corporal expression sport sciences course. *Journal of Hospitality, Leisure Sport & Tourism Education*, 28. Available from https://www.sciencedirect.com/science/article/abs/pii/S1473837621000034?via%3Dihub

Falchikov, N. (2001). *Learning Together: Peer Tutoring in Higher Education*. London: Routledge Falmer.

Fenn, P., and Reilly, P. J. (2020). Problematising the use of Snapchat in higher education teaching and learning. *The Journal of Social Media for Learning*, 1(1), 140–146.

Freyn, A. (2017). Experimenting with Snapchat in a university EFL classroom. *Journal of Education and Practice*, 8(10). www.iiste.org. ISSN 2222-1735 (paper) ISSN 2222-288X (online).

Graves, M. F. (2006). *The Vocabulary Book: Learning & Instruction*. New York: Teacher's College Press.

Halla, M., and Burns, M. (February 2018). Meta-analysis of targeted small-group reading interventions. *Journal of School Psychology*, 66, 54–66.

Hanif, M., Asrowi, A., and Sunardi, S. (2018). Students' access to and perception of using mobile technologies in the classroom: The potential and challenges of implementing mobile learning. *Journal of Education and Learning (EduLearn)*, 12, 644. DOI: 10.11591/edulearn.v12i4.8398.

Hurst, G. A. (2018). Utilizing Snapchat to facilitate engagement with and contextualization of undergraduate chemistry. *Journal of Chemical Education*, 95(10), 1875–1880. DOI: 10.1021/acs.jchemed.8b00014.

Jestice, R. J., and Kahai, S. (2010). The effectiveness of virtual worlds for education. *An Empirical Study*. AMCIS 2010 Proceedings, 512. Available at: http://aisel.aisnet.org/amcis2010/512.

Johnson, C., and Marsh, D. (2014). Blended language learning: An effective solution but not without its challenges. *Higher Learning Research Communications*, 4, 23. DOI: 10.18870/hlrc.v4i3.213.

Jumaat, N. F., and Tasir, Z. (2014). Instructional scaffolding in online learning environment: A meta-analysis. *Proceedings of the IEEE*, 74–77. Available at: https://www.researchgate.net/publication/269033099.

Junco, R., Heiberger, G., and Loken, E. (April 2011). The effect of Twitter on college student engagement and grades. *Journal of Computer Assisted Learning*, 27, 119–132.

Kennedy, M., Kellems, R., Thomas, C., and Newton, J. (2014). Using content acquisition podcasts to deliver core content to preservice teacher candidates. *Intervention in School and Clinic*, 50, 163–168. DOI: 10.1177/1053451214542046.

Literati, I. (January–December 2021). "Teachers act like we're robots": TikTok as a window into youth experiences of online learning during COVID-19. *AERA Open*, 7(1), 1–15.

Lugovics, A. W., and Jocic, M. (2016). Twitter and teaching: To tweet or not to tweet? In *Conference: Contemporary Issues in Economy & Technology at: Split Volume: CIET*. University of Split, Croatia.

Mastropieri, M. A., and Scruggs, T. E. (1987). *Effective Instruction for Special Education*. College-Hill Press/Little, Brown & Co.

Mayer, R. E. (2008a). *Multimedia Learning* (2nd ed.). Cambridge: Cambridge University Press.

Mayer, R. E. (2008b). *Learning and Instruction*. Upper Saddle River, New Jersey: Pearson Merrill Prentice Hall.

McDonald, B., and Boud, D. (2003). The impact of self-assessment on achievement: The effects of self-assessment training on performance in external examinations. *Assessment in Education: Principles, Policy & Practice*, 10(2), 209–220. DOI: 10.1080/0969594032000121289.

Mills, D., and Alexander, P. (2013). *Small Group Teaching: A Toolkit for Learning*. Higher Education Academy Publications.

Nataatmadja, I., and Dyson, E. (July 2008). The role of podcasts in students' learning. *iJIM*, 2(3). Available at: https://online-journals.org/index.php/i-jim/article/view/526

O'Connell, A. J. (2016). Seven blended learning models used today in higher ed. Available at: http://acrobatiq.com/seven-blended-learning-models-used-today-in-higher-ed/. Accessed 18 December 2019.

Pantelidis, V. (2010). Reasons to use virtual reality in education and training courses and a model to determine when to use virtual reality. *Themes in Science and Technology Education*, Special Issue 2, 59–70.

Purvis, A., Rodger, H., and Beckingham, S. (2016). Engagement or distraction: The use of social media for learning in higher education. *Student Engagement and Experience Journal*, 5(1). Available at: https://journals.shu.ac.uk/index.php/seej

Raes, A., Adams, B., Montrieux, H., and Schellens, T. (2016). Using Twitter in higher education: What are students' initial perceptions and experiences. Perceptions and experiences?. In *Proceedings of the 3rd European Conference on Social Media* (pp. 324–331). Ghent Univesity, Belgium.

Rodriguez, B. C. P., and Armellini, A. (2020). *Cases on Active Blended Learning in Higher Education*. Hershey, Pennsylvania, USA: IGI Global.

Schroeder, S. R. C., and Lundgren, L. (2019). Expanding the learning network: How teachers use Pinterest. *Journal of Research on Technology in Education*. DOI: 10.1080/15391523.2019.1573354.

Social Media – Statistics & Facts. (2021). Available at: https://www.statista.com/.

Solomon, S. (2021). Incorporating social media into the classroom: A case study on how TikTok can be immersed into classroom pedagogy. Master of Science in Education | Master's Theses, 39.

Stanford, P., Crowe, M. W., and Flice, H. (2010). Differentiating with technology. *Teaching Exceptional Children Plus*, 6(4), Article 2. Available at: http://escholarship.bc.edu/education/tecplus/vol6/iss4/art2.

Tang, Y., and Hew, K. F. (2017). Using Twitter for education: Beneficial or simply a waste of time? *Computers and Education*, 106, 97–118.

Tomlinson, C. A., Brighton, C., Hertberg, H., Callahan, C. M., Tonya, R., Moon, T. R., Kay Brimijoin, K., Conover, L. A., and Reynolds, T. (2003). Differentiating instruction in response to student readiness, interest, and learning profile in academically diverse classrooms: A review of literature. *Journal for the Education of the Gifted*, 27, 119–145.

Topping, K. (2009). Peer assessment. *Theory Into Practice*, 48. DOI: 10.1080/00405840802577569.

Vygotsky, L. (1986). *Thought and Language* (A. Kozulin, Trans. & Ed.) (No. 2/3, 2003, pp. 119–145). Cambridge, MA: MIT Press.

Wolcott, S. K., and Lynch, C. L. (2001). Task prompts for different levels in steps for better thinking [Online]. Available at: http://www.WolcottLynch.com.

8 Developing academic skills

Students with literacy issues have particular struggles with acquiring and then applying academic skills. These are commonly regarded as the key skills for success at Further Education (FE) and Higher Education (HE) level. In this chapter I hope to isolate some of the main skills and then to suggest ways in which you can support your students to overcome their barriers to success. The three main skills I will discuss are: academic writing, using academic sources and academic presentation.

Academic writing

Academic writing has many conventions. These include being: planned and focused, meaning that the students writing answers the question and demonstrates an understanding of the subject; structured and coherent, so the work is written in a logical order and brings together related points and material, evidenced so that the work demonstrates subject knowledge, supports opinions and arguments with evidence, and is referenced accurately; finally, it is formal in tone and style and uses appropriate language and tenses, and is clear, concise, and balanced.

Many students with language problems struggle with the structural aspects of writing as the selection of appropriate vocabulary, the use of correct grammar, and the creation and development of ideas and thoughts around themes or topics. In practice, some of the barriers faced by students with language issues include the following:

- Defining the purpose of the writing and the audience
- Creating an overall logical structure
- Supporting ideas with secondary sources
- Using the appropriate tone and style
- Using clear and concise language

(Huisman et al., 2019)

DOI: 10.4324/9781003181583-8

Types of academic writing

There are four main types of academic writing: descriptive, analytical, persuasive, and critical. Teachers should ensure that their students are aware that each of these types of writing has specific language features and purposes.

Descriptive

This is the simplest form of academic writing. Its purpose is to provide facts or information. Examples of this would include a summary of an article or a report of the results of an experiment. Learning outcomes for descriptive writing would include the verbs at the lower end of Bloom's Taxonomy: 'identify', 'outline', 'define' and 'state' (Bloom et al., 1956).

Box 8.1 An example of how to teach descriptive writing within a Chemistry class

Teaching reflection

My students have always struggled with writing lab reports and have needed a lot of support. I found that a way to make them more independent writers was to show them a video of and experiment and then model the language to describe what they had just seen with the group. After that I would ask them in pairs to write a lab report based on what they had seen and then to peer assess with other groups. Finally, we would discuss their lab reports with a model lab report I had written. I found that this technique improved the structure of the assignments and the precision of the language.

(Agatha, Chemistry Lecturer)

Analytical

When students write analytically, they will have to describe but also to review, categorise and synthesise the information. The learning outcomes for analytical writing would include the verbs near the top end of Bloom's Taxonomy such as: 'analyse', 'compare', 'contrast', 'relate', and 'examine'.

Planning is central to analytical writing and thus students who struggle with literacy should be particularly encouraged to use different ways to organise their information before they start writing. These might include thought showers, flow charts, tree diagrams, tables, mind maps and colour coding.

> **Box 8.2 An example of how to teach analytical writing in a music class**
>
> **Teaching reflection**
>
> My students all have literacy issues and find it very difficult to write analytical assignments in their music theory modules. I have found that reviewing their essay plans in depth, using peer feedback, and then feeding back on their drafts seems to make a difference to their confidence and their motivation to think deeply about their work.
>
> (James, Music Lecturer)

Persuasive

Persuasive writing combines analysis with individual points of view. Examples of these in academic writing include an argument, recommendation, interpretation of findings or evaluation of others' work. The learning outcomes for persuasive would include the verbs near the top end of Bloom's Taxonomy, such as 'argue', 'evaluate', 'discuss'. In order to write persuasively, students should read widely looking for patterns in the data or references, evaluate the evidence and prioritise several different interpretations. If possible, they should bounce their opinions off someone else and develop their own argument, ensuring that it is coherent and supported by secondary evidence. Any examples, based on clear reasoning, should have valid and relevant assumptions.

> **Box 8.3 An example of how to teach persuasive writing in a Marketing class**
>
> **Teaching reflection**
>
> I find that the best way to develop writing skills with my students is to give them in pairs relevant texts to deconstruct for structure, language, style, layout etc. such as a Marketing brief. And then as a full class I model the key features of the text with the class, and we write one collectively as a group. Finally, they are asked to produce their own Marketing briefs in their pairs. I find they respond well to the different levels of scaffolding and then the opportunity to work autonomously.
>
> (Maria, Marketing Lecturer)

Critical

Critical writing draws on the conventions of analytical writing but tends to provide a variety of viewpoints on a single issue in order to conclude. Examples of critical writing assignments include a critique of a journal article, or a literature review or an annotated bibliography. The learning outcomes for critical writing would include the verbs at the top end of Bloom's Taxonomy, such as: 'critique', 'debate', 'analyse' and 'evaluate'. To do this effectively your students will need to summarise accurately all or part of the work under examination and critically evaluate it, highlighting its strengths and weaknesses and evidencing their arguments with a range of references. Their arguments should be clearly structured paragraph by paragraph and concluded with a clear summing up of their arguments from judgements based on careful reflection and evidence rather than on opinion and prejudice.

Box 8.4 An example of how to teach critical writing in a Psychology class

Teaching reflection

Critical writing is a very complex form of writing which most of my students find difficult to master but which is vital for their success at A Level. I have found that embedding it as a starter every so often seems to work very well for the group as they can develop the skills via repetition and group feedback. I give them all different extracts from two different texts; for instance, two experiments and in pairs they are asked to discuss and to compare and contrast them in different ways, such as in their sampling methods, data-gathering methods and then to evaluate their strengths and weaknesses. Once the pairs have reached their conclusions, they are asked to present them briefly to the rest of the group for group feedback.

I have found that since I have been doing the starters the students use evidence more carefully in their arguments and are better at developing them coherently.

(Damiola, Psychology Lecturer)

Teaching academic writing skills

There are many ways of teaching academic writing. The three main ways are using Product, Process and Genre approaches.

Product

This is the most traditional method of teaching writing. According to Burns and Sinfield (2014), there are four stages of teaching in the product approach: familiarisation, controlled writing, guided writing, and free writing. The focus of the method is mainly on linguistic knowledge. The method is predominantly teacher-centred as the student is encouraged to imitate, copy, and develop their style based on teacher-supplied model texts. Although it has been deemed to be most effective at supporting students who have language and literacy issues. It has been suggested that this approach stifles creativity in students and suppresses their desires to experiment with different styles (Cottrell, 2001).

Process

In this technique the emphasis is on developing writing skills, and it stresses linguistic skills and the processes involved in writing, such as planning, drafting, revising, and editing. The teacher is the facilitator in the process. Their role is to develop individual creativity in the writer. The process approach is cyclical and central to the process is feedback either from teachers or peers and encouraging the student to draft and redraft their work until it reflects their own voice. Some critics argue that it ignores the social process of learning to write, however, and can lack direction and scaffolding for students who are struggling, especially those students who are writing in their second language and who may need models to work from (Neupane, 2017).

Genre

This attempts to blend both approaches. It tries to emphasise on linguistic knowledge and structure in combination with the development of individual style. It also attempts to contextualise writing for audiences and purpose. Students are taught to identify the generic conventions of a specific text and then to replicate and apply them individually. The teacher provides scaffolding initially and then finally allows the students to write autonomously. There are three stages to genre writing: investigating the conventions of a genre; producing texts, and mastering the conventions with the teacher; and then, finally, producing a text independently. This approach can be very effective for students that struggle with writing because it provides structure, but the method assumes a high level of understanding of the rhetoric of texts and may encourage students to write by numbers (Nunan, 1991).

Process/Genre Approach (PGA)

This was developed by Badger and White (2000) and is an attempt to merge the strengths from the Product, Process and Genre approaches to form a coherent, more inclusive model. It aims to develop language knowledge, contexts, and the purposes of the writing, and writing skills. PGA has three stages. In the first stage, the students become familiar with the text organisation, structure, and language used for a specific type of writing. In the second, they are given writing exercises in the skills of planning, drafting, and redrafting and given continued feedback, either from their peers or the teacher. They are also encouraged to self-assess their work (Badger and White, 2000).

Academic language and flow

When using academic language, students need to be concise. It is good academic style to use only main idea per sentence, which should be a maximum of 25 words in length. They should avoid redundant words like "due to the fact that" (because) or "in order to" (to). They should also use formal language based on a blend of active and passive verbs. The latter tends to be preferred in academic writing as it is deemed to be more objective in tone, but the active is more direct and often easier to write and read.

Students also often struggle with organising the flow of their arguments in assignments. Signposting words can help to make clear the direction and flow of your students writing to the reader and to pinpoint the movement and logic of their arguments. For example, they can have a variety of functions, including adding information e.g., furthermore, moreover, additionally, or comparing two similar viewpoints e.g., similarly, in comparison and contrasting viewpoints e.g., however, in contrast, yet. Additionally, they can show impact or conclusion e.g., therefore, consequently, as a result or indicate a sequence e.g., first, second, finally.

(Adapted from Signal words from Clark College, Vancouver)

Encourage your students to use the Manchester Academic Phrase bank as it is a very useful source of signalling words.

The foundation of clear academic writing is paragraphing.

Box 8.5 Paragraph checklist

Teaching resource

I provide my students with a checklist like the following to check their paragraphs against.
 Paragraph checklist

   Does each paragraph contain one main idea or argument?
   Is there a clear point in the first or second sentence of the paragraph to help the reader to follow your line of argument?
   Does the first sentence in each paragraph direct the reader to a change in focus?
   Do you use the rest of the paragraph to expand on this point and provide evidence and examples?

> Does the end of the paragraph to tie up the point and link to the next?
> Do your paragraphs connect in a logical sequence?
>
> Read the first sentence of each paragraph out loud when you have finished the assignment to see whether you can follow the logic of the argument without reading the rest of the paragraphs.

Writing frames

A writing frame is a skeleton outline originally used to scaffold writing in children, but which has been used widely since the 1990s in all levels of literacy learning and has proved to be particularly effective when teaching learners with dyslexia or who have EAL. They consist of a template of starts, connectives and sentence modifiers, depending on the particular genre which is being scaffolded. They provide students with a structure in which they can order their ideas and develop their communication skills (Conteh, 2018).

How can writing frames help students?

They can help by developing an understanding of the generic conventions of texts and can provide models of how texts should be organised and structured and develop a knowledge of ways to link sentences and paragraphs. This can enable students to present their arguments more logically in a coherent structure. They can encourage students to select and think and write what they have understood without wandering off the point, providing opportunities for students to develop their own approaches to form and language. They can be differentiated to help all students achieve the same lesson outcomes but using a different vocabulary and enable students to critically reflect upon their own writing style and the organisation of their own prose.

What to do

The role of the teacher is to teach the writing genres which they want their students to master. The teacher uses the frames to develop independence by supporting their usage in writing by the students across a range of tasks and genres. Once independence has been achieved, the writing frames and scaffolding can be removed slowly, and the students can begin to develop their own writing styles.

Below is a writing frame that was developed by a teacher and her students on a Level 3 Diploma course in Teaching and Learning in order to support learners who were writing an assignment on education policy.

Box 8.6 Writing frame

Teaching resource

This writing frame provides a structure for your policy assignment. Following the guidelines below will enable you to meet the module learning outcomes. You should note the headings and detail required against which you will be assessed. You should endeavour to answer all the questions in the ladder in sufficient detail:

What were the origins of the policy/issue? (150 words)
    What triggered the changes?
    Was it a change in government?
    Or public opinion?
What did it replace or supplement? (150 words)
    What was the former policy or piece of legislation that preceded it?
    What were the policies or laws that it is designed to support or complement?
    What were the shortcomings of this policy or law?
What are the main characteristics of the new policy/piece of legislation? (200 words)
    What were its main aims and objectives?
    How did it attempt to achieve them?
What are the problems in education that it is trying to solve? (200 words)
    What were the main problems?
    What caused these problems?
    What was the impact on education of these problems?
How was the policy/change in law implemented? (150 words)
    Was it piloted in small areas before it was rolled out to the whole country?
    Did it receive initial opposition from other political parties, pressure groups?
How has the policy/law impacted on learners in general? (250 words)
    What are the positive and the negative consequences of the policy change or change in the law on learners in the UK?
How has the policy impacted on teachers in general? (250 words)
    What are the positive and the negative consequences of the policy change or change in the law on teachers and teaching in the UK?
How has the policy impacted on educational institutions in general? (250 words)
    What are the positive and the negative consequences of the policy change or change in the law on educational institutions in the UK?
How has the policy impacted on the curriculum? (250 words)
    What are the positive and the negative consequences of the policy change or change in the law on the curriculum in the UK?

180   *Developing academic skills*

> **How has the policy impacted on your classroom practice? (250 words)**
> To what extent has it helped or hindered your supporting teaching and learning practice?
> Has it made your job harder or easier to do?
> **How has the policy change impacted on your own students? (250 words)**
> To what extent it has helped or hindered your students' learning in class?
> Have they benefited or been disadvantaged by the change in policy/law?
> **Conclusion (300 words)**
> Drawing on the mini-conclusions in the previous sections, answer the following questions:
> To what extent has the policy change/change in the law been a success for education?
> Has it achieved its original aims and objectives?
> Justify your answer with reference to secondary sources.
>
> You should support your arguments in every section with citations taken from valid secondary sources and develop a balanced critical argument in your assignment.

Using academic sources

Academic or scholarly sources are sources which can include books, academic journal articles, and published expert reports. The content in academic sources has usually been peer-reviewed for accuracy and quality before being published.

Why use academic sources?

They have a high level of authority and credibility. They require authors to document and make verifiable the sources of the facts, ideas, and methods they used to arrive at their insights and conclusions. They identify and discuss the merits of alternative explanations and viewpoints for the positions they espouse. It is easier to assess the truth, as well as the strengths and weaknesses, of the claims made in a paper.

What are the benefits to learners of using academic sources?

They give students' work more credibility and authenticity. They offer clarity and conclusions. This helps your students understand strengths and weaknesses of the claims expressed in the journals, from more than one author's viewpoint. They offer evidence for their claims. They provide a wide range of information to work from and can provide case studies and examples to work from. They can promote deep thinking and deep learning, focusing students' own research, broadening perspectives, and enhancing use of academic vocabulary.

Box 8.7 Some different ways of developing students' use of academic sources

Teaching strategies

- Give students Problem-Based Learning (PBL) exercises. Provide a problem or dilemma to your students prior to studying the relevant material. Then allow them to use research to find the answers in groups.
- Provide an initial set of organised sources for students to build upon and also integrate texts from multiple sources during class activities to show students different perspectives that challenge their thinking.
- Allow students to share resources with each other and contribute resources you know to be credible and relevant. In addition, use student-contributed resources in your teaching to validate your students' effort and insight.
- To help students learn to evaluate sources, have them create annotated bibliographies before they write their research papers and also provide students with feedback on their bibliographies, particularly on their assessments of their sources.
- Ask students to summarise each source they include in their bibliographies, as well as to assess the source's credibility and potential use in their papers. In addition, ask students to revise their bibliography to detail why and how they used each source or why they chose not to use a given source.
- Ask students to create visual representations of their topics, in which they depict relationships among ideas and examples; in doing so, they are mapping the big picture.
- Encourage them to use social bookmarking tools and share their favourite web pages with others.
- Ask students to combine and integrate details from two or more texts on a topic to provide a concise summary of a topic and then to compare their work with their peers and an exemplar provided by you.
- Nominate a Google jockey from your student group every session whose role it is during synchronous class meetings (in person or online) to search (using Google or some other search engine) for websites, articles, and other resources relevant to the lecture or discussion.

- Give students an assignment in which they must collaboratively author a document. Collaborative documents, such as wiki pages, GoogleDocs, or even shared concept maps, can help students learn to do this kind of integration.
- Encourage them to join Twitter or some other social network used by professionals or scholars in your field. They could then be encouraged to "follow" those experts and stay up to date with new research etc., as well as others interested in course topics and to create their own Personal Learning Networks (PLNs).
- Engage students in shared thinking using Anchor sources. These can be used as a lens for problem solving or as a prompt for autonomous research.
- Use text-sorting exercises to develop their skills in categorising main ideas from subsidiary ones.
- Stage class debates in which students have to battle in groups taking debating stances using multiple sources to support their ideas.
- Encourage your students to annotate two sources side by side and draw arrows between connecting details. This will develop skills in the close examination of textual details and how those details support the information in another source and enable them to cross annotate sources.
- Encourage them to use the THIEVES mnemonic (T – title, H – headings, I – introduction, E – every first sentence in each section, V – visuals and vocabulary, E – end of source and S – summarise) to analyse texts and to identify multiple sources within the text.

Note taking

This is an essential skill that students at all levels need to master. It is also one of the most complex for students who struggle with English as it demands a clear understanding of the text and the ability to organise and analyse it. Note making helps the student to take control of the information for themselves and then to apply it in new contexts.

Why do students need to take notes?

It can help make them more independent students and less dependent upon PowerPoint slides or spoon-fed lecture notes and develop their understanding of the material. It can save them time and provide a foundation for further reading. It can develop their ability to recall information and build links to other information they have learned. It can help them to self- teach and to peer-teach and help focus attention on what they are reading or listening to and enable them to highlight the most important points.

Students often struggle with note making and some of the obstacles include the following: They find it difficult to understand the content of the text or lecture and/or lack the vocabulary to condense the information adequately. They become overwhelmed by the volume of notes they have taken and/or cannot write fast enough in class. This is particularly the case when they have taken verbatim notes from a session. They find it difficult to read their handwritten notes after a session and prefer to copy and paste and paraphrase afterwards!

Self-reflection and note taking

You could encourage your students to self-reflect on their approaches to making notes from lectures by attempting this note-taking self-evaluation resource task.

Box 8.8 Self-reflection task

Teaching resource

How do you make notes?
  Place these in order of priority from 1 to 22 by adding numbers in the small boxes

---

Read the class slides before the lecture	File handouts away for use afterwards
Identify what is not said	Code references to use as follow-up reading
Compare and revise notes with friends	Try and summarise whilst you are making notes
Print off the slides and annotate them during the lecture	Always note references in full
Underline main points	Make short notes of main points and headings
Turn complex ideas into flow charts	Make short notes on index cards after the lecture for future reference
Ask lecturers to clarify points	Order and file your class notes regularly
Ask questions	Annotate handouts
After the class	
Highlight key points in your work	Revise notes within three days of lectures
Scribble extra questions in margins	Colour code your lecture notes into sections
Write down every single word said by the lecturer	Record the lectures on your phone and transcribe them afterwards

---

  Now compare your choices with two other members of the group and come up with an agreed order of priority and feedback to the rest of the group.

Using a pen rather than a laptop

Mueller and Oppenheimer (2014) have found that using a pen to take notes in a classroom situation is more effective because although laptop users take more notes, hand-writers select, summarise, and synthesise information which makes it more transferable and useable for assignments, revision etc.

Organising notes

Encourage your students to organise their notes whatever the source. This will make them more user-friendly and easier to access when they are writing their assignments or revising for an examination.

Burns and Sinfield (2014) suggest that all notes should contain the following:

- Source information and if taken from a text, a full reference.
- Subheadings which explain the key argument in each section of their notes, highlighted key words, examples, names, ideas, illustrations, statistics, and theoretical concepts.
- Visual signposting using lines, arrows, numbers, letters.
- Colour coding could also be effective. These could all help students link information to the learning objectives of the assignment and prioritise the content when they review their notes later.

In addition, they may make use of: mnemonic triggers which can make their notes more memorable by being strange or amusing, notes on further reading which they need to pursue after they have finished with the current text, annotations which cross-map their notes to the assignment and an overall coding system that links sections of the notes to individual sections of the assignment or assessment criteria.

Types of note-taking strategies

Coded notes

A very simple way system of managing narrative lecture notes is by coding them. Coding notes can help students to structure and extract the essential points made in a lecture. After the lecture, encourage your students to classify them. This should help to stimulate their ideas about the types and relative importance of information, which can be done in several ways. Your students could use a system of asterisks in the margin:

**** Vital
*** Useful?
** Possible
A good idea but not for this assignment, cross-reference to …

They could also try more complex system of coding which distinguishes different types of information:

M Main argument
B Background or Introduction
IT Important theory
C. Conclusion
G.eg. Good Example
I Irrelevant
VI Very important to include
R Reservations – I have 'Yes But' thoughts about this
GP Good point I agree with
D I disagree totally with this
? Not sure about this, need to look at to check it out.

Narrative notes

Many students take narrative line by line notes from lectures and from texts. They are often structured around bullet pointed lists and colour-coded sections. The narrative structure can be an effective way of organising information but is very passive; because of this, it can be a barrier to deep content understanding as it does not make demands on students' criticality.

Question, answer, evidence method

Instead of trying to make verbatim notes, encourage your students to listen actively and paraphrase whilst they are in the session. They will need to take notes based on their own questions, answers provided by the teacher and evidence from the session. This may give them assignment-friendly structured and coherent notes to supplement for their work.

PowerPoint print outs

Printing off uploaded PowerPoint slides with space for notes can enable students to take structured notes as annotations during the session.

Outlining

This uses bullet points and subheadings to organise information into topics and subtopics. Each section of the notes starts with a heading indicating the main topic. Each subtopic and supporting comment is written underneath. Notes written using this method would look something like this:

Main topic 1
Subtopic 1

    Comment 1
    Comment 2
    Subtopic 2
    Comment 1
    Comment 2
    Main topic 2
    Subtopic 1
    Comment 1
    Comment 2

Dual column approach

In this the page is divided down the middle. The right-hand column is used to carry the narrative notes of the lecturer and the left-hand column to carry amendments, annotations, made during and after the lecture.

Cornell notes

The Cornell system is based upon restructuring the page into three sections: one for organising the notes; one for summarising key information; and one for writing a critical commentary or an overall summary of the main points of the lecture or the text.

An example of the Cornell system would contain the following headings:

    Course:
    Module:
    Date:
    Main points   Notes
    Summary and reflection

Concept maps

These are diagrams which show the relationships between different ideas. Ideas are normally represented by shapes and are connected by cross-links such as arrows, wavy lines, etc. They can help students synthesise ideas and organise thoughts and enable them to plot how ideas relate to each other developing their critical analysis of concepts. There are many Concept Mapping applications available for use on Desktops or phones.

Mind maps

These are a very common form of note taking and are very useful for compressing information and generating new ideas. Their free flow structure enables students to draw ideas from other areas and compare visually.

Pattern notes

These are like mind maps. They are non-linear and give students the freedom to make connections between information and to provide critical comparisons between ideas. The most common examples include spider grams, flow charts and tree diagrams.

Post-it notes note taking

Suggest to students that they use Post-it notes to summarise small chunks of information which they then could attach to a blank sheet of paper. Using Post-it notes as mini-summaries of texts or lectures can help them focus their attention on how to condense complex information onto a small space. It can also help them to structure their assignment as they can rearrange the Post-it notes as often as they like.

Audio notes

Students who are struggling to write down information could be encouraged to record summaries of the content and audio reflections whilst they are making notes. They can play these back later and use them to supplement their notes.

Cut-ups

Information is often easier to process if it is in manageable sections or bites. Rather than working directly from reams of notes prompt your students to cut them up either physically or virtually and then to reassemble them according to their essay plan. This can help them to separate the relevant from the irrelevant when they sift through their notes.

Index cards

Students can be prompted to use both sides of the card to summarise key information and concepts with brief explanations. On the front of the card the students would write the date and page number of the source, the subject of the notes and a summary of the assignment. On the reverse, the students would represent important notes linearly with headings and key points in bold.

Tabular note taking

This is an especially useful method if students need to summarise information and compare differences. For example, it could be used to compare different policies or different theorists.

Developing academic skills

Digital note taking

There are also digital applications which can help students with note taking. Two of the most well-known are Microsoft's One Note and Evernote. Digital note-making applications can create, organise, and synchronise notes amongst multiple platforms, facilitating individualised information gathering and user collaboration. They allow students to organise information in a variety of different formats, such as free-form text, drawings, screen edits, and audio notes. Standard features on these applications include the following:

- a text-to-speech facility which can be used for proof-reading and decoding complex text
- a built-in camera for photographing documents, PowerPoint slides, etc. and annotating the image
- a speech-to-text facility which can support writing fluency and speed
- a virtual paper function which allows students to make digital ad hoc notes on a variety of devices
- a web capture feature which allows students to clip and save web clippings

Free-form methods of note taking

There are also more free-form methods of note making such as

Verbalising

Students are encouraged to think aloud during the note-taking process and then to note down what they understand from the text. They can then return to the text, make any amendments, and add quotations, statistics, and additional facts. This can help students understand in more depth what they have written and encourage them to explain the ideas with more clarity.

Pictorial notes

Students could represent information from lectures and texts as pictures, comic strips, or storyboards.

Note pools

When groups of students are struggling together on the same assignment because of the complexity of the reading, for instance, it can be helpful if they are encouraged by the teacher to form study groups. During their meetings students could then divide up the texts on the reading list and allocate them within the group. Students would be required to make notes on their allotted text and then to feedback their analyses to the study group to share their knowledge. The texts could be differentiated so that those students who struggled with reading would be given less complex texts and stronger readers the more complex ones.

Post-class additions

Suggest to your students that they should revise their notes as soon as possible and do the following:

- Use a highlighter to emphasise key parts.
- Check important spellings (names, terms).
- Underline key terms or authors in colour (develop their own colour-coding systems)
- Identify points they want to clarify or follow up.
- Identify points directly related to their assignments
- Add definitions and clarifications.
- Add in key quotations.
- Note down follow-up questions that could be emailed to the teacher

Making notes from texts

According to Haghverdi and Reza (2010). there are two main approaches to note making from texts: passive and active note making. Passive note making is characterised by copying verbatim direct quotes and summarising everything they read. Active note making, by contrast, involves thinking about what the student wants from the text, posing questions and seeing answers from the text, looking for connections across ideas and concepts, exploring the implications of what something means and paraphrasing only what is directly relevant.

- Note making from texts can require a more structured formulaic approach because they are being done under less time pressure and in a more reflective and analytic mind frame. This can also help students who struggle with writing and comprehension. It can help if you encourage your students to pose four questions to themselves:

    - **What do I need this text for?**
    - **What do I know already?**
    - **What do I need to know from this text?**
    - **What don't I need to know?**

Types of active note making

These are classified as: unstructured, semi-structured, and structured note making.

Unstructured note making

There are several approaches to unstructured note making. The most common are annotating while reading, annotating the bibliography, and using sticky notes.

Annotating while reading

The most common ways are highlighting, underlining, or numbering of sections of text whilst the student is working through it and then returning to it to later to paraphrase it. This can be a very lengthy process and can also pose problems for students who struggle with paraphrasing. A more interactive method could be to use the following:

- Read the text
- Then recite the passage orally
- Write down the oral version
- Review it against the original passage to ensure that it is accurate and true to the original
- Move onto the next section

Annotated bibliography method

Students who use this method tend to be more fluent writers as it involves a high level of critical analysis. Students read the text and evaluate its strengths and weaknesses as part of an annotated bibliography which also contains important notes to self.

Using sticky notes

This works well when a student has a pile of texts to go through and wants to survey them first before deciding which ones to focus on. The students bookmark the relevant pages of each text with a coloured sticky note.

Semi-structured note making

Semi-structured note-taking methods tend to be more effective for students who have barriers to writing as it enables them to organise the material more effectively for use in their assignments or examination revision.

Question, Evidence and Conclusion (QEC)

Students divide up their note paper into three sections, Question, Evidence and Conclusion, and work though the text making notes in each section. If this is done carefully, students will create mini-paragraphs of text that

Developing academic skills

can form the basis of their assignments. It can also be made more structured by using predetermined questions and using the text to find answers to them.

Know, What I Want to know and What now I have Learned (KWL)

This is a similar approach to QEC but this time the student divides their page into three sections: What I already Know, What I want to Know, and What now I have Learned. Students then work through the text and complete the three sections.

Copying and pasting under the Learning Outcomes

Students type out the learning outcomes on a blank page using electronic texts, As they read the text if they see that a section addresses an outcome, the students copy and paste relevant sections of electronic texts under the appropriate outcomes. They need to be mindful to ensure that they paraphrase very precisely otherwise they could end up being investigated for academic offences.

Structured note taking

Structured note taking is obviously the most systematic of the methods and is arguably the most effective system for students who struggle with literacy as it provides a uniform structure and organises and signposts information clearly. Some of its major methods include: the alternative index, the triple section approach and the checklist approach.

The alternative index

This is a systematic approach that can be applied to any lengthy text. It can be written directly on the text as an index or separately as the student reads. It should contain page numbers and quotes directly relevant to the student's work that can be easily accessed later. Students should be advised to follow these steps:

- To read the learning outcomes of their assignment and to list how they will address them
- To focus on the topics, the themes, and the ideas most relevant to them as they read the text
- To highlight relevant items: quotes, statistics, ideas, diagrams
- To connect these to themes or an ideas
- To note down quotations
- To note good ideas

- To note these down in blank pages at the text or separately as part of the alternative index
- To write down the page numbers in the index.

The triple section approach

This grid breaks down into three sections, signposting, main points and summary, and creates opportunities for the students to create methodical notes by completing each section starting from their assignment learning outcomes.

Box 8.9 The triple section approach to note making

Teaching resource

Signposting	Notes	Learning outcomes of the assignment
Main points of the text Central ideas Central theories New definitions New vocabulary	Expanded versions of the Signposting notes Main points of the text expressed as: - Bullet points - Diagrams/Charts - Abbreviations - Paraphrases - Outlines	The LOs could either be represented in full or as numbers. The main points of the Note section should be mapped directly against the LOs in this section.
This section summarises all the central information from the text	Summary It should be written after the Notes section has been completed It highlights the most relevant material It can be expanded by adding extra information to it It can be used by the student to expand upon how the content meets the LOs of the assignment	

The checklist approach

This approach is also mainly linear but creates opportunities for the student to reflect upon the content of the article and its relevance to their understanding of the topic.

Box 8.10 A checklist for analysing a research article

Teaching resource

Presentation   **Comments**
Is the information presented and communicated clearly?
Is this information presented clearly?
Is the language appropriate?
Is it succinct?
Can I find what I need here?

Relevance
Is the article relevant to the topic you are researching?
Does this information give me what I want now?
What is it mostly about?
Is it at the right level?
Does it apply to a different context? E.g., Geographical?
Should I save this source as a reserve until later?

Objectivity
Is the article biased, or motivated by a particular agenda?
Is the language emotive? Is there bias in what you are reading?
Are the opinions supported by evidence?
Might the author/s have any hidden agendas?
Have they been selective with their evidence?
Can I trust the conclusions drawn in the text?

Method
Was the purpose of the research clear?
Could you understand its research aims and objectives?
How was qualitative and quantitative data gathered?
Were the methods appropriate, rigorous, etc.?
Was the data analysis rigorous?
Were the conclusions of the research coherent and a valid analysis of the results?

Provenance
Is it clear where the information has come from?
Is it clear who produced this information?
Where does it come from? Whose opinions are these?
Do you trust this source of information?
Who is the author working for?
Would that organisation influence the opinions of the text?
Does the text provide further reading and how valid is that reading?

Timeliness
How up to date is the material?
Is it clear when it was written?
Is it still relevant now?
Can you still use the factual material in the text to support your arguments?

Visual note making

Although this concept can be traced back to the work of Leonardo da Vinci, it has been given a variety of titles, including graphic recording, and, more recently, the concept of the sketch note was developed by Mike Rohde in 2006 (Rohde, 2006). It combines traditional handwritten notes with drawings, symbols, and other creative elements. Arguably, it is particularly useful for students who have difficulties with literacy (Ahrens, 2017).

The potential impacts of using sketch notes as a learning tool include the following. Visual cues can boost memory retention, providing variety and engagement and developing ideas more comprehensively by creating connections between points. It is also compact and easier to review at a glance.

There are four basic steps to designing a set of visual notes: **Listening** – noting detail, quotations etc.; **Processing** – encourage your students to curate their thoughts and be selective; **Writing**; and **Visualising** – adding shapes, lines, diagrams to expand the meaning and cement the content.

The main elements of visual note taking consist of:

Basic handwriting text
Emphasis text – headings, titles, different font styles and sizes of text
Basic shapes – like squares, circles, triangles
Connectors – arrows, lines, links between ideas
Icons and symbols – students can develop their own iconography and personal symbols to represent their concepts
Drawings and illustrations – these can be used to represent conceits and metaphors
Colour systems – these can help to emphasise meaning and to make ideas stand out from the page
Structure – this enables the student to organise and prioritise the content so that the important points stand out and makes the notes more user-friendly.

There is a basic hierarchical structure of elements which enable the student to organise meaning. These are influenced by the rough structure of a newspaper or magazine: Topic, subject etc., at the top of the page and then headlines, subheadings, description text and bullet points.

Patterns of visual note making

There are seven basic patterns to visual note making, but these are often combined to suit the individual student's style of note making:

Linear

This is writing from the top left to the bottom right. It mirrors the pattern of a book.

Radial

This is where text comes out from a central idea in the centre of the page and extends out across the page as a series of strands or extensions of ideas.

Vertical

The notes will flow from the top and the bottom of the page as a horizontal.

Path

The flow of the information is written across the page whether as a horizontal or as a diagonal.

Modular

In this approach, the page is broken down into as areas of sections and each section has its own specific section of information.

Skyscraper

The page will be divided up into a series of vertical panels which the student will use to sub-divide the information and to structure it.

Popcorn

This is a free random note structure which captures information as a series of unconnected parts.

Methods of visual note making

There are many ways in which visual note taking can be used effectively by students (Burns and Sinfield, 2014):

Academic Pictionary

Students can use icons, symbols to represent academic concepts using pictures to deconstruct meanings – for example: Students could draw images to deconstruct the title of an assignment. Firstly, they could illuminate and illustrate the key words of the title with images. Then, link words together with different coloured connectors. Finally, they could describe what they can see and analyse the question. They would need to look at how they have responded to the question and reflect on how they might answer it now.

Collaging essay plans

Assignment plans can form the foundation of successful assignments. Students could collect pictures, headlines etc. from magazines, newspaper, websites etc. And then combined with the students' own annotations to represent themes in the assignment. These will provide an opportunity for students to visually explore concepts and the relationships between them. These can then be explored and developed within the writing of the assignment.

Index card collages

Students could develop assignment resources by collecting images, phrases, etc. from magazines and either collect them physically by sticking them on sheets or use an online site like Pinterest. These can them to be used as visual notes to prompt writing and to help link concepts together before writing them in their assignments.

Digital note making

Using digital technology to make notes is becoming increasingly popular for students who struggle with literacy. It has been argued that they have many benefits including:

- They are faster, neater, more user friendly and more accessible to make notes with.
- They are easier to search, to read, to edit, to save and store, to organise and to use in peer collaboration.
- They can interact with other media and quick to update.
- Arguably, they place less pressure on the student.

Taking pictures on students' phones were the most common uses of note-taking technology. Many students now prefer to use note-taking applications which combine these features with many others to create a more holistic approach to digital note taking. Two of the most popular are Microsoft OneNote and Evernote. Note-making applications in general can be used to help students structure their notes, organise them and then store them efficiently within a cloud system.

Some of the most useful features of these applications include the ability to: record voice memos, take videos and photographs of texts, save screen shots, draw diagrams, store handwritten and typed notes, convert notes into slide shows, insert images into texts, tag notes and store them alphabetically, annotate electronic documents and provide prompts for related notes and news articles.

Handwriting

An increasing number of courses are becoming assessed by written examinations. Therefore, students need to be trained in writing quickly and clearly so that they can achieve maximum grades. Sometimes job application forms must be filled in offline and because of this it is essential that they are written clearly and neatly. Some of the most common handwriting issues include deteriorating handwriting, problem letters, word spacing, size of letters and writing on the straight and narrow.

Box 8.11 Some ways in which you could help your students develop their handwriting skills

Teaching strategies

Self-assessment

In the first instance, students should be encouraged to self-assess their handwriting, first as individual letter formation and then words in paragraphs.

Letter formation

As a homework task your students could write each letter of the alphabet aiming to join every letter and ring each letter with which they most have problems. Then they should practice getting these write before they move onto others.

Words

Encourage your students to copy out passages from textbooks at their normal speeds and analyse some of the following features of their word formation:

- Consistent spacing: Are the words spaced consistently along the lines?
- Slant: Is it consistent to the right or the left?
- Style: Is letter formation consistent?
- Height of letters: Are the heights of upper- and lower-case letters consistent?
- Consistent baselines: Do words line up on the bottom?
- Closing counters: Are the counters of letters like O closed?
- Dotting i's and crossing T's: Are these observed consistently?
- Jumbling upper and lower: Are capital letters mixed amongst cursive letters within words?

Handwriting classroom starters

Many adult learners may regard your handwriting exercises as something they left behind at school, so it is often easiest to embed them in your session. One of the most effective ways to introduce these activities in starter activities. Here are some of the most effective starters to improve handwriting:

Bigger is beautiful

Students copy a passage from a book using thick lined paper to make them aware of the structures of their letter formation and to slow their writing down. Once it becomes more uniform and slower, they can be given ordinary lined paper to write on.

Using ICT

There are a variety of ICT tools both paid for and free of charge which can help develop your students' handwriting skills.
These include:

- YouTube courses such as HEV Project
- Online applications such as freecreativity2019, LazyDog calligraphy and cursive writing practice, Real Cursive – Learn Cursive Writing and Kaligo

Peer assessment from hard copy

Give all students different passages to copy quickly. These could also be differentiated to ensure that all students can access the material at different levels. Once they have finished, learners peer-assess their copies based on their clarity and ease to read.

One problem at a time

Students self-assess a sample of their own handwriting and select a particular problem with their handwriting to work on. They then set targets with you to improve on that area. Once it has been achieved, the student moves onto the next handwriting problem until all the issues have been resolved satisfactorily.

Peer assessment from dictation

Students take dictation notes from each other in pairs and then swop them with other groups to assess them for readability.

Key word practice

Students to practice copying out key words with clarity until they have mastered writing them out at speed.

Reciprocal note taking

All students take verbatim notes from a teacher's 10-minute exposition and then notes are peer-assessed for readability.

Doodle

Give your students time to doodle or free scribble as it develops fluency and flow in handwriting.

Writing revising

Ask your students to attempt an examination question under timed conditions but allowing 5 minutes at the end to correct words that the marker might find difficult.

Effective proof-reading

Proof-reading is an arduous and tedious task even for those students who are confident writers. However, ESL/EFL learners' errors are different from the ones produced by the native-English speaking learners (Ferris, 2002). For example, ESL/EFL learners' errors have patterns, and those patterns occur frequently. However, it should be noted that these patterns vary from one student to another, depending on several factors such as L1, the proficiency level, the amount of time devoted to learning English, and students' traits, e.g., motivation, learning styles, time, and energy (Ferris, 2002).

It is especially complicated for those students who struggle with written work. It is essential that all students proof-read before handing in their assignments to ensure they have no spelling or grammar mistakes and that what they have written makes sense to the people reading it. It can be a problematic task to master because it is too easy to focus on the content or read what they think is there rather than what is present in their assignment. Central to this process is to encourage your students to make their proof-reading strange (Burns and Sinfield, 2014).

As Mark Twain said: "The difference between the almost right word and the right word is a really large matter – it's the difference between the lightning and the lightning bug."

Some suggestions that could help improve your students' proof-reading

Use fresh eyes

Remind them that it is a good idea to leave proof-reading until the day after they finish their assignments which means they will be looking at their work with fresh eyes, rather than simply seeing the words they think they have written. Proof-read at the time of day when they are most alert to spotting errors. They could also ask someone else to proof-read for them.

Do things one at a time

Suggest to them that they look through their work for spelling mistakes, then go back and look for sentence structure, then go back and look for punctuation and so on. It will make it easier for them to locate each problem. They need to circle them each time to ensure that they have not missed any errors. Encourage your students also to use the find feature when they come across errors to check whether this is a common problem and then to eradicate it in the whole document before moving forward.

Make sure that the facts or figures used are accurate

If they are quoting people, ensure they know who they are, how they support their work and that their names are spelt correctly.

Printing their work out and proof-reading from the hard copy

This will give them opportunity to read the words closely and to mark or highlight any mistakes with a pen or pencil. They might also print the assignment out in a different layout. The six-inch lines of text can make reading closely a struggle. It can be helpful to change the layout size – perhaps to 4 × 8 inches – or use double columns to make the width of a line shorter. This can help your students see their errors more clearly.

Reading their work out loud

When students have read something a lot, the words can start to blur, and they may not see their mistakes. People tend to read in a different way when reading aloud and may hear mistakes that you would not have otherwise noticed.

Using the PC's spellchecker

Remind them to be aware of American spellings and homonyms. The spellchecker should be a part of, not the whole, of their proof-reading task.

In addition, if they know they make certain mistakes regularly then think about creating your own checklist. They could note down all of their specific problem areas and check through those first, before proof-reading for any other problems. Remind your students also to run a full spellcheck at the end of proof-reading to ensure that they have not made further errors in correcting their work.

Focussed proof-reading

Tell them to cover their assignments with a sheet of paper and read the assignment through one sentence at a time, or they proof-read from the end of the assignment to the beginning or also proof-read from the bottom of the page to the top.

Use standardised copy-editing symbols

When they are proof-reading longer assignments and drafts, they might want to use proof-reading symbols such as the ones used by copy-editors. Such as:

TRS, transpose words
UC, upper case
LC, lower case
Stet, Leave as it is

Conclusion

In this chapter we began to discuss the development of academic skills as a priority area. We showed how a range of skills from core ones, such as note taking, to more complex ones, such as academic writing, could be advanced using practical exercises. This discussion will be concluded in the next chapter, which will examine how to develop students' critical reading and critical analysis skills.

Box 8.12 Over to you!

Storyboarding essays

In the first instance, tell your students to thought shower their assignment and devise the key questions that have to be answered. Then ask them to draw images, motifs, and pictures to cover each question. These need to be drawn on separate sheets of paper. Students then need to organise the visuals to answer each question to provide a pictorial narrative of the essay. This could then be used to storyboard the answer to the essay and to provide a structure for the reading behind the assignment and ultimately to provide the directions of analysis for them.

> **Box 8.13 Take away self-reflective questions**
>
> Have you got enough information about the problems your students face with their academic skills?
> Do you think here is enough emphasis in your programmes on developing basic academic skills?
> How will you inspire your students to spend more time on developing their academic skills?

References

Ahrens, S. (2017). *How to Take Smart Notes: One Simple Technique to Boost Writing, Learning and Thinking for Students, Academics and Nonfiction Book Writers*. Columbia (SC): CreateSpace.

Badger, R., and White, G. (2000). A process genre approach to teaching writing. *ELT Journal*, 54. DOI: 10.1093/elt/54.2.153.

Bloom, B., Englehart, M. Furst, E., Hill, W., and Krathwohl, D. (1956). Taxonomy of educational objectives: The classification of educational goals. *Handbook I: Cognitive Domain*. New York, Toronto: Longmans, Green.

Burns, T., and Sinfield, S. (2014). *Essential Study Skills. The Complete Guide to Success at University*. London: SAGE.

Conteh, J. (October 2018). Translanguaging. *ELT Journal*, 72(4), 445–447. DOI: 10.1093/elt/ccy034.

Cottrell, S. (2001). *Teaching Study Skills and Supporting Learning*. Basingstoke: Palgrave Macmillan.

Ferris, D. (2002). *Treatment of Error in Second Language Student Writing*. Ann Arbor: The University of Michigan Press.

Haghverdi, H., and Reza, B. (2010). Note-taking strategies and academic achievement. *Journal of Language and Linguistic Studies*, 6(1), 75–109.

Huisman, B., Saab, N., Broek, P., and Driel, J. (2019). The impact of formative peer feedback on higher education students' academic writing: A meta-analysis. *Assessment & Evaluation in Higher Education*, 44(6), 863–880. DOI: 10.1080/02602938.2018.1545896.

Mueller, P. and Oppenheimer, D. M. (2014). The pen is mightier than the keyboard: Advantages of longhand over laptop note taking. *Psychological Science*, 25(6), 1159–1168.

Neupane, P. (2017). Approaches to teaching english writing: A research note. *Studies in Foreign Language Education*, 39, 141–148.

Nunan, D. (1991). *Language Teaching Methodology: A Textbook for Teachers*. Upper Saddle River, NJ: Prentice Hall.

Rohde, M. (2006). *The Sketchnote Handbook: The Illustrated Guide to Visual Note Taking*. Hoboken, NJ: Peachpit Press.

9 Reading comprehension

Reading comprehension is the interaction between reader, text, and task. It is a skill that is central to academic achievement because it underpins the accessing and the application of learning. It is also one of the most difficult to develop in students and to measure and to research (Elleman and Oslund, 2018).

Barriers to reading comprehension

There are many linguistic abilities, cognitive processes, and knowledge factors which can create barriers to reading comprehension amongst students who struggle with reading and writing. According to Lenz (2005), these include the following: students' lack of previous knowledge of target topic (schemata), knowledge of language, knowledge of text structure and genres, knowledge of cognitive and metacognitive strategies, reasoning abilities, motivation to read. In addition, there are issues related to the quality of the reading material in terms of the way the text is organised and the writing itself, level of engagement with the text, lack of ability to decode and recognise words, lack of language skills and strategies and the type of instructions given by the teacher (Bouchard, 2005). They can be categorised into teacher-related, student-related, and writer-related factors.

Many researchers agree that teachers should focus on developing background knowledge, vocabulary, inference, and comprehension monitoring skills in students to overcome some of these issues (Elleman and Oslund, 2018). One of the most well researched and debated is SQ3R.

SQ3R and SOAR

SQ3R

SQ3R is a method designed to improve reading comprehension based on five steps, survey, question, read, recite, and review, and was developed in Robinson's 1946 book *Effective Study*. It is a systematic approach presenting

DOI: 10.4324/9781003181583-9

a detailed step-by step model to reading comprehension. Robinson (1941) claimed SQ3R is efficient because it can help the students to read faster, to isolate the important points, and to memorise the content.

Supporters of the method argue that it presents an efficient and active approach to reading textbook material by creating mental frameworks of a subject into which the student can fit information and that in the long term students can develop effective study habits by engaging in the pre-reading, during-reading, and post-reading steps of this strategy (Carlston, 2011).

Some studies suggest that SQ3R helps enhance comprehension and retention of information. It places students at the centre of the learning process. It is deemed to be metacognitive in nature in that it is a self-monitoring process which can increase student autonomy and engagement with the text as students are involved in actively consuming information to answer self-generated key questions regarding the subject content. In doing so, it can help students to set their own study goals (Elleman and Oslund, 2018).

Other studies argue that it can also improve the speed of reading and the pace of understanding in students that struggle with reading. In addition, it can encourage peer collaboration and discussion (if done in groups or pairs), raise the level of motivation to read by developing confidence, improve note making and summarising skills and develop oral communication skills (Klingner et al., 2007).

SQ3R can be applied in three different ways but researchers are divided over which is the most effective: teacher-directed, independent study and teacher-facilitated and feedback. Some believe that SQ3R is most potent when students can use it independently (Tadlock, 1978). Huber (2004), however, concluded that SQ3R is most effective when scaffolded and that, therefore, students must be informed of its purpose, the technique must be logically related to the text materials by the teacher, students must receive feedback, and students must be given sufficient amounts of both guided and independent practice using SQ3R.

The five steps of SQ3R

Survey (S)

In the first stage, survey or skim, students should be encouraged to go through the text and note the headings, subheadings, and other outstanding features, such as figures, tables, marginal information, and summary paragraphs for about 3–5 minutes. The student should identify ideas and formulate questions about the content of the chapter and create an outline or mental framework for the content. Key words should also be extracted to develop a stronger working vocabulary.

Question (Q)

In the second stage students need to generate questions about the content of the text based on its headings and subheadings. As part of this pre-reading process, they can also formulate more general questions such as: What is the overall text about? What question(s) is this text trying to answer? How can the information in this text aid my understanding? An alternative approach is, instead of the students formulating their own questions, they use the ones in their textbook (if they have one?). Or they use previous examination questions (if they are studying for an examination?) which will help them read with purpose (Richardson and Morgan 2000).

Read (R1)

In this phase students build upon the foundations laid in the previous two stages to begin reading actively. Students should be reading in order to answer their own questions, to understand unknown or unfamiliar words, and to investigate references in the text. As they progress through individual sentences, they should also be processing individual meaning units within sentences, inferring the relationships between clauses, and making connections across sentences as in integrative processing (Klingner et al., 2007).

Recite (R2)

R2 is known as either the Recite or Rephrase stage. Using their own words encourage students to recite from memory and formulate and conceptualise the material. Major points from the headings and the subheadings and answers from the self-generated questions should be identified in either an oral or written format. This could help to develop verbal communication skills, comprehension of the text and long-term memory.

Review (R3)

Review is the final stage of the process. Students should survey the text and review the questions and make sense of the text section by section. This can either be done by mind mapping all the central points and the connections they make to each other or by peer discussion which should help them to connect their new learning to their prior knowledge and to make greater sense of the whole picture. During this process they can also add new material to expand their understanding (Cunningham, 1982). If the text has been used for examination purposes, SQR3 should be combined with spaced repetition whereby the students test themselves on the content of the text after a week, then two weeks etc.

Box 9.1 A SQR3 template

Teaching resource

Survey

This is the Scanning stage.
Read to get the general idea of the text and the concepts that will be examined in it.
Map it out in your head.
Survey important headings, subheadings, images, diagrams, graphs, maps, title, front and back cover information, contents, and/or abstract.
Scan the introduction or preface to find over all what the text about is.
Check the topic sentences (first line) of each paragraph to work out the argument in each.
Look at the headings, diagrams, graphs and conclusions.
Read the title and headings of the sections.
Read and familiarise yourself with words which are bold or italicised.
Read any questions you have been set about the reading.
Decide if this text will give you the information you are looking for.
If not, move the reading to one side – you might need to come back to it later.

Question

This is the pre-reading stage.
Write down any How? Who? What? Why? When? Where? questions that you want to ask from the text.
Reflect on its relevance.
Think about what exactly you want to learn from it and what level of detail do you need.
Think about your level of prior knowledge and the level of the text.
Do you know enough or would reading a more basic overview first help me understand the topic more?
Focus on the subheadings of the text.
Rewrite them as questions which may help you better understand how the text is relevant to your studies.
Make notes on any apparent connections between this text and what you currently understand by the subject area.
Identify any gaps between the two.
Reflect on any questions you have may be around definitions of key concepts, examples of practice and/or theoretical perspectives.
Try to compare and contrast them with your own examples.
Prepare one question per paragraph.

Read

This is the first read stage.
First read right through the text and see how much you understand.
Read to find the answers to the questions as important facts and details.
Re-read the text one section at a time.
Identify key phrases, concepts, examples, citations and ideas.
Pay attention to any words which are bold or italicised.
Pay attention to any charts and diagrams.
Re-read any sections on which you are not clear.
Make marks on the text.
Underline/highlight/annotate/colour code.
Apply critical thinking skills and make notes which fit your main questions.

Recall

The self-questioning stage.
Reflect on to what extent have you answered your questions from the text.
What are the key points?
Are your notes clear?
Teach the text to a peer for feedback.
Use examples to help you recall the details.
Answer your questions using OneNote.
Explain any terms you did not know and had to look up and record them as audio or as written notes.
Narrate the arguments of the text and show how they fit together and flow.

Review

This is the 'pulling it all together' stage.
Re-read the text and your notes.
Create a mind map of all the important points and how they relate to one another.
Review your questions and the answers you have noted down.
Write a summary of not only what you have read, but also its relevance (or not) to your current studies, including any other literature you have read.
Reflect on how you might respond to the reading you have done.
Think about whether you need to expand your existing notes to answer different dimensions of the questions.

> Put in page numbers and add in key quotations (particularly important if you are reading for an assignment as you will need to reference your sources).
> You should have answers for the questions you started out with.
> Reflect on whether your reading has triggered new questions to answer.
> If you are reading to revise keep list of questions to test your memory.
> Test yourself at frequent intervals, for example, a week later etc.

SOAR

Another commonly used approach is SOAR, which stands for Select, Organize, Associate, Regulate (Kiewra, 2009). Some critics argue that this is a far more flexible and contemporary version of SQR3 that is more user-friendly and is better suited to develop metacognition in students (Mayer, 2008). There are very few studies that have compared them head-to-head, however (Kasson, 2012).

Each of the four steps of SOAR was designed to address and correct a common strategy error by students, such as piecemeal learning, and poor note taking and each of the corrective strategies is supported by research (Kasson, 2012).

Select

In this stage, students write a set of notes that provides them with complete study materials.

Organise

Students then convert notes into charts or other graphic organisers that make relationships within the information apparent (Kiewra, 2009). The Organise step of SOAR corrects the disorganised or linearly organised materials problem by employing the use of graphic organisers. There are four main types of organisers described by Kiewra (2009): hierarchies, sequences, matrices, and illustrations. Hierarchies reveal superordinate/subordinate relationships. Sequences reveal step-wise relationships. Matrices reveal comparative relationships; and illustrations reveal positional relationships.

Associate

During this stage students relate noted ideas to each other (associations within the material) and to previous knowledge (associations outside the material). Essentially, association works by linking pieces of information to each other and to information students already know. Not only does association facilitate encoding (Mayer, 2008), but it also improves understanding of the material and aids in the retrieval process (Mayer and Wittrock, 1996).

Regulate

Students construct and answer potential test questions that cover various learning outcomes.

Differentiating the learning of specialist vocabulary

A lack of academic vocabulary places one of the most significant constraints on EAL students' comprehension of written and spoken language in the classroom Vocabulary learning has grown out of text-based activities that focus predominantly on learning strategies for developing background knowledge (Burgoyne et al., 2011).

Marzano suggests that the more times we engage information in working memory, the higher the probability that it will be embedded in permanent memory. Background knowledge manifests itself as vocabulary knowledge; therefore, teaching vocabulary can be seen as synonymous with teaching background knowledge (2004). There are many ways that this can be done effectively by differentiation:

Modelling

This can best be done in class through helping your students build a word bank of ambiguous and low-frequency subject specialist vocabulary.

Immersion

Encourage students to use the words in context. For example: in their assignments, in presentations, when they read out aloud from PowerPoints or handouts or when they are researching and making notes.

Interactions

Subject specialist language should be promoted as much as possible in class so that it becomes part of their everyday usage. For example: in class discussions, in group work and when they ask questions or respond to them.

Direct instruction

Complex terms and their meanings may have to be taught explicitly. You might want to consider the following as more interactive ways. For example, devising wordsearches or crossword puzzles, role play dialogues, cloze handout exercises, visualising the word as a picture or linking words to visual images.

Encourage students to read diverse texts

This can be achieved by introducing a range of texts onto the prescribed reading list or providing your students with handouts drawn from a range of sources in class.

Use summary frames

Summarisation helps to build confidence in using new terminology. Ways to develop this skill include pair summaries in which students read extracts from the same text and provide a verbal summary to their partner (Brown and Day, 1983). Alternatively. providing sentence starters can help to promote the use of the words in context.

Help students translate from academic language to everyday language

This can be achieved by modelling and demonstrating to your students how to write or to say something in a more academic way, paraphrasing exercises in which students have to paraphrase a complex text into everyday layman's terms or modelling paraphrasing as part of the feedback on students' formative assignments.

Design scripts for academic routines

This can provide initial scaffolding until the students are confident enough to develop their own. For example: 'The aims and objectives of my presentation are to -----------------------.' 'In the first section of my essay I would like to discuss the main characteristics of the -----.'

Dynamic introduction of new words

Introduce new terminology in an interesting and interactive way which will help them recall it at a later time. For example: introduce it via a clip from a film or TV programme, package it as part of an entertaining anecdote or encourage students to come up with their own definitions before giving them the standard one.

Develop students' abilities to deconstruct the meanings of words

This can help them to own the words and improve their reading comprehension and writing fluency. Ways this can be done include matching the word with the definition card exercises, asking the students to compare and contrast the meaning of different words, or multiple choice quizzes in which the correct term is missing from the text (Kintsch and van Dijk 1978).

Marzano's six steps of subject specialist language development (2004)

In **step one** the teacher provides a description, explanation, or example of the new term to the students. In **step two**, the teacher asks the students to restate the description, explanation, or example in their own words and include it in their word bank or academic glossary. During **step three**, the students construct a non-linguistic representation of the term using a mind map, diagram, or storyboard.

In **step four**, the teacher reinforces their understanding of the terms by asking students to do activities periodically to complement their knowledge of the new material. These can include some of the following: comparing, classifying and researching the history of terms, generating metaphors and analogies using terms, revising initial descriptions or pictorial representations of terms by comparing them with their peers' representations and breaking down the words into their roots and affixes to deepen knowledge of the term.

In **step five**, the teacher encourages the students periodically to use the term in group discussions, role plays, debates; finally, in **step six**, the students engage in games based on the new terms to develop their understanding.

Game ideas

Box. 9.2 Using game starters to develop your students' vocabulary

Teaching strategies

Game ideas

Here are some game ideas that could be used as starters or plenaries for developing vocabulary:

Connect four

Students choose four subject specialist words and connect them by meaning. For example – Erosion = abrasion, attrition, hydraulic action and solution.

Word Jenga

Students are given a word and have to provide a list (a stack) of words that relate to the longest list (tallest tower wins).

Amazing anagrams

Using anagram software like wordsmith.org produce anagrams of key subject specialist words and ask your students to unscramble them.

Balderdash

In groups, students define the meanings of obscure words and points are given to those who guess the correct definitions as in the classic board game. This can also be done online using Zoom or MS Teams.

Taboo

Divide your group into two opposing teams and allow them to battle it out defining words restricted by taboo words which they cannot use on their card.

Six degrees of vocabulary

Give your students an initial vocabulary item based on their current assignment, such as 'global warming', and a sixth word of connection, such as 'floods'. Tell your students to connect the sequence by providing four vocabulary items in between the words. Then they need to explain and to justify their sequence. As an extension exercise, they could then write a paragraph using all the six words and read it out to the class for peer assessment. This will also help to develop the vocabulary and the use in context to write their assignments.

Pre-reading identification

Before getting your students to study a new text in class ask them to identify any new terminology and research a definition to write in their own words. Finally, they could annotate the text with their own definitions. The teacher then could check for understanding using questioning.

A to Z

This can work as a strong recap of topic terminology. In pairs, students could write an A to Z using 26 subject-specific words and their definitions. As an extension activity, students could then select 6 of those and write a paragraph around them.

Heads I win

This is based on a well-known party game where people guess words or names stuck on their forehead. In the classroom version, students use Post-it notes with concept words written on them and have to decide what they mean based on clues given to them by the rest of the group.

Word sneak

There are a variety of different ways this can be done according to whom you read on the internet, but it originated in the US on the *Tonight Show*. You will need to do the following:

Organise your class into pairs seated facing each other. Select 10 key words from a topic and give each student 5 words. Each student has to 'casually and seamlessly' drop the word into a sentence without it appearing to be forced whilst being assessed by his peer. The winner is the one who has successful sneaked his words first.

The game could also be done online using MS Teams or Zoom using small groups in the breakout rooms or as one large group using pairs of competitors and the rest of the group as an audience as in the original TV programme.

Critical/useful/interesting

This is a review task to test how students view and understand the relevance of subject specialist terms. For example, if you were teaching Law you might ask your students to complete the following terms and rankings table:

Term	Ranking
Defendant	1
Plaintiff	1
Charge	2
Liability	2
Offence	1
Testify	2
Witness	1
Credibility	3
Custody	2
Jury	1

1. *Critical to know.*
2. *Useful but not critical.*
3. *Interesting but not critical.*

Once you have collected these in you could use this as a basis for a revision session or question and answer follow-up to determine how much they understand about each term in the context of the course and whether they appreciate how useful it is in terms of the course.

Roots and affixes Bingo

Understanding the building blocks of words via their roots and affixes is crucial to interpreting the meaning of new words. Central to the teaching of these is to focus on a small number of the most commonly used (Oxley and Topping 1990). The most common prefixes used to form new verbs in academic English are: re-, dis-, over-, un-, mis-, out-. The most common suffixes are: -ise, -en, -ate, -(i)fy. By far the most common affix in academic English is -ise.

The game is structured like standard Bingo. Each student is given a different Bingo card containing different root words and affixes. The teacher reads out a key word and if a student believes that they have the correct root or affix on their card, they can mark it off. The winner of the game has a completed card.

Word generation

This can help develop the range of their vocabulary through morphology as students are asked to generate as many words as they can from a word root or prefix. For example, the Latin root word Miss (send) would become missile, missionary, mission etc.

Word mapping

Involving the group in this process could help them to see the connections between words and concepts.

Vocabulary quick draw

As in the game Pictionary, students compete in pairs to represent words as visuals under time pressure.

Storyboarding

Students are given printed storyboards to represent verbs/processes/models as a series of actions.

Freeze frame

In a variation of role play, students could be given a term and asked to represent it as a series of frozen poses.

Alien invasion

Ask your students to script an explanation of a given term for an alien who has just landed in Trafalgar Square. They have only a limited understanding of English and little knowledge of human culture so the explanation can be drawn, acted, sung and mimed as well as verbally explained. The scripts could also be performed with members of the class and filmed and used for peer feedback and class revision of the words.

Rap attack

Divide up the class into threes and give each team a different term. Ask them to compose a short rap to explain the meaning of a term. Each pair will then battle it out with their opposite number to see who has the most creative and accurate definition. This will be judged by a member of the opposite team.

Working word wall

Having a permanent display of working vocabulary in the room helps to provide an affixed reinforcer. Students should be encouraged to update this themselves. Every lesson one student could add another team which they found particularly useful to the display. The rest of the class will have to write a sentence using that word correctly.

Pairs

In this matching card game, students in groups will be asked to match the term with the correct definition. To make this more challenging, however, you might want to include slightly inaccurate definitions.

Jargon Jeopardy

In this game, the teacher or group leaders (If done in small student groups) provide the answer and the students have to state what the question is. For example: a History question might be; 'A levy on a defeated country forcing it to pay some of the war costs of the winning countries.' Answer: 'What is reparation?'.

Odd one(s) out

This is a paired activity in which students are given lists of words and their meanings in groups of three. They then test each other's understanding of either the word or its definitions. They have to guess which word/words are not linked or associated with each other. You can devise many variations on the links between terms or definitions. For example:

- The terms could be part of the same process. For example: Photosynthesis –absorption of light, electron transport, generation of ATP, oxidation, conversion of CO_2 into carbohydrates.
- They could part of the same model. For example: The Marketing mix – product, price, promotion, place, proposition, people, process, physical evidence.
- They could be antonyms or synonyms of the same word. For example: Inertia – Momentum, Indolence, Laziness, Energy, inherent.
- They could involve misspellings, For example: Isosceles, Isossceles, Isocselees
- The definitions could be incorrect. For example:

Autism. 'a developmental disorder of variable severity that is characterised by difficulty in social interaction and communication and by restricted or repetitive patterns of thought and behaviour' (OED, 2017).

Autism. 'a developmental disorder of variable severity that is characterised by difficulty in physical interaction and communication and by restricted or repetitive patterns of thought and behaviour.'

Autism. 'a developmental disorder of variable severity that is characterised by difficulty in social interaction and communication and by restricted or repetitive patterns of thought.'

Draw it in five

This is a paired activity in which students will need to think of a term and draw five images/diagrams to illustrate it for the other pair member to guess.

Last student standing

Students in a circle throw the ball to each other and pose questions related to terms and definitions based on a specific topic, If they get a question right, they can throw it to someone else, if wrong, they have to stand down. Students can also choose their own topics to add variation to the task. This activity can also work as an ice breaker or as an initial diagnostic.

Target terms

Using table groups give each one sheet of flip chart paper and a target term. Each group member takes a turn to write a word on the paper

> related to the target term. When you call time, the last student on each table to write on the flip chart has to explain to the rest of the class how the words are related to the target term.

Using mnemonics

Mnemonics are techniques for improving memory. Although. there is still much debate about their effectiveness as compared with other forms of self-teaching like re-reading, spacing and retrieval practice, they have been used in different ways, ranging from simple acronyms to help specific ideas to complex strategies that have been used to recall numbers by recoding them as distinctive words and phrases (Dunlosky and Rawson 2013). Many researchers believe that mnemonics work because they capitalise upon naturally occurring cognitive processes like visual memory, coding, and schematic organisation (Higbee, 2001).

The purposes of using mnemonics

They have many purposes which can support the learning of students who have EAL and dyslexia. These include the following. They enable students to learn basic facts which can help enhance higher-order learning and help to develop recall of lists of words which can help improve knowledge of vocabulary and terminology (Dunlosky and Rawson 2013). They can help students improve the spelling of words, especially of those that are irregular, and learn more complex blocks of information from lecturer notes for examinations. They can help improve motivation to study by making learning more creative and fun and reinforcing learning of a topic once mastery had been reached. (Fisher et al. 2007). They can help students revise more efficiently for examinations. They can also help teachers recap learned material (Worthen and Hunt, 2011).

The two main types of mnemonics are: single use in which mnemonics used to learn specific information for a specific period such as for examination revision and extended use which is where mnemonics function as a cueing structure that can be applied in different longer-term contexts such as language learning. Mnemonics can also be distinguished by cognitive function. There are organisational mnemonics, which is where they are used to provide a mental structure/map which serves to organise new items to be recalled like items on a shopping list (Bloom and Lamkin, 2006). Alternatively, there are encoding mnemonics, which is where items to be remembered are given a specific code before memorising and then recalled by triggering the code.

Types of mnemonic system

According to Putnam (2015), there are many types of mnemonic systems. These include:

Link method

Students use mental visual images to represent words or concepts and link them together in a chain. When they retrieve one item in the list, the next will be cued.

Method of loci

Students create a mental map of a structure/building and then store items in various parts of the building. These items can then be retrieved by visiting the appropriate areas. For example, one way to learn the names of the bones of the skull could be to place each one in a different room of the house such as the occipital in the living room, the zygomatics in the bathroom, etc.

Peg system

Students pre-memorise a list of words that are easy to associate with the numbers they represent (1 to 10, 1–100, 1–1,000, etc.). Those objects form the "pegs" of the system. They then use concrete visual imagery to combine the items with those in the list. Students can then retrieve the item by thinking of the number which then triggers the specific item. The peg system is very effective at learning lists in sequence. A common form of this is using a rhyme system. For example, if a student on a Catering course wanted to learn the basic ingredients for making a chilli, they could use the following process:

Peg number	Recipe item	Visual imagery
1. Sun	Beef	A cow sunbathing
2. Shoe	Tomatoes	Trainers covered in tomatoes
3. Tree	Chilli beans	Beans in cans growing on trees in a garden
4. Door	Onions	A string of onions attached to a front door
5. Hive	Fresh chillies	Fresh chilies hanging next to a beehive

Key word method

Arguably this is an effective way of learning the meaning of the word and especially new vocabulary as it involves finding a familiar key word that sounds like the meaning of an unfamiliar word and giving it a mental image. Once the mental image is triggered, the meaning of the word becomes clearer. For example, a student wanted to remember the definition of the word chic might link it with the word chick and imagine a chick dressed in designer dress.

Phonetic system

This is a good method of learning large numbers. Students link each number to a consonant sound and add additional vowels if necessary and this means that numbers can be decoded as words.

Acronyms

The first letters of a list of words are used to create a new word. Each letter serves as a retrieval cue for the target items. The following could be used to learn the carpal bones for A Level Biology:

Some – Scaphoid.
Lovers – Lunate.
Try – Triquetrum.
Positions – Pisiform.
That – Trapezium."
They – Trapezoid.
Can't – Capitate.
Handle – Hamate.

Acrostics

The first letters in a list of words serve as the first letters in a new sentence or phrase. A classic example used to structure paragraphs is PEEL:

Point
Evidence/example
Explain
Link

Songs, stories, and rhymes

Students can join words to be learned together as a coherent narrative or a song. They can also be encouraged to learn standard rhymes like I- before -E -except- after- C to invent their own.

How to use it

Students need to be trained to use the technique. This can be done in the following steps: Firstly, you will need to model the specific technique and then discuss it amongst themselves. Secondly, either provide the students mnemonics or encourage them to develop their own using mental maps, key words, or acrostics of their own. Thirdly, students should be given tasks to practice using the mnemonics either individually or in pairs.

Literature circles

This is a method that incorporates collaborative learning and independent reading, both of which are the most important concepts in education. It can benefit students who struggle with literacy in a variety of different ways. It can provide students with a more global understanding of a text via group discussion and enable deeper textual connections as students are given the freedom to question, to investigate and to interpret what they read. Students can develop a more autonomous approach to learning because the circle is student-directed (Covert, 2009),. It can help create a social environment for reading and, thus, reading can become more purposeful and relevant to students as it can be linked directly to assignments or examinations.

Students can develop skills in reflection through discussion and the exchange of ideas and grow in understanding from seeing the text or the ideas expressed in the text from several different ways. They can also develop writing and note-taking skills and skills in textual analysis and in understanding the conventions of different genres of writing.

They can benefit students who have EAL in many different ways. Students who have EAL can contribute different 'funds of knowledge' based on their own culturally divergent knowledge and skills to the textual discussions which will broaden the understanding of all students in the groups and create a more inclusive class dynamic (Ahrens, 2017). Their use of their first and second language can be valued and respected in small groups. They are given time to practice, to develop new vocabulary and to internalise their use of English. Students that speak the same first language can support each other in small groups to understand and to analyse the text (Samway and Whang, 1996). Literature circles can develop skills in cross-curricular understanding as students have the opportunity to draw upon their subject knowledge in other areas.

They can develop the confidence in students to ask questions and to interrogate texts. Students who struggle with expressing their ideas on paper can draw inspiration and ways to represent ideas from their peers and, in addition, can develop confidence in those students who struggle to express themselves orally in front of the whole class (Daniels, 2002). Literature circles can develop the motivation and the confidence in students to read more widely and to draw connections between different texts and can facilitate peer support and peer feedback for assignment writing and examination revision (Klingner et al. 2007). Peer feedback can enable students to become more aware of those areas of reading comprehension they need to develop.

Literature circles consist of 12 key components:

Students choose their own reading materials (from a pre-selected series of options) and form small, temporary groups based on book choices. Groups read different books and meet on a regular, predictable schedule to discuss reading. Written and drawn notes produced by the groups are used to guide students' reading and discussion. Students generate discussion topics and because group meetings are open, natural conversation about books, personal opinions are welcome. Discussion roles are rotated, and the teacher is a facilitator, not a group member or an instructor. Assessment is conducted predominantly by peers but supported by teacher facilitation, which means that focus and energy are maintained in the classroom. Upon finishing books, readers share with others, and new groups form around new reading choices (Daniels, 2002).

Roles change often so that students can respond to the text in a variety of different ways. Usually, the most interesting roles are student-generated, as it can allow students to feel more ownership over the process (Covert, 2009). According to Daniels (2002), these are the central role descriptions but in smaller groups the roles can be combined

- Discussion Director: to develop a list of questions that will facilitate group conversations.
- Literary Luminary: to locate sections of the text the group would like to hear read aloud.
- Illustrator: to draw some kind of picture related to the reading.
- Connector: to find connections or links between the book and something outside the text.

These previous four roles offer students four different reactions to the text: analytical (discussion director), oral (literary luminary), associative (connector), and symbolic (illustrator). In larger groups, the following roles can also be added. Summariser, whose role is to prepare a brief summary of the day's reading; Vocabulary enricher, who locates important or unusual words that appear in the text; and Investigator, who provides background information as to the text and its author.

Box 9.3 Here is an example of a literature circle conducted in a class of EAL students on a Level Two Nursing course

Case study

I provided my students with some novels about hospitals and nursing which included *One Flew Over the Cuckoo's Nest* (Ken Kesey), *Middlemarch* (George Eliot) and *Regeneration* (Pat Barker) and asked them to choose one and form their own literary circles based on their choices. I wanted them to broaden their understanding of nursing and to develop their skills in collaborative learning because working in small groups is an important feature of health care work. They met every week for 20 minutes each session over two terms. I found they engaged very quickly with this as it was something completely unrelated to their assignment-driven course and a different type of classroom activity. During the sessions there was a lot of really good independent learning taking place. Some of the students became a lot more confident about using spoken English when they discussed their ideas on the books. When they struggled with vocabulary, they looked up the words and wrote in their notebooks different ways of using it. Some of the less extrovert students became quite happy to draw on their own personal experiences of hospital treatment. They all gave good feedback and

> praised each other's contributions when they changed roles. Overall, they learned a lot more about hospitals through this type of activity than I anticipated. I found out by listening to them that through their discussions they were learning about the historical contexts of hospitals, different types of hospitals in different contexts and roles, responsibilities, and relationships in hospitals. (Josephine, Lecturer in Nursing)

Critical Analysis skills

Critical Analysis is a form of writing that involves exploring academic theories, discussing evidence, evaluating main themes, and drawing conclusions based on a variety of perspectives (Chamot and O'Malley (1996).

Why is it an important skill to acquire?

It enables students to maintain objective positions in their assignment work. It demonstrates high-level thinking and helps to develop the ability to evaluate evidence and make reasoned judgements based on this. It can help them to identify relevant information, analyse analogies, to create categories and classify items appropriately (Mayer and Wittrock, 1996). It can also enable them to construct and recognise valid deductive arguments and to test hypotheses and to recognize common reasoning fallacies and finally to distinguish between evidence and interpretations of evidence.

How to develop Critical Analysis skills in your students?

Description and Critical Analysis

Box 9.4 Description and Critical Analysis comparison exercise

Teaching resource

Students often confuse description and Critical Analysis in their writing. So I find it can be useful as a teaching exercise to cut up the following statements and ask students to sort them in the two categories.

Descriptive	*Critically analytic*
States what happened	Identifies the significance
States what something is like	Identifies the significance
Gives the story so far	Evaluates strengths and weaknesses
States the order things in which things happened	Weighs one piece of information against another Makes reasoned judgments
Says how to do something	Argues a case according to the evidence

(Continued)

(Continued)

Descriptive	Critically analytic
Explains what a theory says	Shows why something is relevant or suitable
Explains how something works	Indicates why something will work best
Notes the methods used	Identifies whether something is appropriate or suitable
Says when something occurred	Weighs up the importance of the component parts
States the different components	Evaluates the relative significance of details. Structures information in order of importance
States options and lists details	Shows the relevance of links between pieces of information
Lists in any order	Draws conclusions
States links between items	Identifies why the timing is of importance
Gives information	Gives the reasons for selecting each option

Adapted from University of Bradford Academic Skills Unit.

Textual comparison

Provide students with two texts about the same topic, one which is Descriptive and the other Analytic, and ask them to compare them.

Drafting and re-drafting

Learners could be encouraged to re-draft their previous work editing the material, adding extra material, clarifying the points made and identifying what they would change now. This will develop their ability to self-assess and reflect on the own work.

Categorising theories/arguments

Box 9.5 Theory checklist

Teaching resources

Draw up a checklist of the different generic types of theory and ask learners in pairs to analyse the contents of a broadsheet newspaper such as *The Guardian* or *The Times* using the categories. The checklist could include the following categories:

> Aesthetic Cultural Economic: Educational Ethical Historical Humanitarian Legal
> Philanthropic Philosophical Political Scientific Sociological Sophistical.
>
> (Cottrell, 2005)

Box 9.6 Task prompts/sentence starters for critical analysis

Teaching resource

Involve your students in debates about how knowledge is produced by asking them to compare two forms of news coverage relevant to their subject, for example, a right-wing tabloid and BBCTV News. Here are a series of task prompts/sentence starters for better Critical Analysis (Wolcott and Lynch, 2001). The prompts are broken down in stages from the lowest (Foundation – Knowledge and Skills) to the highest cognitive stage (Integrate, Monitor, and Refine Strategies for Re-addressing the Problem.

Step 1: Identify the Problem, Relevant Information, and Uncertainties (low cognitive complexity tasks)
When students need to repeat or paraphrase information from textbooks, notes and to reason, to single "correct" solution, perform computations, etc., they could use the following prompts:

Tasks:
Calculate_____
_____.
Define_____
_____.
Define in your own words_____
_____.
List the elements of _____
_____.
Describe_____
_____.
List the pieces of information contained in _____
   (specific narrative/paragraph/text).
Represent the arguments about _____
_____.

When students need to identify problems and understand why there is no single correct solution and to identify relevant information and uncertainties embedded in the information, they could use the following prompts:

Tasks:
Explain why people disagree about_____
_____.
Explain why _____ cannot be known with certainty.
Identify aspects of _____ in which uncertainty is a major factor.

Explain why even an expert about _____ cannot predict with certainty what will happen when _____ _____.

Provide a list of information that might be useful in thinking about ___
_____.

Outline the main arguments used to explain why:
Create a list of issues related to _____
_____.

Create of list of different viewpoints related to _____
_____.

Identify a range of possible solutions to _____
_____.

Provide information and identify a given solution to _____
_____.

Step 2: Explore Interpretations and Connections (moderate cognitive complexity tasks)

When students need to do the following tasks, they could use the appropriate prompts such as interpret information, recognise and control for their own biases, articulate assumptions and reasoning associated with alternative points of view, qualitatively interpret evidence from a variety of points of view and organise information in meaningful ways to encompass problem complexities (Herrell, 2000).

Tasks:

Discuss the strengths and weaknesses of a particular piece of evidence related to _____
_____.

Interpret and discuss the quality of evidence related to _____
_____.

Interpret and evaluate the source related to _____
_____ from different points of view.

Compare and contrast the arguments related to two or more solutions to _____
_____.

Identify and discuss the implications behind the assumptions and prejudices related to ideas about _____
_____.

Identify and reflect on your own experiences about _____
_____.

Organise information and research in ways to help you think more thoroughly about _____
_____.

Step 3: Prioritize Alternatives and Communicate Conclusions (high cognitive complexity tasks)
When students need to do the following tasks, they could use the appropriate prompts below:

- develop and use reasonable guidelines for prioritizing factors to consider and choosing among solution options
- communicate appropriately for a given audience and setting

Tasks:
Prepare and defend a solution to _____.

Identify which issues you weighed more heavily than other issues in arriving at your
conclusion about _____.

Explain how you prioritised issues in reaching a solution to _____.

Describe how the solution to _____
might change, given different priorities on important issues.

Explain how you would respond to arguments that support other reasonable solutions to _____.

Identify the most important information needs of the audience for communicating your recommendation about _____.

Explain how you designed your memo/presentation/_____to effectively communicate to your audience.

Describe how you would communicate differently about _____ in different settings.

Step 4: Integrate, Monitor, and Refine Strategies for Re-addressing the Problem (highest cognitive complexity tasks)
When students need to do the following tasks, they could use the appropriate prompts below,

- acknowledge and explain limitations of endorsed solution
- integrate skills in on-going process for generating
- and using information to monitor strategies and make reasonable modifications

Tasks:
Describe the limitations of your proposed solution to _____
_____.

- Explain the implications of limitations to your proposed solution to _____.
- Describe conditions under which you would reconsider your solution to _____.
- Explain how conditions might change in the future, resulting in a possible change in the most reasonable solution to _____
_____.
- Develop strategies for generating new information about _____
_____.
- Establish a plan for monitoring the performance of your recommended solution to _____
_____.
- Establish a plan for addressing the problem strategically over time.

Critical Analysis starters

Effective starters are short purposeful, whole-class, interactive teaching opportunities to involve all pupils in developing new skills, preparing learning for the new session, or reinforcing previous learning. Starters normally provide a mental 'warm-up' for the lesson and can build challenge into the session.

Here are some critical analysis starters:

- Present the students with a new concept and encourage them to complete a strengths and weaknesses table in pairs and then discuss their ideas collectively.
- Devise role plays to teach students how understand and represent points of view that they may not hold. Ask them to reflect afterwards on how this felt.
- Provide the students with scenario-based work where there are no right solutions to the problems only a series of alternatives. Ask them or debate with their peers. This will help to develop their ability to see multiple solutions and outcomes to complex scenarios.
- Ask students to construct their own moral dilemmas and then answer them.
- Give students a list of five random words, pictures and numbers and ask them to show how any or all of them connect to and influence one another and suggest how they might link to the learning. They could then mind-map the connotations of each and then analyse the links between them. And finally summarise their overall significance in a single paragraph (Frey et al. 2003).

- Recap a theoretical model that your students just learned and ask them to apply it to a real-life case study in groups. Ask them to discuss the relevance of the model to their case study and then to evaluate the strengths and the weaknesses of the model.

Critical Analysis plenaries

Plenaries should draw together the learning of the whole group and the individual and link carefully to the objectives, outcomes, and success criteria of the lesson. Central to the plenary is bridging which refers to the process by which students apply what they have learned and the way they learned it to a new situation (Mayer and Wittrock, 1996).

Here are some Critical Analysis plenaries:

- Ask your students to draw a character cloud with key vocabulary to sum up the main points about the character. Alternatively, encourage them to write an acrostic to sum up the main themes of the text they are studying.
- Write an important key quotation from the text on your paper or whiteboard. The class composes a statement to introduce the key quotation.
- Distribute KWL cards to all your students, ask them to complete the "what I have learned" part on individual cards and distribute it to other students in the class. They can then read each other's ideas, compare with their own and explain the similarities and differences.
- Pose a problem at the end of the lesson about a text for other students to solve ready for the next lesson as a form of flipped learning
- Mask a picture used in text from the lesson. Invite students to talk about the range of different possibilities beneath the masked picture.
- Tell the students to write three subheadings for the main areas explored in the lesson today and to prepared to say how they summarised different parts of the lesson.
- After your students have finished a classroom debate, ask them to change perspective and develop a line of reasoning that is contrary to their previous one. Remind them that their new perspective must rebut all the key points they initially.
- Give students a moral dilemma to debate. Then ask them to adopt a different point of view.
- After having completed a particularly topical session, ask the student to role play based on the ideas and the views of the participants referred to in the session. The bravest ones could hot seat their views in front of the rest of the class and be cross questioned by them.

Conclusion

This chapter concluded the discussion about to develop academic skills by highlighting approaches to teaching specialist vocabulary, reading comprehension and critical textual analysis.

> **Box 9.7 Over to you!**
>
> **Battle of the theorists**
>
> In pairs ask your students to stage a series of one-on-one debates between major theorists about a single topic. They will script each of their responses and battle it between themselves. When they have finished, they will reflect upon the outcomes and feed them back to the rest of the group for peer feedback. This will develop skills in research and in understanding different perspectives on a single issue.

> **Box 9.8 Take away self-reflective questions**
>
> How do you encourage your students to draw distinctions between description and analysis in their assignments?
> Why is critical analysis a major problem for many students?
> How do you persuade your students to read more widely to improve their reading comprehension?

References

Ahrens, S. (2017). How to take smart notes: One simple technique to boost writing, learning and thinking for students, academics and nonfiction book writers. *Journal of Writing Research*, 9(2), 227–231. DOI: 10.17239/jowr-2017.09.02.05.

Bloom, C. M., and Lamkin, D. M. (2006). The Olympian struggle to remember the cranial nerves: Mnemonics and student success. *Teaching of Psychology*, 33(2), 128–129. DOI: 1207/s15328023top3302_8.

Bouchard, M. (2005). *Comprehension Strategies for English Language Learners*. NY: Scholastic Inc.

Brown, A., and Day, J. D. (1983). Macro rules for summarizing texts: The development of expertise. *Journal of Verbal Learning and Verbal Behavior*, 22(1), 1–14. ISSN 0022-5371. DOI: 10.1016/S0022-5371(83)80002-4. Available at: https://www.sciencedirect.com/science/article/pii/S0022537183800024.

Burgoyne, K., Whiteley, H. A., and Hutchinson, J. M. (2011). The development of comprehension and reading-related skills in children learning English as an additional language and their monolingual, English-speaking peers. *British Journal of Educational Psychology*, 81(2), 344–354.

Carlston, D. L. (2011). Benefits of student-generated note packets: A preliminary investigation of SQ3R implementation. *Teaching of Psychology*, 38(3), 142–146. DOI: 10.1177/0098628311411786

Chamot, A. U., and O'Malley, J. M. (January 1996). The cognitive academic language learning approach: A model for linguistically diverse classrooms. *The Elementary School Journal*, 96(3), Special Issue: The Language-Minority Student in Transition, 259–273 (15 pages). Available at: https://www.jstor.org/stable/1001757

Cottrell, S. (2005). *Critical Thinking Skills: Developing Effective Analysis and Argument*. Basingstoke: Palgrave Macmillan.

Covert, K. (2009). Literature circles and their effects on student motivation and reading comprehension. Education and Human Development Master's Theses, 450. Available at: http://digitalcommons.brockport.edu/ehd_theses/45.

Cunningham, J. (1982). Generating interactions between schemata and text. In J. A. Niles, and L. A. Harris (Eds.), *New Inquiries in Reading Research and Instruction* (pp. 42–47). Washington, DC: National Reading Conference.

Daniels, H. (2002). *Literature Circles: Voice and Choice in the Student-Centred Classroom*. York, ME: Stenhouse.

Dunlosky, J., and Rawson, K. A. (January 8, 2013). Improving students' learning with effective learning techniques: Promising directions from cognitive and educational psychology. *Psychological Science in the Public Interest*. DOI: 10.1177/1529100 612453266

Elleman, A. M., and Oslund, E. L. (2018). Reading comprehension research: Implications for practice and policy. *Policy Insights from the Behavioural and Brain Sciences*, 6(1), 3–11. DOI: 10.1177/2372732218816339.

Fisher, B., Cozens, M. E., and Greive, C. (2007). Look-say-cover-write-say-check and old way/new way – mediational learning: A comparison of the effectiveness of two tutoring programs for children with persistent spelling difficulties. *Special Education Perspectives*, 16(1), 19–38.

Frey, N. Fisher, D., and Hernandez, T. (December 2003). What's the gist? Summary writing for struggling adolescent writers. *Voices from the Middle*, 11(2), 43–49.

Herrell, A. L. (2000). *Fifty Strategies for Teaching English Language Learners*. Upper Saddle River, NJ: Merrill/Prentice-Hall.

Higbee, K. (2001). *Your Memory: How It Works and How to Improve It*. Boston, MA: Da Capo Lifelong Books.

Huber, J. A. (Summer 2004). A closer look at SQ3R. *Reading Improvement*, 41(2), 108+. Gale Academic OneFile, link.gale.com/apps/doc/A119850552/AONE?u=anon~bca0ecb9&sid=googleScholar&xid=14ff528f. Accessed 26 October 2021.

Kasson, S. C. (2012). Which study method works best? A comparison of SOAR and SQR3 for text learning. Unpublished Thesis. University of Nebraska.

Kiewra, K. A. (2009). *Helping Students SOAR to Success*. Thousand Oaks, CA: Corwin.

Kintsch, W., and van Dijk, T. A. (1978). Toward a model of text comprehension and production. *Psychological Review*, 85(5), 363–394. DOI: 10.1037/0033-295X. 85.5.363.

Klingner, J., Vaughn, S., and Boardman, A. (2007). *Teaching Reading Comprehension to Students with Learning Difficulties. What Works for Special-Needs Learners*. NY: Guilford Publications.

Lenz, K. (2005). *An Introduction to Reading Comprehension*. University of Kansas. Available at: http://www.specialconnections.ku.edu/cgibin/cgiwrap/specconn/main.php?cat=instruction&section=rc/main.

Marzano, R. J. (2004). *Building Background Knowledge for Academic Achievement: Research on What Works in Schools*. Alexandria, VA: ASCD.

Mayer, R. E. (2008). Old advice for new researchers. *Educational Psychology Review*, 20, 41–56.

Mayer, R. E., and Wittrock, M. C. (1996). Problem-solving transfer. In D. C. Berliner, and R. C. Calfee (Eds.), *Handbook of Educational Psychology* (pp. 47–62). New York: Macmillan.

Oxley, L., and Topping, K. (1990). Peer-tutored cued spelling with seven-to nine-year-olds. *British Educational Research Journal*, 16(1), 63–78. DOI: 10.1080/0141192900160106.
Oxford English Dictionary (OED) (2017). Available at https://www.oed.com/
Putnam, A. L. (2015). Mnemonics in education: Current research and applications. *Translational Issues in Psychological Science*, 1(2), 130–139. DOI: 10.1037/tps0000023.
Richardson, J. S., and Morgan, R. F. (2000). *Reading to Learn in the Content Areas* (4th ed.). Belmont, CA: Wadsworth.
Robinson, F. P. (1941). *Effective Study*. New York: Harper and Row, Publishers.
Samway, K. D., and Whang, G. (1996). *Literature Study Circles in a Multicultural Classroom*. York, ME: Stenhouse Publishers.
Tadlock, D. (November 1978). Q3R--Why it works; based on an information processing theory of learning. *Journal of Reading*, 22(2), 110–112.
Wolcott, S. K., and Lynch, C. L. (2001). Task prompts for different levels in steps for better thinking [online]. Available at: http://www.WolcottLynch.com
Worthen, J. B., and Hunt, R. R. (2011). *Mnemonology: Mnemonics for the 21st Century*. Hove, UK: Psychology Press.

Afterword

My original intention behind this book was to fill in a gap in the literature by showing how to meet the needs of post-16 EAL learners with dyslexia. Many of the practical difficulties and barriers to learning which these students experience can be linked to both dyslexia and EAL characteristics and underlying difficulties. Everyone working in the post-16 sector, and the students themselves, can benefit from understanding these multi-dimensional learning preferences.

In order to determine whether a student has signs of dyslexia, this book has advocated that a holistic approach must be taken, considering factors such as the student's educational history, and whether their difficulties go beyond those expected of an EAL student, and consider problems that go beyond language, such as issues with organisation and time management and the working memory. It has tended to highlight four major areas of approach. These have been:

- How to develop independent learning skills and metacognition
- How to enhance strategies to academic reading and writing skills
- Differentiated approaches to teaching, learning and assessment and feedback
- Using technology to supplement text-based resources

The book has considered many specific difficulties students with EAL and dyslexia might experience and some teaching strategies that can be particularly useful. As well as using highly proven multi-sensory techniques that are often used with dyslexic students, it has also shown that an explicit metacognitive approach which can help the EAL student to build compensatory strategies. The importance of activating the EAL student's 'schema' through pre- and post-reading exercises was also highlighted in several chapters as a possible strategy to make learning material more meaningful and increase comprehension. Meaning was also shown to be a key factor in securing knowledge for the EAL learner, helping them to transfer information from short-term to long-term memory, thus increasing automaticity.

This book was designed to provide practical ideas and activities that could be used in the class that would also benefit all learners and to discuss much of the theories which underpin them in a jargon-free way. The book deliberately highlighted in each chapter the incredible work done by fellow professional colleagues to support students in different colleges which should have helped to demonstrate why the best ideas come from observing, discussing, and ultimately sharing good practice. It has also focussed on the importance of developing different levels of academic writing and research skills which are obviously vital to the learners' success in post-16 education, and which has tended to be overlooked in the literature because of its attention traditionally paid to younger learners.

The book should have demonstrated how you can play to your students' strengths by recognising and exploiting what they bring individually to their learning, rather than relying on pre-packaged 'magic solution' sets of teaching and learning strategies. It should have shown how using principles taken from the Universal Design for Learning can be used to create opportunities for inclusive learning, no matter how diverse the cohort.

Inclusion is currently a key theme in education, and this presents considerable challenges to teachers, particularly those with some responsibility for students with specific literacy difficulties to overcome. The chapters of this book have provided some central approaches to supporting students in FE, but clearly each student is unique, and each offers an individual set of challenges to teachers and colleges.

One of the key aspects is the acknowledgement of self-esteem and every effort should be made, irrespective of the setting, to boost the self-esteem of neuro-diverse students who have EAL. This can be achieved through success, and it is crucial that personalised teaching strategies are used attainable goals are set in order that success can be achieved in some form. An understanding of their literacy issues, knowledge of the student and of their own approaches to learning is necessary to help achieve this. I have found that by developing their literacy abilities students have discovered new strengths within themselves, such as analytical skills, imaginative writing skills and design skills which they never realised they had which has had a great impact on their motivations to learn.

Appropriate and effective teaching and assessment is always at the heart of this. It is possible, however, to deal with this effectively with support, understanding and collaboration at all levels. This should involve the school management team, parents and all aspects of practice and policy. Many students with EAL/dyslexia find themselves making transitions into work roles which may be well below their capacity, because they are unable to show qualifications which map to English requirements. Consequently, this means they may need particular support to enable them to reach their potential. It is recognised that people with dyslexia, for a range of reasons, often find it challenging to make appropriate transitions from education to employment and in career progression (Bell, 2010), and this is likely to be even more of a problem for those who also have EAL.

It is the responsibility of the individual college and one that needs to be shared by all. This is consistent with the theme of this book, and it is hoped that teachers and management will appreciate the need for training and collaboration, in order to provide all staff with an awareness of the needs of EAL students who have dyslexia and consider the implications of this for teacher education, curriculum development, the classroom environment and educational policy.

Index

academic language 177, 210
academic pictionary 195
academic skills 7, 12, 172–202; self-reflective questions 202
academic sources 180–181; teaching strategies 181–182
academic writing 172–178; barriers for students with language issues 172; conventions 172; flow of argument 177; frames 178, 179–180; structure 172; teaching reflections 173–175; teaching resource (paragraph checklist) 177–178
academic writing skills (teaching) 175–177; genre approach 176; process approach 176; process-genre approach (PGA) 176–177; product approach 175–176
academic writing (types) 173–175; analytical 173, 174; critical 175; descriptive 173; persuasive 174
Accelerated Cognition (AC) 20–21, 38; aim 20; case study (Psychology) 21–22
Accelerated Cognition (stages): 1. concrete preparation 20, 21–22; 2. cognitive conflict 21–22; 3. social construction 21–22; 4. metacognition 21–22; 5. bridging 21–22
Access to Education students 49, 85
action and expression 11
action plans 102; student self-evaluated 110
Active Blended Learning (ABL) 146–148, 155; benefits 146; components 146
Adey, P. 20
age 124
A Levels 21, 31, 46–48, 52, 175, 219
alien invasion game 138

alphabet games 138
alternative index (structured note-taking) 191–192
anagrams 58, 211
analytical rubrics 80–81; steps 81; use in business class 81
Anchor Charts: characteristics 36–37; definition 36; implementation 37; purposes 36; subcategories 37; teacher-student collaboration best 36; teaching reflection 38; use of content chart in dance class 38
Anchor sources 182
annotated bibliographies 82, 91, 135, 175, 181, 190
annotation while reading 190
anxiety 21, 76, 88, 143
applications (on mobile phones) 90
Art 47
assessment and feedback 12, 69–86; comprehension tasks 69–72; Cued Spelling 78–80; Dictogloss 76–78; peer assessment 82–85; questioning 72–76; using rubrics 80–82
assistive technology 143–168; characteristics 143; definition 143; differentiation strategies 143–144; examples 143; interactive online facilities 149–151, 152; mobile learning 156–158; remote teaching 154–155; self-reflective questions 168; social media and differentiation 158–167; virtual learning 155–156
assumptions 44, 49, 174, 225
asynchronous teaching 154–155
atomisation: central concept in fluent reading 34; definition 34; teacher input 35; teaching examples 34–35
Attributional Retraining (AR) 26–27; feedback 27; independent mindset 27;

Index

positive messages (internalisation) 27; role play 27; student modelling 27; teacher modelling 27
audio feedback 10, 106
audio-visual media 10–11
augmented reality 165
automatisation 34–35
autonomy 10, 204

Badger, R. 176
Baratta, A. 60
barrier activities 118
BBC 224
Bell, S. 3
Bereiter, C. 29
big picture 55, 125, 181
big questions 73, 75, 167
Biology 52, 219; self-assessment using traffic light system 89–90
Bird, M. 29
Blended Face to Face learning 145
Blended Learning 143–148; flexible model-enriched virtual 145; SAMR model 146; types 144–146
Blended Learning Environments (BLEs) 146–147; support for EAL students 147
blogs 125, 154
Bloom's taxonomy 28, 72–73, 160, 162, 173–175
Blunkett, Sir David 47
Bottle Neck theory 34
Boud, D. 88
bridging 21, 22; definition 228
British Sign Language 10
Brubaker, J. 146
BTEC courses 45–49
buddy systems 25
bulletin boards 24
Burns, T. 175, 184
Business Studies 51, 66, 81; breaking down terminology 136–137; Twitter 167
buzz groups 75

card games 24
Carpenter, P. 159
case studies 126
catering 106–107, 218; meaning triangle 134
charades 137
Chat facility (MS Teams) 149, 149–150
Chemistry 73; teaching reflection (descriptive writing) 173
Childcare 27–28, 119–120, 151

Churchill, D. 147
Clark, R. C. 153
classroom culture 82
Cognitive Acceleration through Science Education (CASE) 20
cognitive conflict (Piaget) 21–22
community of practice approach to learning 24
comprehension activities 69–70; critical responsiveness 70; drawing inferences 70; literal comprehension of text 69; use of text for purposes additional to understanding 70
comprehension questions 61
comprehension tasks 69–72; different activities 69–70; teaching reflection 70–71
concentration span 4, 7
concept maps 56, 186
connection questions 61
constructivist theory 56, 61
Content Acquisition Podcasts (CAPs) 152–153; case study 153–154; characteristics 152; definition 152; design guidelines 152; impacts upon learning 152–153; instructional practices 153; role 152
content chart (subtype of Anchor Chart) 37; use in dance class 38
Continuing Professional Development (CPD) 1–2
cooperative learning theory 61
Cornell note-taking system 186
Cottrell, S. 223
COVID-19 106–107, 148, 149, 154, 160–161
credibility 44, 108, 180, 213; components 44; evaluation 43, 181
critical analysis: definition 222; versus 'description' 222–223; self-reflective questions 229
Critical Analysis skills 222–228; alternatives and conclusions 226; development 222–223; drafting and re-drafting 223–228; importance 222; interpretations and connections 225; plenaries 228; problem identification 224–225; starters 227–228; strategies for re-addressing problem 226–227; task prompts and sentence starters 224–227; teaching resources 222–227; textual comparison 223; theory checklist 223
critical reading 42–53; definition 42

Index 237

critical reading skills 42–50; credibility evaluation 43, 44; ideas (separation of main and subordinate) 42–43; identification of power relations 50; questioning of author's assumptions 49; support for arguments (judgements about) 44; teaching resources 45; textual elements (identification of patterns) 42
critical thinking 55, 60–65, 121, 129; metacognition 60–61, 62–63; self-reflective questions 67; small group seminar activities 63–65
critical writing: critical reading, thinking, and exercise 60; 5Ws and H model 59; graphic organisers 53–56; relationship with critical reading 59–60
cross-cultural barriers 123, 156
crossover groups 63–64
Cued Spelling 78–80; benefits 78–79; definition 78; effective use (tips) 80; student feedback 79; teaching strategies 79; ten steps 79
cumulative learning 37

Dance 38, 47, 93
Daniels, H. 221
da Vinci, L. 194
De Bono, E. 83
Demetriou, P. i
Dewey, J. 124
Dialogic Teaching 31–33, 38; classroom organisation (five ways) 32; definition 31; impacts 32–33; principles 31–32; repertoires 32; scaffolding (use of questions) 33; teaching example (biology class) 33–34
Dictogloss 76–78; assessment activities 77–78; benefits 76; case study 76–77; debate 78; definition 76; elaboration 78; examination model answer 78; genre 78; negotiation 77; scrambled structure 78; self-selected 77; student-student dictation 77
differentiated teaching and learning 115–140; experiential learning 124–125, 126; gamification 128–130; metalinguistic awareness 130–135; paired thinking 122–124; peer teaching and learning 119–120; Reciprocal Teaching 120–122; scaffolding 115–117; self-reflective questions 140; Self-Regulated Learning 126–127; small group work 117–119;

translanguaging 138–140; *see also* peer teaching and learning
differentiation 12; definition 115; importance 115; nature 115
digital activities 11, 143, 146, 151, 154, 157, 159, 162
Digital Design 48
digital environment 147, 155
digital media 2, 147
digital note-taking 188, 196
Directed Activities Related to Texts (DARTs) 51–52, 150; teaching example 53; types 52
discussion (active encouragement) 23
Do Now activities: definition 56; examples 57–59; functions 57; piece the puzzle 58–59
Doyle, C. 143
Drama 101
Driskell, J. E. 19
Dweck, C. S. 23
dyslexia 46, 53, 65; adult learners with and EAL 2–4; indications (holistic approach required) 232; note-taking 56; overlapping issues 3; prevalence 3; transition from education to employment 233
dyslexia (impacts on language learning and studying) 4–5; concentration span 4; memory 4–5; metacognition 4; processing ability 4; self-confidence 5; self-organisation 5

EAL and dyslexia (challenges faced by students) 5–7; academic skills 7; oral skills 6–7; reading 5; writing 6
EAL (English as Additional Language) 1–4, 46, 65
EAL students 54–55; core principles for supporting 7–8; difficulties and strengths 232–234
Early Career Teachers (ECT) 1
Early Years class 34–35, 53, 129
Economics, reciprocal teaching 121–122
Edmondo (mobile application) 157
engagement 9–10
engineering, metalinguistic awareness 133–134
English as Additional Language *see* EAL
English class: Dictogloss case study 76–77; ideas storming 64; using self-assessment 93
enquiry-based learning (EBL) 65–66; benefits 65; characteristics 65;

238 *Index*

small-scale investigations and projects 66
Enriched Virtual delivery 145
enrichment 63
Erarslan, A. 159
essay planning 56, 196
essay storyboarding 201
expectations 7, 9, 21, 25, 95
experiential learning 124–125, 126; benefits 125; effectiveness 124; teaching example 126; uses in classroom 125
extended reality (XR) 156

Facebook 144, 158
facts 20, 44, 83, 173, 180, 188, 200, 207, 217
failure 25–27, 99, 128
feedback 24, 27, 97–107, 124; aim, definition, importance 97; answers to three key questions 98; ethical principles 98; levels 98–100; online 105–106; reflection and comparison 96–97; self-assessment and 88–112; self-reflective questions 112; teaching example 106–107; teaching reflection 101; teaching strategy 99–100; three-stage process (FRRFF) 96; types 97; *see also* assessment and feedback
Feedback about Processing of Task (FP) 99
Feedback about Self as Person (FS) 100
Feedback about Task (FT) 98–99
Feedback at Self-Regulation Level (FR) 99, 99–100
feedback (central principles) 100–102; one-minute papers 101; self-designed checklists 100–101; self-selection 100; student evaluation 101–102; swopping by peers 101; transparency of assessment criteria 102; use of exemplars 102
feedback on feedback 112
feedback podcasts 106–107
feedback priorities checklist table 109
feedback tutorials 106
feedback (way of closing gap) 102–105; feedforward 103; modelling answers 102; online pop quizzes 103; oral feedback 103–104, 104–105; providing work-in-progress feedback 102; reviewing action plans 102; student voice 103; teaching resource (self-assessment checklist for students) 104–105; teaching strategy 104; written feedback 105
feedforward 96–97, 103, 117, 127
fill-in-blanks game 138
Film Studies 35, 163
fishbowl activities 17, 64, 119–120
flashcards 138, 151, 165
flexible learning 65, 90, 146
flip charts 64, 77, 81, 85, 216–217
flipped classroom 145
flow charts 52, 173, 183, 187; definition 54
formative assessment 11, 20, 36, 69, 86, 148, 167; gamification (media theory) 129–130; use of graphic organisers 56
formative feedback 159; definition 97
Freyn, A. 164
friendship 124, 159
frustration control 116
Functional Skills 152
Further Education (FE) 1, 46, 172

game ideas, vocabulary development (teaching strategies) 211–217
gamification 128–129; applications to learning environment 128; benefits 128; multiplayer (collaborative) 129; multiplayer (competitive) 129; quizzes and puzzles 128–129; replayable scenarios 129; strategy 129; teaching example 129–130
García, O. 139
gender 115, 124, 127, 140
genre chart (subtype of Anchor Chart) 37
Geography 56
Geva, E. 3
goal-setting 89
Gombert, J. E. 130
Google 181–182
Google Classroom 96, 154
Goudvis, A. 37
Grammarly (software) 96
graphical scaffolding 116
Graphic Design 47
graphic organisers 53–55, 136; benefits 54–55; definition 53; designs 53–54; essay planning 56; formative assessment 56; serial maps 55; structure 54; teaching reflections 55–56; types 53; uses 54–55
Graves, K. 135
group assessment 89
group discussion 20, 22, 24, 69, 75, 76, 81, 140, 155, 211

group feedback 98, 107, 175
growth mindset development 23–24; bulletin boards (inspirational) 24; feedback 24; practising phrases that promote 24
growth mindset exit tickets 24
growth mindset vocabulary 24
Guardian 223

Haghverdi, H. 189
Hair and Beauty 79
handwriting skills 197; bigger is beautiful 198; classroom starters 198; doodle 199; using ICT 198; key word practice 199; letter formation 197; one problem at time 198; peer assessment 198; reciprocal note-taking 199; revision 199; self-assessment 197; teaching strategies 197–199; words 197
Harvey, S. 37
hashtag challenge facility 161
Hattie, J. 98, 120
Health and Social Care 47–48, 55, 64, 125
Healthcare 72, 165
Henderson, M. 107
Hertzberg's theory of motivation 71
Hew, K. F. 166
Higher Education (HE) 1
Hillier, Y. 105
History 18, 60, 215
holistic rubrics 80
Horney, K. 22
Hotel Management (RASE model) 148
Huber, J. A. 204
Hughes, G. 96
Huisman, B. 172
Hungwe, V. 140
Hutchings, M. 7

ideas storming 64
ideas wheel, definition 54
IMPROVE method 61; case study 62–63; components 61; comprehension questions 61; connection questions 61; strategic questions 61
inclusion 8, 128, 158, 166, 233
inclusive teaching 9–11; multiple means of action and expression 11; multiple means of engagement 9–10; multiple means of representation 10–11
independent learning skills 16–40; self-reflective questions 38
independent mindset 27

index cards 187, 196
individual feedback 97–98; preferred by EAL students 98
informal feedback, definition 97
information gap activities 118
information transfer 70
Inoue, L. 4
INSET 2
Instagram 158–160; teaching reflection (Performing Arts) 160
Instagram Creation 158
interaction styles 124
interactive online facilities 149–151, 152; case study 151; differentiation using communications platforms 149–150; Moodle Forum 151; teaching reflections (use of Chat facility) 149–150
internet 140, 145–147, 157; interactive facilities 149–151, 152
ipsative assessment 94–97; benefits 95; goal 94–95; online software, quizzes, tests 96; origins 94
ipsative assessment (uses) 95–97; feedback (reflection and comparison) 96–97; league table grading 95; teaching example 95
ipsative tutorial feedback 104

jeopardy game 137
jigsaw activities 66–67, 118, 123
journalism 43
judgements 44
Jumaat, N. F. 25
justified lists game 137
Juwah, C. 100

Kahoot! 96, 103
Kennedy, M. 153
Kiewra, K. A. 208
King, A. 28
Kolb, A. 124
Kolb, D. 124
Kramarski, B. 61–62
KWL system 17, 53, 191, 228

Law 70–71, 213
league tables 95, 129
learner independence 23; teaching strategies 8–9
learning activities, variation 10
learning contracts 92
Learning Outcomes (LOs) 91, 132, 161, 173, 191, 192; copying and pasting text 191

Learning Support Assistants 2
learning talk 32
learning targets for today 58
Lenz, K. 203
lesson recapping 57
literacy, fluency in (main indications) 3
Literati, I. 161
literature circles 219–222; benefits 219–220; case study 221–222; components 220; role variation 221
Locus of Control (development) 26–27, 27–28; self-reflection 26; strengthening internal LOC 26
Locus of Control (LOC) 22, 25–27; external versus internal 25–26
L1 (first language) 2–3, 7, 199
Long-Term Memory (LTM) 4, 7, 18, 205, 232; *see also* memory
L2 (second language) 2–3, 5–7

Manarin, K. C. M. 42
Manchester Academic Phrase Bank 177
mandala design, definition 54
Marketing 216; experiential learning 126; teaching reflection (persuasive writing) 174
Mark the Words 152
Marzano, R. J. 209, 211
Massive Open Online Course (MOOC) 145
mathematics 61
Mayer, R. E. 153
McNair, S. 98
meaning triangles 134, 134
medals 111
Media Studies 35, 56; gamification 129–130
memory 3–5, 7, 194, 205, 208–209, 217; *see also* Short-Term Memory
metacognition 4, 20–21, 22, 55, 79, 232; benefits 60; central technique 60; definition 60; IMPROVE method 61
metacognitive questioning 61, 62, 74
metalinguistic awareness 130–135; checklist approach 131–132; development tasks 130; improvement 131; meaning triangles 134; multiple meanings 133; 'no single definition' 130; origins of term 130; other ideas 135; reverse comprehension 132; subdomains 130; teaching reflection 133–134; teaching resources 131–132, 134; triple section approach 132
Mevarech, Z. R. 61, 62
Micro Learning 157

Microsoft Evernote 188, 196
Microsoft One Note 188, 196, 207
Microsoft Teams (MS Teams) 106–107, 144, 149, 154–155, 157, 212–213
Millar, A. 22
mind maps 51, 55, 186, 205, 207, 227
mindset words 24
Miranda, J. N. W. 55
missing links 58
missions 111
M-learning *see* mobile learning
mnemonics 217–219; purposes 217; training 219; types 217
mnemonic strategies 78, 153
mnemonic systems: acronyms 219; acrostics 219; key words 218; links 218; loci 218; pegs 218; phonetics 218; songs, stories, rhymes 219
mobile learning (M-learning) 156–158; definition 156; differentiation 156–157
Molden, D. C. 23
Moodle Forum 149, 151; resources 151
More Knowledgeable Other (MKO) 25, 119
Mortimore, T. 7
motivation 124; feedback and 107–108
Mraz, M. 37
Mueller, P. 184
Multiple-Choice Test (MCT) 63, 159, 210
multi-sensory teaching 19–20
Music, teaching reflection (analytical writing) 174

NALDIC 7–8; key to abbreviation 8
newspapers 42
Norton, B. 2
notes from texts 189–193; approaches 189; initial questions 189
notes from texts (active note-taking) 189–193; semi-structured 190–191; structured 191–192, 193; unstructured 190
notes from texts (passive note-taking) 189
note-taking 7, 9, 31, 38, 50, 51, 56, 139, 156–157, 164, 182–189; obstacles 183; organisation 184; pen better than laptop 184; purpose 182; teaching resource (self-reflection task) 183
note-taking (free-form methods) 188–189; note pools 188–189; pictorial notes 188; post-class additions 189; verbalising 188

note-taking strategies 184–188; audio notes 187; coded notes 184–185; concept maps 186; Cornell notes 186; cut-ups 187; digital note-taking188; dual column approach 186; index cards 187; mind maps 186; narrative notes 185; outlining 185–186; pattern notes 187; Post-it notes 187; PowerPoint print outs 185; question, answer, evidence method 185; tabular note-taking 187
nursing 221–222

Occupational Therapy 48
O'Connell, A. J. 144
Office for National Statistics 2
one-minute papers 101
online feedback 105–106
online forums, differentiation using 150–151
open-ended issues 65, 122, 144
Oppenheimer, D. M. 184
oral feedback 103–104, 104–105
oral questions (types) 72–74; big questions 73, 75; eavesdropping questioning 73–74; focus and funnel questioning 73; high-challenge questioning 72–73; hinge questions 73; metacognitive questions 74; staged questioning 73; 'thick' versus 'thin' questioning 73; translanguage questioning 74
oral skills 6–7
overlearning 18–19; benefits 19; use as part of teaching 19

Padlet (mobile application) 157
Pair and Compare 123
paired thinking 122–124
pairs 76–77, 78, 79, 84, 121, 151, 152–153, 173–174, 198, 212, 214, 216, 227, 229; mixed-ability 162
paragraphing 177–178; use in metalinguistic awareness 131
pattern notes 187
peer assessment 82–85, 86, 88, 150, 157; Twitter 166; underlying condition of success 82; usefulness 82
peer assessment methods 82–85; feedback (warm and cool) 83; five bullet point summary 85; one question, one comment 84; peer-created questions 84; sixty seconds 84; teaching resource (I, you and we table) 84; thinking hats (De Bono) 83; traffic lights 83; two medals and mission (basic and advanced) 82–83
peer feedback 150, 151; benefits 151; definition 97; online 107, 151
peer questioning 49
peers, competency levels 124
peer teaching and learning 124, 129; benefits 119; example 119–120; peer learning 125; peer teaching 8, 9, 11, 16, 61, 63, 76, 78, 118, 121, 127, 147, 149, 157; *see also* teaching and learning
Pelling, N. 128
performing arts 38, 89, 160, 160
Personal Learning Networks (PLNs) 182
Petty, G. 82
Physics 73
Piaget, J. 20
Pinterest 158, 162–163, 163–164, 168, 196; mini resource inventory 163; teaching reflection (Politics class) 163–164; teaching resource (Film Studies) 163
plagiarism warning 191
podcasts 106–107, 152–154
points, badges, leaderboards (PBLs) 128
Politics 44, 67, 144, 161, 163–164; critical reading example 45–49
posters 24, 38, 96
Post-it notes 84, 91, 187, 212
PowerPoint 19, 107, 117, 136, 146, 157, 162, 182, 185, 188, 209
power relations 50
praise 23, 80, 99, 99, 100, 103, 108, 222
prediction, use in metalinguistic awareness 131
pre-reading 16–18; benefits 16; concept mapping 17; definition 16; example (GCSE History class) 18; first paragraphs 18; fishbowling 17; identification of textual features 17; KWL charts 17; listen, read, discuss 18; list, label, group 17; mind mapping 17; quotations 17; TPS 17; true or false questions 18; uses in class 17–18
prior knowledge 23, 92, 124, 205, 206
Problem-Based Learning (PBL) 65–66, 148, 156, 181; subcategory of EBL 65; teaching reflection (Business Studies) 66
problem-solving 61, 62–63, 116, 119–120, 129

procedural chart (subtype of Anchor Chart) 37
process-genre approach (PGA), academic writing skills 176–177
processing ability 4
Project-Based Learning (PBL) 129
proof-reading 152, 199–201; accuracy of facts and figures 200; copy-editing symbols 201; focussed 201; fresh eyes 200; one thing at time 200; printouts 200; reading out loud 200; spellchecker use 200–201
Psychology 13, 21–22, 31, 94; teaching reflection (critical writing) 175
Public Service courses 86
punctuation 52, 57, 109, 111, 200
Putnam, A. L. 217

Question, Evidence, Conclusion (QEC) 190–191
questioning 72–76; oral questions (types) 72–74
questioning techniques 74–76; assertive questioning 75; buzz groups 75; nominees answer 74–75; pair checking 75–76; teaching reflection 75; volunteers answer 74–75
questions, types 33
Quick Response (QR) codes 158
Quizlet (interactive study sets) 162
quizzes 58, 103, 128–129, 154, 157

Race, P. 82, 91
reading comprehension 203–229; barriers 203; battle of theorists 229; Critical Analysis skills 222–228; learning of specialist vocabulary 209–211; literature circles 219–222; mnemonics 217–219; self-reflective questions 229; skills 42, 43; SOAR approach 208–209; SQ3R method 203–205, 206–208
reading skills 5
reading speed 204
Reciprocal Teaching (RT) 120–122; definition 120; effectiveness 120; example (Economics class) 121–122
Reciprocal Teaching (strategies): clarifying 121; predicting 120; questioning 121; summarising 121
remote teaching 154–155; asynchronous versus synchronous 154–155; characteristics 154
representation 10–11
resource-based tasks 119

Resources, Activity, Support, Evaluation (RASE) model 147–148; principles 147; teaching example 148
reverse comprehension 132
Reza, B. 189
Robinson, F. P., *Effective Study* (1941) 203–204
Robson, K. 143
Rohde, M. 194
Rohrer, D. 18
role play 27, 64, 125, 228; use of Instagram 159
roundtable reviews 59
Rubistar website 157
rubrics 80–82, 111, 151; definition 80; integration into assignments 82; marking 82; teaching example 81; types 80–81
rubrics (effective use) 81–82; inter-rater reliability 81; transparency 81

Sainsbury Review (2016) 45
scaffolding 89, 120, 122; awareness factors 116–117; CAPs 153; components 115–116; definition 115; differentiated teaching and learning 115–117; Pinterest 162; RASE model 148; specialist vocabulary 210; SQ3R 203–204; strategic use 25; teaching example 117; timing and scale 117; Twitter 167; types 25, 116; writing frames 178
Schoonmaker, A. 132
Science 52, 59, 73, 90; Self-Regulated Learning (SRL) 127; terminology teaching 138
Screencast-O-Matic 158
Second Life 155
self-analysing success 38
self-assessment: benefits 88; criteria 88; and feedback 88–112; before formal submission 92; as goal-setting 89; as part of group assessment 89; as part of learning contracts 92; prior knowledge (determination) 92; RAG rating table 94; self-reflective questions 112; tools 56
self-assessment approaches 88–94; annotated bibliographies 91; integrated peer and tutor feedback 89; Learning Outcomes 91; model answers 93; peer assessment, then self-assessment 88; positive evaluation 91–92; reflective questions 91; teaching examples 89–90, 93;

using technology 90; three-minute pause 94; today's targets 90–91; traffic light system 89–90; workshop review 92
Self-Blended Learning 145
self-confidence 5–6, 9, 76, 123, 144
self-confidence (building) 22–25; buddy systems 25; community of practice approach to learning 24; contextual background 23; discussion 23; expectations (realistic) 25; form and function relationship 23; growth mindset 23–24; learner independence 23; praise for accomplishments 23; prior knowledge 23; scaffolding (strategic use) 25; teaching example 27–28
self-development 11
self-directed learning 48
self-efficacy 38, 60, 65, 98–100, 126, 155
self-esteem 5, 107–108, 233
self-evaluation 20, 24, 82, 110, 125, 127, 164
self-feedback, definition 97
self-organisation 5
self-questioning: independent learning skill 28–29; three-stage cycle 28
self-reflection 26; note-taking 183
self-reflective feedback 104–105
Self-Regulated Learning (SRL) 11, 95, 120, 126–127, 157; barriers 127; development through differentiation 127; scaffolding 127; teaching example 127
self-regulation 9, 99, 99–100
sensory scaffolding 116
serial maps 55
Shamsulbahri, M. M. 52
Shayer, M. 20
Short-Term Memory (STM) 4–5, 29, 232; *see also* working memory
simulations 64, 119
Sinfield, S. 175, 184
skill self-assessment 57
small group reading: benefits 50; case study 51; skills developed by 50
small group seminar activities: definition 63; impacts 63; teaching reflection (ideas storming) 64
small group seminar activities (types) 63–65; crossover groups 63–64; fishbowl 64; ideas storming 64; project-based work 65; role play 64; simulations 64

small group work: barrier activities 118; and differentiation 117–119; jigsaw activities 118; optimum group size 117; qualities 118; resource-based tasks 119; simulations 119; split texts 119
SMART 25–26, 109, 143, 154
smartphones 156, 164; 'phones' 55, 57, 85, 90, 93, 107, 154, 157, 159, 186, 196
Snapchat 164–165; feedback feature 165; Geofilters 164–165; Question and Answer 165; Story feature 164; teaching example (Healthcare) 165; tutorials 164
Snowballing 63–64
SOAR approach 208–209; 1. Select 208; 2. Organise 208; 3. Associate 208–209; 4. Regulate 209
social construction 21, 22
social interaction 79–80, 118, 216
social interactive scaffolding 116
social media 146, 158–167, 168; characteristics 158; critics 158
socioeconomic status 85
sociolinguistic theory 50
Sociology 13, 75, 99–100
software 35, 47, 96, 138, 143, 211
Spain 161
Special Educational Needs and Disabilities Coordinator (SENDCO) 2
specialist vocabulary 209–211; deconstruction 210; direct instruction 209; immersion 209; interaction 209; Marzano's six steps 211; modelling 209; new words (dynamic introduction) 210; reading of diverse texts 210; scripts for academic routines 210; summary frames 210; teaching strategies 211–217; translation into everyday language 210
specialist vocabulary development (game ideas) 211–217; alien invasion 214–215; anagrams 211; A to Z 212; balderdash 212; connect four 211; critical-useful-interesting 213; draw it in five 216; freeze frame 214; heads I win 212; jargon jeopardy 215; last student standing 216; odd one out 215–216; pairs (card game) 215; pre-reading identification 212; quick draw 214; rap attack 215; roots and affixes Bingo 214; six degrees of vocabulary 212; storyboarding 214;

taboo 212; target terms 216–217; word generation 214; word mapping 214; word sneak 213; working word wall 215
Special Needs teachers 2
Speed Reviews 78, 80
Spelling, Punctuation, and Grammar (SPaG) 52, 109
split texts 119
Sports 63, 86, 95; CAP session 153–154
Sports Science 91, 161
SQ3R method 203–205; teaching resource 206–208
SQ3R method (five steps) 204–208; 1. Survey (S) 204, 206; 2. Question (Q) 205–206; 3. Read (R1) 205, 207; 4. Recite (R2) 205, 207; 5. Review (R3) 205, 207–208
sticky notes 83, 190
storyboarding 214
strategic questions 61
strategic scaffolding 25
strategic thinking 55
strategy chart (subtype of Anchor Chart) 37
structured note-taking 191–193; alternative index 191–192; checklist approach (teaching resource) 192, 193; triple section approach (teaching resource) 192, 192
student feedback 110
student voice 103
study groups 188–189
Substitute, Augmentation, Modification, Redefinition (SAMR) model 146
summary frames 210
summative feedback, definition 97
synchronous teaching 155

taboo game 137
Tang, Y. 166
Tasir, Z. 25
teachers' feedback: effective use 108–111; four questions 110–111
teachers, recently-qualified 46–49
teaching activities using comprehension texts 70–72; comprehension tweeting 71; concept comparison 71; DIY 71; information transfer 70; minding gaps 71; question time 71–72; summary 70; summary by deletion 70–71; teaching example 72; theory to practice 71
Teaching Adult Learners with Dyslexia 1–15; afterword 232–234; book aims 1–2; book background 2–4; book design 232–233; content (selection criteria) 13; key notion 13; nine central areas 13; original intention 232; structure 12; teaching and learning themes 11–12; toolbox 12–13
teaching and learning 1, 7, 13, 50, 66, 156, 178, 180, 233; themes 11–12; *see also* differentiated teaching and learning
Teaching Assistants 2
teaching talk 32
technology 90; *see also* assistive technology
terminology: correct usage (importance) 135; differentiated teaching of 135–138; teaching reflection 138
testimony 44
text organisation, patterns 42
text-sorting exercises 182
textual analysis, basic tools 44
THIEVES mnemonic 182
thinking aloud: concurrent versus retrospective 29; independent learning skill 29–31; process 29–30; using recorded comments as basis for essay draft 31; strategies 29; teaching example (fashion class) 30; teaching reflection 31
thinking hats (De Bono) 83
Think, Pair, Broadcast, Share 123
Think, Pair, Broadcast, Vote 124
Think, Pair, Share (TPS) 7, 122–124, 149; clarity of modelling 124; conditions impacting effectiveness of 124; extensions 123–124; scaffolding 124; selection of tasks 124; time allocation 124
Think, Pair, Square 123
TikTok 93, 157–158, 160–162; teaching example (grading videos) 161
time management 6, 7, 47, 232
Timperley, H. 98
T-Levels 45, 46, 48
Tomlinson, C. A. 143
Toohey, K. 2
Topping, K. J. 97
trainee teachers 46–49
translanguaging 23, 74, 120, 127, 138–140; definition 138–139
translanguaging (classroom uses) 139–140; academic skills development 140; glossaries (bilingual and multilingual) 139; group discussion 140;

metasemantical analysis 139; note-taking 139; research in first language 139
transparency 102, 121
Tudhope, E. 3
Twain, M. 199
Twitter 90, 123, 158, 165–167, 167, 182; Direct Questions function 167; post-class discussion 166; teaching reflection (Business Studies) 167; use by teachers 167
Twitter Chat 166

United Kingdom 2–3, 27, 43, 127, 154, 159, 179
United States 76
Universal Design for Learning (UDL) 8–11, 233
University of Northampton 146

verbalising 29–31
verification 63
video feedback 106
videos 130, 157, 173; Snapchat 165; TikTok 160–162, 161
video self-assessment 93
virtual learning 155–156
Virtual Learning Environment (VLE) 22, 38, 96, 146, 154–155, 157, 161, 167
Virtual Reality (VR) 156
virtual worlds (VWs) 155
visual aids 116
visual note-making 194–196; elements 194; methods 195–196; patterns 194–195; steps 194
vlogs 38, 127, 146
vocabulary 9, 11, 52, 57, 71, 76–77; *see also* specialist vocabulary
Vocabulary Planning Framework 153
vocabulary programmes (components) 135–138; extensive reading to expand knowledge 135; instruction in specific words 136; instruction in word-learning strategies 136; teaching reflection 136–137; word consciousness and word-play activities 137–138
vocational education and training 44, 45–49
Vygotsky, L. S. 20, 88, 117, 119

Wajnryb, R. 76
WhatsApp 123
wheel of fortune 140
White, G. 176
Who Wants to be Millionaire? 103, 129
wiki 147–148, 150, 157–158; pages 182
Wiliam, D. 82, 110
Wolf Report (2011) 45
Wong, B. Y. L. 28
Wood, D. 115
word banks 118, 135, 209, 211
word Bingo 137
word consciousness 137–138
word identification 34
Wordle 138
word-play activities 137–138
working memory (WM) 4, 6, 232; *see also* Long-Term Memory
workshop review 92
Write, Pair, Share 123
writing frames 178; teaching resource 179–180
writing skills 6
written feedback 105

YouTube 158, 162–163
YouTube HEV Project 198
YouTube videos 125, 136, 154

Zone of Proximal Development 119
Zoom 107, 154–155, 157, 212–213
Zulkiply, N. 52